A Good Look at Evil

A Good

Look at Evil

Abigail L. Rosenthal

TEMPLE UNIVERSITY PRESS
Philadelphia

Temple University Press, Philadelphia 19122
Copyright © 1987 by Temple University. All rights reserved
Published 1987
Printed in the United States of America

The paper used in this publication meets the minimum
requirements of American National Standard for Information
Sciences—Permanence of Paper for Printed Library Materials,
ANSI Z39.48-1984

Library of Congress Cataloging-in-Publication Data

Rosenthal, Abigail L.
  A good look at evil.

  Bibliography: p. 231
  Includes index.
  1. Good and evil. I. Title.
BJ1401.R59 1987   170   86-14535
ISBN 0-87722-456-0 (alk. paper)

For my father and mother

CONTENTS

PREFACE

A Good Look at Evil takes a view of good as the working out of one's own life story, and a contrasting view of evil as the deliberate thwarting of that work, whether in oneself or in another.

The sorts of worked-out life stories that are advocated here are not to be thought of as fictions. Ideally, they exhibit a serious commitment to practical reason. However, in Chapter One, the rationality of what we call here an ideal story is distinguished not only from fiction but also from that sort of rationality which is mere shrewd economy in the choice of means that get one to incorrigible goals. Nor does the book support a mere thoroughgoing pragmatism, in which means and ends would become mutually and endlessly corrigible, in the style of John Dewey. What is emphasized, rather, is the emergent picture one works to gain of what one has been all about, oneself. The life story meant here is the story *of someone,* whose self-interpretations remain the central effort of it.

The setting forth of the peculiar kind of nonfictional rationality that belongs to the living of an ideal story, and the defense of that ethical standard from objections to a naturalistic ethic, are the topics of Chapter One.

In Chapter Two, the method is explained by which the book's concepts will be shown to have practical application in concrete cases. For each sort of evil, a "pure type" will be constructed, a hypothetical agent who will *aim at* that sort of evil—not merely stumble into it—and who will show an ongoing involvement in the implications of that particular aim. Since those hypothetical agents are, in each case, living a sort of mistold narrative and abandoning their own ideal stories, the method of evil "pure types" calls for comparison with some other narrative views and with the virtue ethics that has seen recent, partial revival along with them. Since these recent revivals tend to be some-what relativistic, whereas the view here presented is not so fundamentally, it will also be the task of Chapter Two to deal with objections on the score of relativism.

Chapters One and Two together form Part One, "Conceptual Foundations."

In Part Two, "Evil Under Wraps," the method of pure types is applied to its first two cases. Chapter Three, "Going to the Bad," is about personal dissolution. Chapter Four, "Selling Out," concerns institutional corruption. In these two chapters the careers of the pure types will be most intelligibly followed within the setting provided by representative governments, where there are maximum legal and institutional safeguards against mutual predation. In that setting, where the evil chosen is either illegal, or at least unsanctioned by public opinion, it will be easier to see the careers of the evil agents as expressive of personal processes of decision. Here the evil that is done must be done covertly. It is not the official expression of state policy. It is under wraps.

In Part Three, "Evil in the Daylight," what is under study is genocide, which cannot ordinarily take place without the sanction of an entire culture or its government. The moral assessment of agents who do evil at the behest of their culture or government is a very difficult thing, but it must be carried through nevertheless, if moral standards are not to collapse relativistically into mere cultural norms, norms that may themselves sanction genocide. Chapter Five, "The Types of Genocide," tries therefore to set forth and resolve the special difficulties involved in the struggle to rediscover and mark out the universal moral lines in that place where cultures confront and challenge each other's right to exist and to flourish—the vast and obscure place of the human imagination called "history." Chapter Six, "Banality and Originality," focuses on the Holocaust. It deals partly with objections to such a focus, objections on the alleged ground that the Holocaust is not a special or extreme case of the evil of genocide. It is also concerned to take up some themes associated with the name of Hannah Arendt: the partial delegitimation of the Nuremberg and Eichmann trials, the alleged ordinariness of the Nazi, and the alleged moral complicity of his victim. The purpose of dealing with Arendt's themes is to prepare the way for consideration of the Nazi as a free agent of evil, not merely as a victim of state bureaucracy, or as someone who cannot—even for the purposes of analysis—be lifted free of a morbid syndrome in which his victim is equally implicated. Finally Chapter Seven, "Thinking Like a Nazi," deals directly with the Nazi as the pure type of genocidal evil, by whom the ideal stories of persons embedded in their nations and in history are deliberately and consciously destroyed.

The pure types in Chapters Three through Seven are not meant to be exhaustive. They have been selected in order to show the explanatory power of the book's concepts of good and evil. But perhaps a further word should be said at this juncture about the method of pure types itself. I am not the inventor of the method. Plato uses it. We find it in Hegel's *Phenomenology of Mind.* Kierkegaard uses it repeatedly. Sartre uses it in *Being and Nothingness,* for example, in his discussions of bad faith. What makes the method of pure types work? And what sort of work does it do? Is it literary work, or philosophic work?

When we find the method at work in Plato, Kierkegaard, Hegel, and others of philosophic stature, what it gives us is insight into a fact about human nature—that people steer their courses, petty and large, people live and people die, partly in thrall to ideas. We simply understand a view better when we see what a person who holds it will do with it. And we understand a person better when we get some purchase on his or her views.

But this does not tell us what Plato, Kierkegaard, and Hegel (for example) are *doing.* Is it merely "literary"? Or are novelists also doing something fundamentally philosophic, in showing how ideas may be felt and implemented by people? In the nominally philosophic writers, as opposed to the novelists, there is a tilt toward showing the idea in its most legible human form. Thus, when Thrasymachus bursts upon the stage of the Platonic piece of theatre called in translation *The Republic* and takes issue with the whole Socratic effort to get at a definition of ideal justice, he does not merely remark, "justice is the interest of the stronger." First, he does a lot of *shouting.* In one sense, as Plato shows us, Thrasymachus tries to stop the whole discussion about justice because—as Thrasymachus sees it—discussion is irrelevant to the understanding of the term. We will understand the term "justice," Thrasymachus believes, when we take note of the fact that it is generally found in the mouth of the bigger bully, as his rationale for his bullying.

Now, if what Thrasymachus wants is to stop the discussion, why does Plato have him merely shout? A real bully might in fact beat up Socrates and put his point across even more memorably. But that *would* stop the dialogue and in consequence make the bully less legible to Plato's readers. Plato needs to have him do all that a bully can do, *while still remaining intelligible to us.* Thrasymachus is a pure type, in the sense that he is the type most nearly serviceable to Plato's pedagogic purpose—which is to bring out important implications of defining justice as the interest of the stronger.

By contrast, when the novelist George Eliot wants to depict a bully, say, the tyrannical husband Grandcourt in *Daniel Deronda*, she shows us a man who would never stoop to the use of force on his wife, and who would never be so ill bred as to raise his voice. This is not because exquisite manners are an important implication of the bullying aim. It is, rather, because modern novelists *don't* show us the "pure"—that is, the most legible—type. What they do show us is a simplified facsimile of a real human being, someone whose ambiguous and contradictory motives coexist in the same mortal frame. The real man dies of his contradictions, perhaps. Or at least they constitute a danger to him, unseen by him, with which the novelist will surprise him by and by. Whereas the Platonic man lives his one mistake eternally, and we regard him from all sides contemplatively, at our leisure.

So the standard of "purity" is essentially pedagogic. Judge William, who represents the Ethical Stage in Kierkegaard's *Either/Or*, is a judge and not a businessman or a minister, perhaps because a judge would have most legibly represented the respectable social stabilities to Kierkegaard's readers. Extraneous factors are kept out of it—in the business case the fluctuations of the market, in the clerical case the fluctuations of the human negotiation with the divine. But there is nothing *merely* tautological about Judge William's way of embodying the concept of living according to the received cultural norms. It unfolds consistently with the concept but informatively, and we could easily imagine the concept's being embodied in some other way. In Kierkegaard's version of the embodied concept, it is Judge William who lives out the implications of his respectable aims. Yet in another culture, where judges were more bribable, for example, the illustration would not do. A different embodiment of respectable aims would have to be found and would show those aims better to that other readership.

For all that—the fact that his pure type does not exhaust the domains over which his concept applies—the Judge is too much a creature of a single aim, too much an embodied abstraction, to be a good fictional character. Kierkegaard has not written any sort of modern novella. Furthermore, Kierkegaard's character is instructive to us in a way that fictional characters are not always. We don't only need to see those almost-real people which modern fiction delivers to us, people living the fragments of their conflicting ideas. We also need to see what one such idea would look like, if a person tried to carry out all its implications, and what a person would look like, if he tried to subordinate his whole life to one of its aims. In sum, we also have a need, a philosophic and moral need, to understand *our ideas* as well as we can. This the method of pure types can help us to do.

Still another difficulty that may arise for the reader in connection with the method of pure types is that all these types are types of evil *agent,* whereas the reader may feel that most people who do the wrong thing do it somewhat passively. Most people don't jump into an abyss freely. Like Adam, they are unfairly persuaded (or feel that they are) to fall. The important factor of unfair persuasion (which converts the pure type into a mix of contrary types, part agent and part victim), is dealt with rather briefly in the Epilogue to this book. Here it is enough to say that our expository concern is with evil, which is most legibly itself when the freedom of the agent is studied in isolation from the other elements in his or her psyche and situation. Perhaps it is for the novelists to sketch the whole—and more realistic—picture. But if they are to give it interestingly, the grounds for a moral assessment will still be wanted. Otherwise, their stories and ours will have no plot—no good to strive for, no evil to escape.

A word on the vexed question of the proper pronoun of common gender. The most committed sexual egalitarian (and I would put myself in that number) may still find "he or she" arhythmic. "He," which in English has traditionally been the pronoun of common gender as well as the masculine pronoun, cannot but sound a bit masculine. Some consequently now favor "she" for common gender, notwithstanding its even more noticeably feminine connotation. Until our language has evolved beyond this impasse, the best counsel still seems to me the simplest: "he" as the singular of "they." In the same spirit, and without pretending to complete consistency here, I some-times use "man" in the traditional generic sense of "the human being." Readers who disagree, as some surely shall, are invited to read "he or she" wherever "he" is not obviously masculine.

I should like here to pause and express my appreciation to some of the friends and colleagues who gave me their philosophical help and their personal encouragement. With John Bacon first of all, I enjoyed long hours of discussion that greatly refined my sense of these problems and directed me to important sources all along the way. His help was indispensable. Much of the research for this book was done during my sabbatical year 1982–83, when I was a research affiliate at the Department of Traditional and Modern Philosophy of the University of Sydney. The generous hospitality and guidance offered me that year were of much assistance to my thinking through the problem of conceptual foundations, especially in the invigorating context of tireless philosophical give and take at staff club luncheons and departmental colloquia. Also beneficial that year were several talks with members of the Department of General Philosophy of the University of Sydney. In Sydney, it is a pleasure to thank particularly David M. Armstrong, David C. Stove, and Lloyd Reinhardt. Elisabeth Gross kindly met with me on several occasions to discuss the post-structuralist movement. The philosophy colloquia at Brooklyn College and at the University of North Carolina at Chapel Hill provided early opportunities to read sections of the first two chapters, and to get expert criticism. My colleagues at the Philosophy Department of Brooklyn College gave me the chance to work through some of the puzzles of this book in a congenial and informed environment. Among colleagues in The City University of New York, at Brooklyn College particular thanks go to Malcolm Brown, Elmer Sprague, Paul Taylor, Mary Wiseman, and, at Hunter College, to Joan Stambaugh. For enlightened reflections on the connection between legal and ethical issues, I am much indebted to Milton Schubin.

As footnotes may partially indicate, many others were supportive, in very many ways. Sandy Deak was a tactful and impeccable typist. Jane Cullen, whom it has been my good fortune to have as editor and friend, has been a disciplined, keen-sighted, and all the while profoundly encouraging guide. To all these people, and some I have not mentioned here, who taught me that philosophy is a form of friendship, and that friendship is enhanced by philosophy, I want to express my gratitude.

PART ONE

Conceptual Foundations

CHAPTER ONE

Getting Round to the Story

Ideals, Fictional and Rational

WHAT IS EVIL about human actions, I will contend, is that aspect of them that intentionally obscures, disrupts, or deflects the ideal thread of plot in human lives. To deserve to be called "evil," the doer must in some degree detect the ideal story line that could belong to his victim. Agents are good, then, insofar as they try to realize the ideal stories that belong to themselves, or to anyone affected by them. These notions of good and evil obviously concern the character of persons. They have to do with the effects of actions mainly insofar as these help shape the characters of those affected, or rebound on the agent to help shape him.

The ideality of the thread of plot in a life story is not conceived here as a merely fictive component of the agent's self-interpretation. Rather, the influence of the thread of plot that the idealistic agent tries to make out in his life is rational, in that it makes optimal sense of its materials, and active, in that it continues to guide the series of his actions. The rationality envisaged in the present context should be distinguished from its acquisitive sense of economy of means in the realization of ends arbitrarily sought or retained.

When one discerns an ideal thread of plot, whether in someone else's life or in one's own, one is not simply trying to get that life segment to fit the pattern of a favorite novel, poem, epic, myth, or arrangement of icons. In other words, the ideal does not become one on account of merely aesthetic preferences in the idealist. To clarify the point, we might try to characterize the merely aesthetic preference, omitting reference to aesthetic *judgment*, which does not necessarily come into account here.

3

Aesthetic response may in part be reductively explained as enjoyment in the exercise of biologically innate capacities to transform perceptual stimuli into useful information.[1] Insofar as it is only that, aesthetic responsiveness would be one key instrumentality of a life story, but the important thing would be the further use one made of the "information." If such is aesthetic response in the minimal sense, far more complex aesthetic resources are put in play when one settles down to the enjoyment of a good book from the period of the novel's heyday. Consider a book by Jane Austen, Charles Dickens, or Henry James. The more sympathetic (i.e., the good) characters in such books have to be understood partly in the light of their relatively admirable purposes. Suspenseful plots work out the question of whether those purposes shall be thwarted or realized. In such a reading experience, the characters are represented as having already transformed and put to exemplary further uses the perceptual information of *their* lives. To have aesthetic preferences for one such story over another is something different from liking an abstract painting. It is to stand, as it were, in the margin between entire shadow lives, and apparently to choose between them. One gets the luxurious impression that lives one might have lived could have been lent beneficent influence in just that way, or villainously robbed of it in just this way.

Part of the pleasure of reading Austen, Dickens, or James comes from the sense that these stories are already given to us. Apart from the price of the book and a little attention, we don't have to pay for them. On the question of the novel's appeal, Henry James writes, "man combines with his eternal desire for more experience an infinite cunning as to getting his experience as cheaply as possible. He will steal it whenever he can" (James, 1900, p. 33). By the vicarious ease with which they are enjoyed, and the uncertain light they shed on the reader's efforts to sum *himself* up, fictional idealizations of life stories can be distinguished from their nonfictional counterparts.

The contrast we have drawn is a rough-and-ready one. One can imagine a science-fiction case where the distinction between the story of one's own life and the story inside the covers of a novel would collapse. If one were to browse in a bookstore and notice, thumbing through a new novel by chance, that it told the page-by-page story of one's own life, getting purposes, secrets, and reveries letter perfect, and if one experienced this discovery with the compressed suffering, surprise, relief, joy, or whatever that one had actually gone through over a lifetime—well, then, *this* rough-and-ready distinction between real stories and fictional stories would collapse.[2] It sometimes does happen that one has the uncanny, exalted feeling of reading one's own story in a novel. When that happens, the distinction does collapse.

But, unlike the science-fiction example, it collapses only in part and momentarily for the normal reader.

The distinction also collapses in part when one considers the kind of work that goes into writing a good piece of fiction. Picture the serious writer who has ransacked memory for stored impressions that can become fragments of incipient stories. By a different effort of controlled, attentive *letting go,* he releases these fragments to assemble and live out their unknown plot lines. Sometimes he supervises his production from above, sorting and changing in conformity with canons of aesthetic judgment. But at other times he feels surprised, overpowered, and dragged behind the self-moving substances he has released. He may be very worried as to whether he can spring free when they have crossed the finish line. And his worries may be well founded, psychologically. But it must be said, when all the writer's genies have come out of all his bottled memories, that no actual person has been created by him, to have the fictional character's impressions, form his intentions, or be held accountable for his actions. The only actual story that has been put in jeopardy is the writer's real and nontransferable life story, whose shaped happenings he has taken apart and reconverted into raw material for fiction.

In other words, fictional stories are not made or tested the same way as real stories. If it were not so, both fictional stories and real stories would require a different analysis than they presently do. In the science-fiction case, the supposed fictional story was *not* one and should not have been placed under "novels" in the rack. If the story had been written by the browser's ex-wife, or psychoanalyst, the browser would perhaps be entitled to sue. But if the story was committed to paper in good faith, then we can make the science-fiction supposition that the unknown author was himself the victim of a queer mixup, setting down what he *believed* were the inspired fancies of his muse, but what was in fact the videotape of someone else's life, telepathically replayed on the author's mental screen. So the science-fiction case is not an exception to the rough-and-ready rule that differently combined causes are at work in making real and fictional stories, and that different consequences result from making the one or the other. We conclude that a distinct sort of understanding is relevant to each, though we may not be able to make the distinction precise in every detail.

The kind of story that lends ideality to a human being's life has here been distinguished from fictive stories by the *nonvicariousness* of its enjoyment and its production. The kind of story that one would do well actually to live would also be a distinctively *rational* story. But the rationality here in view is not the kind exhibited by those who act with maximal efficiency to implement purposes that have already hardened in the mold. Ruthless consistency is fully compatible with evil, as has frequently been noted. It has affinities too with settled aesthetic preferences, in that one holds fast to one's course, no matter what prompted it to be chosen in the first place.[3]

There are different types of livable rationality. The relevant contrast to draw here is not between ruthless consistency, on the one hand, and behaviors and purposes that make no conscious effort whatever at consistency, on the other. If there are behaviors and purposes like that, which the agent remembers over time but disclaims from moment to moment without apology, they would be decidedly atypical of human behavior as a whole, probably dangerous to the agent and his fellows, and at worst a sort of limiting case of practical unreason. In sum, the relevant contrast to draw here is not the one between economic reason and madness. The contrast is, rather, between the rationality of hardheaded consistency and the rationality of corrigible, forward-and-backward-looking approximations to an ideal thread of plot in one's life.

By progressive and corrigible approximations, the agent makes a reasonable effort to save whatever made sense about his earlier purposes. One saves the sense of them by integrating them within a wider fabric of purposes. The successor purposes make one better able to handle what one intended to handle earlier, and also better able to explain one's earlier purposes. There is plenty of evidence that this is how normal people behave anyway.

(Some of the experimental evidence that even young children overcome impulses, solve problems, make plans, *and have a pretty good idea how they do all this,* is discussed in Mischel and Mischel [1977, pp. 52ff]. In the same volume on moral psychology, one can compare too Alston's finding that there is enough continuity between an agent's discrete motivations to warrant talk of at least two "motivational systems," rational and sensual, hierarchically ordered [1977, pp. 83, 86]. Alston holds that the principles by which the agent controls lower-level wants must be rationally *regulated,* even if his ethical principles were acquired irrationally. Similarly, Wolf, another essayist in that volume, finds essential to psychological well-being the conscious effort to integrate desires in a "highly complex configuration . . ." [1977, pp. 212, 216]. The same sort of reference to the person as crucially involved in the conscious integration of his purposes is in McCall, another contributor, who describes those complex purposes as a "dynamic, hierarchically organized system of social identities . . ." that experimental subjects "will knowingly pay a very high price" to maintain [1977, pp. 278, 281]. Even Gergen, the contributor who thinks the effort at accurate self-conceptualization hopeless, reads his conclusions off the evidence of frequent and blundering attempts at it [1977, pp. 155f, 165f]. Indeed, if those attempts were to stop *because* one became convinced of their futility, the sincerity of them would be only underscored thereby.)*

In this effort to make sense of our purposes, what is it that any of us want, finally? Is it to do something, or to grasp something? Or is it to understand something? Or again, is it to become something? Can we find out, by holding on to any Ariadne's knotted thread of recollected motivations, how any of us got to the place where we are now? What was it that any of us *wanted* to begin with, that got us all the way to here? When one tries to answer such questions, one sees first the doings and the graspings that one is now involved in. These get referred back to earlier remembered attempts to grasp-by-doing or grasp-by-refusing what one's parents or guardians wanted for one, and concomitantly for themselves. There is no earliest memory without its freight of guesswork, having reference to a complex situation that one was trying, with inadequate means, to size up. The primitive graspings and doings that set one on one's present course could not have been *persisted in* as mere insignificant behaviors, or raw surges of feeling. However one arrived at one's earliest interpretations of self and world, whether these were partial translations into natural and gesture language of inferential abilities encoded in the young organism, or introjections of socially proffered inferences as to what one was up to, or both, the past has to be reconstructed out of its interpretations.

The precise questions of how the interpretive layering process works in children, or by what stages it proceeds, are in the last analysis empirical. But there seems to be a measure of agreement among experimental and philosophical psychologists that the child is early launched on a lifelong task of figuring himself and his world out, a task that can be done well or badly, but cannot be bypassed. (Cf. Fodor, 1975, pp. 65, 88–94, and Merleau-Ponty, 1960, pp. 109ff, 136f, 151–55.) One need hardly add that this consensus is introspectively plausible as well. Finally, the point about interpretations or hypotheses, childish or other, is that they are not ordinarily self-encased. Rather, any set of them will soon require further interpretations or hypotheses, whose generalizations are broader, whose applications are more detailed.

---

*I am grateful to Graeme Marshall for bringing the Mischel volumes in moral psychology to my attention.

It stood to reason that one moved, and was propelled, beyond the parental orbit and up through the successive layers of skilled interpretations made accessible in the culture. The penalties for not accepting this course of education would have been severe. Nevertheless, one was not absolutely forced to accept it. In fact, the degree of self-monitoring and self-encouragement that was required was far from negligible. Remembering all that was really involved, the miserable and tedious climb, it is plausible to say that one moved to the level of cultured interpretations *deliberately*.

But what in the world did one want, in all this desperate (that is, half-deliberate, half-forced) striving, to pass one's exams, to jump one's hurdles, and—at last, at last—get what was coming to one? Surely it was not the objects of these doings and graspings that were wanted, *originally*. However, one recalls that no definite state of affairs was or could have been wanted originally. At the outset, one was surrounded by what others believed, wanted, and could implement, but what could scarcely be fathomed by oneself. Also, one was finely netted in one's own not-yet-interpreted, malleable propensities. In sum, it is only over the long term that the question of what one wanted at the outset could have an answer. The answer to the question of what we wanted at the outset can only lie in what we *have done* with what we wanted at the outset.

Unfortunately, even this method of decoding lifelong intentions promises frustration. The same string of impressive achievements might have been straightforwardly intended by one agent and deployed as a device of self-concealment by another. So it is not enough to look just at what we have done in the world, particularly where what is being decoded is the hidden thread of purposes in the outward works. On the other hand, it has just become apparent that we could not decode the initial purposes, from which the rest follow, except *in terms of* the outward works. So we seem to be at an impasse.

The present impasse feels both mysterious and a little fateful. The questions (What in the world do I really want? and What, in that connection, have I been up to?) do not seem inconsequential. On the other hand, they do not seem to have answers, not really deep-going answers. It's perfectly possible to find such questions boring, ridiculous, and insoluble. But in so finding, one has made a certain choice as to how one wants to deal with one's own purposes and works, namely, *without trying to get to the bottom of them*. It is also possible to keep the impasse firmly before one's mind, without trying to gratify the curiosity that first led one to the impasse. One cannot tell what one purposed except through one's works. But the works by themselves are not transparent as to the purposes that lay behind them.

In confronting the impasse without exiting from it, one keeps alive to the possibility of mystical, aesthetic, or other nonrational exits. The trouble with such exits, if they are taken as exits from the more ordinary channels of information, is that they not only do not necessarily facilitate one's getting to the bottom of one's purposes and works, they may involve one in the abandonment of both. No matter how attractive the rewards for the sake of which one loses grasp on one's story, the loss of such grasp cannot itself be recommended. One would have no standpoint (or only a covert standpoint) from which to make even prudential judgments.

If one were a certain type of mystic, aesthete, or existentialist, one could conceivably put in brackets norms by reference to which people are helped to help each other, and discouraged from harming each other, on the grounds that these norms are merely sanctioned by convention. Illustrative of this possibility might be some of Heidegger's vagaries, as reflected on in the interesting biography of Hannah Arendt by Young-Bruehl (1982, pp. 69, 218, 443f). Nevertheless, to try to discredit the founders of existentialism solely on the grounds of their irresponsible political flights or erratic personal tendencies would be to overwork this point. Humdrum examples will serve just as well or ill to put the point across, the point being that it is perilous to try to uncover the purposes of one's life by predominantly non-reasonable means. (For philosophical examples of Heidegger's over-subtle blurring of the distinction between consciencelessness and authenticity, there is however also *Being and Time* [1927, pp. 328f, 333f].) Putting the case of Heidegger or Sartre aside, even if (as a closet mystic, say) one retained conventional standards in a provisional and prudential way, one could be partly self-subverted by a felt gap between one's matter-of-fact account of the day's business and one's anomic sense of where one really stood personally. In any case, and however one resolves the question, it still seems that *attitudes taken toward the question* of what one really wants in life can be themselves extremely consequential.

The first two attitudes have involved partial frustration of the question's literal intent, which was *to get an answer*. In the first frustrating attitude, one drops the question by finding it unanswerable. In the second frustrating attitude, one bypasses the question by allowing it to open one to predominantly nonrational responses. There is, however, a third possible attitude that seems worth considering here. One might *persist in a lifelong curiosity* about what one has really been up to. If one did persist in it, how could this curiosity be gratified? Since neither works nor intentions, taken by themselves, can shed sufficient light on the question, the thing to do may be to take the entirety of a life as a persistent effort to decode itself, or as a persistent renunciation of that effort, or as something in between. In other words, the key intention is the forward-and-backward intention of self-knowledge. Curiosity, or the lack of it, is perhaps the one thing one *can* confidently trace back into one's remotest beginnings. Puzzling incidents will tend to stand out in memory. The way one combined one's forces to keep curiosity alive at such moments, or to shelve it, has had its extensions into the present moment of retrospection. One either has the heart to try to remember, or one does not, and either fact tells much about the past-become-present.

Suppose, then, one finds that one is able to view one's own life as the living out of lifelong curiosity about oneself. The curiosity felt in the present moment strikes sparks of curiosity along the way into the past. The following remarks from Buber serve to illustrate the third possible attitude:

> What we are dealing with here is generically different from what is called self-analysis in modern psychology. The latter, as is the case in general with psychological analysis in our age, is concerned to penetrate "behind" that which is remembered, to "reduce" it to the real elements assumed to have been "repressed." Our business is to call to mind an occurrence as reliably, concretely and completely as possible, which is entirely unreduced and undissected. Naturally, the memory must be liberated from all subsequent deletions and trimmings, beautifications and demonisations; but he can do this, to whom the confrontation with himself, in the essential compass of the past, has proved to be one of the effective forces in the process of "becoming what one is." (1952, pp. 64f)

In the case of the third attitude (namely, with lifelong curiosity), what was it that we wanted, in all of our graspings and doings? Surely all of them were merely the long way, the roundabout way, the permissible way, to get to the point. The point was to do what we wanted. Or rather, it was to want and to do what it belonged to us uniquely to want and to do. All we could have wanted was to be ourselves, in other words.

(Contrast this with the science-fiction case of the self for whose functional parts machine replicas have been carefully substituted, and which then goes through all the replicable paces of the original. Recall, for example, Dennett's reflections on such a science-fiction case:

> Now if subtracting the supposed self-symbol and feeling of personal consciousness left [human-looking automaton] Ralph's control structure basically intact—so that we on the outside would never be the wiser, for instance, and would go on engaging Ralph in conversations, enlisting his cooperation, and so forth—we would be back to the beginning and the sense that there is no *point* to a self-symbol—no work for it to do. . . ." (1981, p. 267)

The science-fiction case seems to be one that completes in imagination the partial predicaments of real individuals when they go through their daily chores mechanically, the heart being elsewhere. Aside from flattering the contemporary sense of illimitable technical virtuosity, the science-fiction case also flatters cynicism, by suggesting that if one could simply go through life minimally conscious, everything as routinized as possible, all would be well; nostalgia and anxiety would be calmed. One might call this particular way of not wanting to be oneself *machine-envy*.)

In sum, if one still has curiosity about oneself, then chances are one has always had it. One hasn't let it get killed. It has been the animating fire of one's life. Again and again, one has come back to that curiosity. That was why one wanted to get to the bottom of what was originally asked of one. One couldn't get to the bottom by taking a nosedive, though that was tempting. The self does not actually become more accessible to itself by dropping out of and under the stages of acculturation. On the contrary, it becomes more manipulable, heavy with the freight of other people's unflattering interpretations of what it has done, and awkward from having constantly to react to others' initiatives. The picture is prettied up in nihilist fiction, as in the Russian novel *Sanine* by Artsybashev (1907), which closes with its nihilist hero leaping off the train by which he has left the town and striding into the untamed landscape. Of course the would-be real-life counterparts to Sanine would have found out sooner or later about broken ankles, local constabulary, effects of riotous living, effects of prolonged sophistry, and so forth. In real life, the self is outnumbered. It cannot play the noble savage. There is no subcultural self-knowledge.

Given the cultured character of achievable self-knowledge, and its reliance on the continuity of curiosity about the self, one can now draw the real contrast between rationality of the ideal type, and the type that we have called "economic." Rational life in the ideal sense here meant is lived between memory and the projected future, as between two connected continents that must maintain and safeguard diplomatic relations. By contrast, what the man of economic reason has done is simply sever connections with his origins by fiat, henceforth exempting himself from having to find out how near or far he is to what originally wanted. Once one recognizes that the effort at self-knowledge must make its way through the layers of interpretation and skilled implementation made accessible only in culture, one must not then forget to check back to the past in order to see whether what one wanted earlier is indeed getting progressively better expressed, recollected, and clarified in terms of what one is doing now. What once seemed executive of early intentions may come to appear partly subversive to them, when it has been tried, in act, thought-experiment, or both. Suitable modifications are called for, if one is to remain true to what one wanted in the first place. What goes on is not just a self-correction as to means, but also a self-correction as to purposes, insofar as the latter prove dependent on discredited means, or in some other way inadequately qualified. On the other hand, the man of economic reason shows just that sort of contempt for what he wanted in the first place that severs the living connection between his origins and his contemporary strivings.

To sever that connection is minimally to become—with a sort of sad-sack exemption from further appeal—one more adult in the prosaic world of adults. This is just what most of us must have once hoped, Peter Pan fashion, never to become. (On the other hand, the man of childlike homesickness for origins has also disappointed his early hopes, since what he wanted at the start surely went beyond what he then *was,* an unformed being in his parents' shade.) In the minimal, or sad-sack case of severed connections, we can suppose some degree of passive acceptance of conventional goals, which in turn suggests that the sad-sack adult has at least purposed to keep alive in himself title to wistful affection for some of the adults who first modeled human values for him. At least he does not utterly repudiate them. We can say that such loyalty-by-default is itself a kind of wordless purpose. One could do worse. The man of economic reason has done at least somewhat worse, and at most a lot worse.

We have characterized the man of economic reason as having cut himself off from curiosity about his early purposes, in order no longer to have to find out how his present projects clarify or obscure his earlier ones. His present projects, therefore, have the air of being launched *from the present* and taking only the present circumstances into consideration. As he carries less baggage, the man of economic reason moves faster than his memory-laden, self-interrogating counterparts. Naturally, he can often be more effective than they in particular projects. Viewed from inside, however, his course is not a reasonable one.

It is unreasonable to bring all one's cleverness to bear on doing something over the long term that one can't be sure one wants to do. Since one can no more get rid of one's deep-lying preferences and puzzlements by succeeding at an adventitious project than one can get rid of one's shadow by flying off to foreign parts, the more reasonable thing to do would be—first and constantly—to seek an accommodation with one's self. After all, one's self won't go away in any case. Perhaps if one *could* become a machine, that might solve matters. But unfortunately, one doesn't become a machine just by so acting as to put other people in mind of one. One's "hardware" is still flesh. One's memories still cling closer than a shadow. One is still who one is, and not a machine. *Wherefore, seeing we also are compassed about with so great a cloud of witnesses,* it seems pretty clear that the life of merely economic reason is not a counter-example to the claim that the storylike life is more fully the reasonable one.

For clarification of the distinction I am drawing here between economic reason and the rationality of backward-and-forward approximations to an ideal story, one might compare Charles Taylor's similar distinction between "weak" and "strong evaluation" (1977, pp. 104, 107, 115). For Taylor, what he calls "weak evaluation" is prompted by a concern with pleasurable outcomes, and "strong evaluation" by a concern with the sort of person I should be. However, what I have called "economic reason" can operate even where one makes Taylor's strong evaluations. For example, if I act shrewdly on a fanatical ideal, or an implacable sense of what is due me, such actions may be prompted by the rigid desire to be a certain kind of person and may show hedonic restraint, both characteristics of Taylor's strong evaluation. Yet such actions would show the efficiency in pursuit of fixed goals that I have called "economic reason." Of course Taylor's discussion rules out by implication that the hardhead or fanatic could illustrate "strong evaluation" in his preferred sense. But to show why, I think one must not merely note the difference in the outcomes sought, as Taylor does, but also mark a difference in the *kind of rationality* invoked. That is what I have tried to do here.

If the nonfictional aspect of an ideal life story has been at least provisionally underscored here, and its dialectically rational aspect distinguished from merely economic or acquisitive reason, we can move on to a further question. What precisely is storylike about a rational life? What do we mean here by a "story," and how can we recognize one? At minimum, a story is a purpose transformed into enough experience to allow that purpose to understand itself a little better.

Does one live a story, then, when one finds or fails to find a proof in logic? Let us distinguish among purposes here. A computer may be given formal symbols to manipulate in accordance with effective rules. This is not a story, although a story contains elements analogous to the computational procedure. A medical technician can intend to test for results predicted by a hypothesis about normal electrical activity of the brain and accordingly administer the required electroencephalogram. This is not a story either, although something partly like that happens in a story. A lawyer can intend to defend his case, or a philosopher his views. These are not stories, not even when carried out, though either enacted purpose may figure in a story. One can put to the test the intention of tying one's shoelaces. That is not a story. Usually, it is not even a conscious intention, though it is a happening that goes without saying in real stories.

All the purposes we just mentioned above are rational. And they all may figure in stories. Yet they are not, in and of themselves, storylike. To live entirely in terms of such purposes as these would be humanly possible only if a human being were very much like a machine. One could also attempt it insofar as one were given over to such fixed purposes as are served by economic reason, but it is not clear how successful (as opposed to persuasive) one could be in all the given cases. It is difficult to want nothing more than effectively to exercise a skill. Even if one could want to do only that, doing only that is not storylike.

Does one live a story, then, if one lives *dramatically,* springing surprises, capturing stage center, involving others in one's caprices and intrigues? No. This gets nothing done that was originally one's own. It is third-hand stuff, life imitating fiction. But how can one recognize a story, then? The answer is that one can't immediately. A story plays itself out over time. It is a long, drawn-out thing, often a hidden thing. It involves its own mistakes, as to its own proper course. But whether one is living one's own story or has lost it is pretty obvious introspectively to oneself, and can become fairly clear over a course of longer close acquaintance or friendship with another. In sum, the rational purpose that is storylike is the purpose to become (and incidentally to find out what is involved in becoming) *a certain kind of person,* namely, one's original and ongoing self. A story in our sense is *that* purpose, transformed into enough experience to allow it to understand itself a little better, or possibly a lot better.

What shall we make of "senseless" tragedies, then, whether in fiction or in life? How shall we characterize the accidental disruptions of formed purposes that, however unexpected, happen so frequently in natural and social life? Don't such disruptive happenings make stories, too, "absurd" stories, as they are called today? And if they too make stories, why does a story need a rational component? Hasn't contemporary art itself got mostly beyond a commitment to story telling, or even the display of decipherable purposes?

That art has got beyond the point of giving tacit support to certain kinds of purposes (say, some of the conventional ones, or some of the ones that can be sustained over a long stretch of time) is itself a thesis about art.[4] It is not a typical thesis in the long history of the practice. It is unlikely to have moved to their colors the cave painters of the Upper Paleolithic. Nevertheless, it has been voiced by some of the artists and critics in our time and can itself be seen as *a purpose with respect to art*. To take the thesis as true, or the purpose as also one's own, because it has been announced by some working artists and some critics is to suppose that art making and its appreciation draw on sources of insight that are unique and incorrigible (or at least are so for artists and critics who hope to separate art from decipherable purposes and story telling; the rest, despite their numbers, would be presumed not to be speaking *ex cathedra*).

This is an occasionally tempting, but I think doubtful, suggestion about authorized art and its votaries. It has a history, or anyway there are precedents for the suggestion. Thus, the view that artistic genius made truth incarnate was current in the Renaissance and shared by a number of outstanding artists then. It had its place in the hermetic program to treat man the savant, artisan-inventor, and potential magus as a conduit to the divine, separate from and equal to the clergy. The influence of the hermetic movement on artists and their works is discussed in Yates (1964, pp. 76f). Graff (1979) traces a more recent development, from post-Kantian Romanticism, which credited the artist with access to noumena, to the late nineteenth-century view that made art autonomous because the artist was the last repository of values elsewhere discredited. As art feeds off itself, daredevil fashion, the theory of it now starves it further. In formalism, art is "secularized"; art works refer only to themselves. Finally, in postmodernism, they do not even do that. What this history suggests is that art in the West had latterly been assigned too many offices, offices such as that of contacting the real and the sacred, earlier performed by metaphysics and by theology. In reaction, art, or at least some of its votaries, got disburdened of too many offices.

If we reject as implausible the view that art (and purposeless art in particular) is a key to life, what view would be likelier to be the right one? The answer is that the selective perception that goes into art, like sense perception itself, is laden with the rudiments of interpretation. This is not to say that the interpretive aspect of good art is "made up" on the spot, any more than clear and striking perceptual moments are. Such incipient interpretations as surround artistic seeing or hearing may themselves have arisen from arduous, cultivated, and *controvertible* meditation on the world and the self. In sum, a claim about art or life is not warranted merely because it has been seconded by an artist or an art critic. Therefore, the deconstructionist claim about coherence between purposes (that such coherence is either adventitious with respect to the individual or accepted by the individual because he is deluded) should be examined on its own terms. It is not right merely because it may have talent to vouch for it.

Taken in its extreme and overliteral form, the claim is obviously wrong and self-refuting, since it takes active meshing of purposes even to get to the end of the sentence "I have no good-faith, coherent purposes." The larger point is that we are already born into multiply expanding networks of human purposes. To shrug any of the major ones off is therefore a purposive act, taken with regard to a counter-vailing, socially inscribed purpose, and usually defended by an elaborate rationale. (The rationale can be provided by an aesthetic theory, say, deconstructionism; a psychological theory, say, Freud's; an economic theory, say, Marx's or some other source. But provided it must be, if one is to hope to make one's way safely *out of* any prevailing network of purposes.)

There are purposes that know their own price and reward. There are purposes that do not. One has both kinds. What one does not have are purposeless tracts of time. That is, one does not have those insofar as one is mentally furnished in the usual style with long- and short-term memory, a cultural context, biological and social require-ments, technical skills, perceptual and rational capacities.

We make too much of despair. In the thick frameworks of human life despair is a *negative relation* to a context of purposes. It is not, for all that, a purposive void. The gratuitousness that has been claimed for purposes in modern fiction and experience is itself a thesis about purposes, upheld by tendentious rewritings of bygone purposes and their record of attempted enactments, which one must then work overtime to forget.

A few seasons back Jacques Derrida, the deconstructionist, gave a talk to a packed hall at the Graduate Center of The City University of New York. His talk was meant to illustrate the general claim that a wealth of insights into texts is made available by the deconstruc-tionist assumption that texts have indefinitely many possibilities for decoding, one superimposable over another, none having priority, and that life situations are not different in principle from other "texts." Such was his purpose in giving the talk, I take it. Now, the talk was unhappily marred by amplified voices from another part of the build-ing that came into the auditorium over a malfunctioning sound sys-tem. Derrida, though he certainly confronted the mishap with humor and grace, was understandably in the condition of a man restraining annoyance.

For a deconstructionist, the moment was "senseless"—but not in the sense that the deconstructionist meant before this happened. A theory that asserts the relative insignificance of the author's inten-tions to the decoding of his text cannot make sense of its author's frustration when his intention to assert *that theory* is interfered with.

What had become senseless in day-to-day terms was in fact his theory, and the author's fate at that moment could only become senseless because at that moment the author *had* a theory. So, even in this case, the "absurdity" depends on the story that the author told himself before the crisis with the sound system occurred, and it can only be recognized in terms of that story.

That the story that Derrida had told himself, about the insignificance of the author's intention and its irrelevance to the decoding of texts, might itself have been a kind of fiction, functioning at a stylized academic or bohemian distance from his real story, is a further complication, which we need not delve into at present. (What it raises is a further question about relativism—and how we can tell truth from error—fuller consideration of which will be reserved for Chapter Two.) For the present, it is enough if this illustration can help paradoxically to show that the life of the typically furnished individual is already a story, whether a true one or a false one. If "senselessness" overtakes that story, or "arbitrary" interpretations beset it, we understand that in terms of the story, as senseless (extrinsic to the story) or tragic or wicked (inimical to the story.).

How to Miss the Story

In the living out of a story there are two ways to be in default on what the story promised. The first way is the default on ideality, to be more precise, the failure to see the further story. The other way is the deliberate thwarting of the story. The latter is what I take to be evil. The former seems merely banal. Merely to fail to see ideality and actively to thwart it are not the same thing. It is quite possible to be banal and decent. It is not possible to be banal and evil, in the same respect. If one thinks it is possible, I believe that one has just not looked closely enough at one's subject.

Hannah Arendt's influential study (1964) takes the feature of "banality" to be important to the understanding of evil, at least in its totalitarian setting. A further consideration of her views is in our Chapter Six, "Banality and Originality." Here it may be remarked that although Arendt regards as *sincere*, if mindless, Eichmann's self-portrait on the stand as an *ordinary* fellow just following orders, against this stands her own assessment of "a complete lack of consistency in his thoughts and sentiments" (p. 63)—not an ordinary trait surely—and his having added to lies, self-deceptions (e.g., pp. 28f, 46ff, 49), and convenient memory lapses (e.g., p. 201) the *lie* that he could not safely have asked for a job transfer (p. 91). If, as Arendt thinks, Eichmann had an untroubled conscience, that may only show that the more warranted self-condemnation is, the more uncomfortable it gets, till finally it is too uncomfortable to be felt. So one should not confuse the ordinary person's failure to envision ideality with the subjective numbness that sets in when one has actively obliterated ideality on every hand. It is likely that Arendt's Eichmann was actually in the second condition.

The first sort of failure, which is not precisely a moral one, will detain us for the rest of this chapter. Since there are no strict experimental controls on story living or story seeing, failures to see the stories of human lives can be by-products of the broad investigative programs of the social sciences and experimental psychology, which try where possible methodically to *bracket out* such observational data as cannot be replicated under controlled conditions. These bracketed ways of seeing can be instructive up to a point. Beyond that point, such methodologically bracketed ways of seeing may be at least subjectively incompatible with the kind of seeing that goes into ideal stories. (For example, it would be hard to conduct an experiment in which information relevant to a specified choice were so disguised that subjects were led to make their choices on irrelevant grounds, *while continuing to regard one's experimental subjects primarily as persons* whom it would be wrong to manipulate.) The question of how such experiments might be conducted so as not to demean experimenters and subjects is one for ethical casuistry on the one side, and for psychological or social-scientific theory on the other. As such, it is perhaps not an absolutely insoluble question. Reasonable guidelines can be proposed. For this reason, it is not necessary to take issue directly with methodological bracketing of narrative coherence, where this is done for some instructive, presumptively scientific purpose. But, insofar as the failure to see the story forms part of a philosophical view about goodness, it deserves a closer look here.

In the English-speaking philosophical world the objection to our sort of view might sound roughly like this: "You are making an evaluative claim" (so runs the objection), "and supporting it by pointing out certain features of human experience. Since, however, not all experiences mirror the sort of thing you want to recommend, you have been forced to pick and choose your illustrations. What guides your choice of illustrative matter is a particular value judgment. You judge those linked segments of purposive behavior that meet your definition of 'stories' to be good, commendable, preferable, and so forth. What you overlook is that no quantity of illustrative material, whether drawn from fiction, autobiography, or biography, can suffice to *justify* a value judgment. On the contrary, it's your value judgment that has conferred on what you call storylike lives the title of 'good lives,' and likewise conferred on story-spoiling lives the title of 'bad' or 'evil.'

"You hope to bring additional support to your value judgment with a psychology whose most familiar textual supports would seem to be nineteenth-century novels, ignoring the Freudian evidence that many of our purposes are unconscious, also ignoring experimental evidence that people often do not know why they do what they do.[5] You seem further to maintain the essential unity of the self, something that is not introspectively evident, as Hume clearly showed. Nor has the unity of the psyche been assumed in all cultures, nor at all stages of our own culture. Nor is it presupposed as further advances in neurophysiology make more evident the merely *contingent* identity between mental events and brain events.[6]

"Your judgment of what to call 'good' and 'bad' conflicts with the ordinary meanings of such ethical terms. A few examples will make this clear enough. If your lexicon entry for 'good' were approved, it would follow that a person who had lived a useful life, made important discoveries in immunology, let us say, would not be 'good'—unless he had also become a certain kind of person. For argument's sake, let's equip our medical researcher with an array of constructive motives. Let's say he wants no other trophy for himself than the sheer joy of fathoming nature. Or let's say that he wants, quite single-mindedly, to improve the health of his fellows. By your lights, this exemplary citizen would not even be a 'good' person, because his life would lack that self-reflective quality that you happen to prize. The most selfless life would not even qualify as a 'good' life, according to you, unless the saint in question were making a constant effort to see his present purposes as a clarified realization of his earlier ones.

"In sum, you ask of your 'good' person a degree of self-involvement that might make it hard for him to do anything else *but* be a student of himself. While we are about it, I might say that the notion of 'story' seems odd, in a moral theory. There must be a reason—with some recent exceptions—it hasn't appeared in one before. We all know that a life can be filled with dramatic incident, and yet be a bad life, with damaging consequences. We know too that a life can be terribly dull and unvarying, but very good.

"Your psychology is controversial and (we suspect from your choice of novelists) goody-goody, but perhaps not more controversial than many of the going baddy-baddy ones. Your way of using familiar ethical terms is nonstandard, but perhaps you didn't mean to be giving a justification of ordinary usage. When all is said and done, one can only come back to the first point. You *can't* begin with factual premises and end up with evaluative conclusions. Not by any valid inferential argument known to man. David Hume has shown that. Sidgwick and Moore and Hare and many others have underscored the point. Moore's 'naturalistic fallacy' still *is* one, when all is said and done, and there's an end of it.

"Now what you should have done, had you wished to recommend to us a style of life, was first of all to admit that that's what you wanted to do, and taken the responsibility for it. If you had but put into the words the absurdity of your preferences, the sense of anxiety and dread that you possibly feel in committing yourself to them, and so forth, then we would have understood you. The influence of Sartre and Beckett has made itself felt over here, in the thought of R. M. Hare and some others. We might have thought your way of expressing the view somewhat at variance with its standard literary accompaniments, in Gide, and so forth. But we would not have felt obliged to oppose you on *philosophical* grounds, as we must now do. We could just have consulted our own equally absurd preferences on the question. The question of whether one wants to live like a character in a story is not an ethical question, after all."

The outstanding questions here concern the relation of evaluative terms to factual terms in general. Once that question is settled, the others can sort themselves out. The kind of psychology that is presupposed or ruled out by our criteria of good and evil is not a question that poses conceptual difficulties for our view, though it could conceivably raise empirical problems for it. (For example, certain brain states might prevent goodness from being intended; still others might allow it to be intended but prevent it from becoming visible in the world.) Likewise, a *détente* can and will be negotiated between extremist implications of the present view and common-sense views about ethics as reflected in ordinary usage. One of the tasks of the chapters on applications of this theory (Chapters Three through Seven) will be to show how familiar to common sense the theory is, when applied to concrete cases in all their detail. Indeed, it may turn out—without Berkeleyean paradox—to be the most commonsensical view of all, the view we always took, the prose we always spoke, did we but know it.

There is no coherent ethical view that does not occasionally create problems for common sense, and no common-sense view that is both internally coherent and responsive to every ethical challenge. The reader might find that for him or her, the climb between the present view and common sense is an arduous one in the coming chapters, but it cannot be found blocked *a priori*. On the other hand, the claim that the path between factual and evaluative terms is blocked *is* an *a priori* claim, and must be confronted directly and forthwith.

We have first of all to determine how factual and evaluative terms are different in kind. In the same vein, what are the links between them, and how are these links ordinarily deployed? For this purpose, let us consider the use of evaluative terms in contexts that are neither moral nor aesthetic, but strictly epistemic. Let us look at a graduated series of such contexts. On what is perhaps the simplest level, would one want to say that an *evaluation* is in play when one describes a red patch in one's sensory field as "red"? Possibly it is. The correct application of a descriptive term requires a *matching operation* between the English word "red," the property to which it refers, and the appropriate sensory stimulus. That this matching operation, or judgment, must be either wrong or right does not mean that the outcome of the judgment can be produced while bypassing the judgment itself. Perhaps a machine could make the judgment, and a feedback loop could insure that it made the right one. Nevertheless, even a machine can make a wrong judgment, calling the red stimulus "yellow." If this *possibility of error* is to be the deciding component of judgments that are evaluative, then we might be able to say that the machine makes an evaluative judgment. On the other hand, if it is held that *intentionality,* in some irreducibly conscious sense, must belong to evaluation, then perhaps we must conclude that a machine cannot make an evaluative judgment about such things as having a red patch on its "visual" buffer or internal scanner. Only a man can.

We move on to the domain of things in the world, where the intentionality of consciousness has bearing. Suppose one judges that the red patch is really "out there," is not just a sensory datum but an intentional object to which there corresponds a real flag, waving redly over Red Square, where one affirms inwardly that one is now standing. The judgment that something really is the case involves all the previously mentioned components of judgment, the matching operation, the possibility of error and intentionality, as well as the weighing of new evidence of various kinds. One remembers having got a visa, taken a plane, heard the Russian language spoken ubiquitously, seen photographs of a place looking like this in newspapers and travel brochures, located Moscow by spinning a model of the globe in one's study prior to getting packed, and so forth. It all adds up. The flag is not a hallucination. It is real and it is red. All this seems more like an evaluative judgment.

One could go further, subsuming statements about matters of fact under empirical generalizations and theories, according to criteria of simplicity, deductive confirmation from above, having test implications, and so forth. Such matchings and fittings seem even more obviously evaluative.

But what do we mean by the *evaluative* component in all this? What marks it off from other sorts of judgment, in whole or in part? Perhaps we mean that an evaluative judgment fulfills an aim and in doing so allows some room for free play of the mental powers. Thus the judgment "This (visual patch or waving flag) is red" is not evaluative in any important sense, because there is no legitimate way to differ on the point. This either is or isn't red. One is either right or wrong in saying it is. The judgment is compelled. Therefore it is not evaluative.

But aren't all judgments at least partially constrained? For example, although one has some obvious leeway in making prudential judgments, are not these constrained by one's aim in making them? If I want to get to Scotland, I might take the high road and I might take the low road. But I must go north, from London. I cannot take the road to Cornwall and preserve my aim. Similarly, if I want to help my team to win an American-style baseball game, I might try a line drive to center field. I might try to hit a home run. I can't simply strike out and preserve my aim. Within games, academic disciplines, or social conventions I have some evaluative free play. Yet it is a free play constrained by the aim of the game, discipline, or convention, and its rules.

Likewise, if I aim to be a certain kind of person, or to live a certain kind of life, some evaluative free play is involved. Yet these evaluations too will be constrained by the tools and options I must choose between, or refuse, and by how much I am willing to pay for choosing either way (or am *able* to pay, while preserving my aim). Again, the range of options is something that I cannot determine at will, nor the cost of trying to modify that range. That is, I cannot decide the cost of trying to affect my culture. Furthermore, should I wish to put to myself the question *What is the most reasonable of the ways I could choose to live?* or the other question *What is the most self-defeating of the ways I could choose to live?* there would again be certain constraints on my answers. The constraints would come from the nature of human life, viewed biologically, socially, intellectually, and so forth, the choices it in fact offers at a given historical and cultural moment, and the costs of its choices. If the ultimate choices are the ones that follow from confronting the answers to the last two questions, then they must fall on or between what really are the most reasonable or self-defeating ways to live a human life. If the choice falls on either extreme (on the most self-defeating or the most reasonable way to live), then it is a choice of what we have already called "evil" or "good."

We are now in a position to correlate moral with epistemic evaluation, at least in a rough-and-ready way. The failure to see a red sensory stimulus as "red" would have as its moral counterpart the failure correctly to identify any one of my own discrete purposes. Again, the more complex epistemic failure to notice that the red flag I see and name is out there, fluttering over Red Square, can be correlated with the moral failure to see that some introspected intention of mine has really been implemented or has not been implemented, in a series of actions I performed in the world. Furthermore, my still more complex epistemic failure to fit experiential patterns into the relevant empirical generalizations is roughly like the moral failure to see that a certain thread of connected and implemented purposes could yet be the plot of my ideal story. Finally, my epistemic failure to subsume empirical generalizations under appropriate theories would be like a moral failure to find and apply the common criteria of story-living (such as keeping curiosity about oneself alive, making earlier purposes make as much sense as they can reasonably do, and so forth), which common criteria have long-term and wide implications for my own life, and for human life generally, its analysis, and the handling of its incessant emergencies. And so likewise for the corresponding epistemic and moral successes.*

The present view, then, is that the evaluative character of assessments of fact is not different in principle from evaluation in moral matters. The evaluative criteria can be said to be "hard-wired" in Fodor's sense, or transcendental in Kant's sense, or intrinsic to human intelligence in some other sense. But, since the matching operations that link such criteria with phenomena take place at every epistemic level, we have, for all practical purposes, no raw facts at the start in any case. The problem is not, and never has been, to get by inference from raw facts to evaluative criteria or "values" and back again. The problem, on the epistemic and the moral side of the water, is to get from lower level facts-cum-evaluative operations to more general facts-cum-evaluative operations. And the proper way to do this is, inevitably, by inference—with its inductive jumps and deductive constraints.

It is true that in the epistemic case one is coming to a conclusion or a hypothesis about objective matters, whereas in the moral case one is coming to a conclusion about what to do in the light of the sort of person one decides to become, that is, the sort of story one is trying to live. But, although ethical views affect one's character and the course of one's story, one doesn't merely—as it were—"exist" one's

---

*I am indebted to Kenneth Gemes's paper, "Causal vs. Epistemic Explanation in Quine" (1983), and to the discussion afterward, for first bringing to my attention the possibility of correlating moral and epistemic value judgments and for showing some of their structural similarities (not the ones I have emphasized here).

ethical views. First of all, one holds them, *as* views. (They are the *reasons* one thinks it better to try for one story rather than another.) There are decipherable disagreements between people who hold different ethical views, and each of the conflicting views is at least in part and in principle open to argument. Where the argument breaks down, one can usually show *why* it has. A book like this one (that is, a book on moral theory) would be inconceivable if ethical disagreements were in principle impermeable to reasoned argument. But if they are permeable to reasoned argument, then moral views are, like epistemic views, views about what is true—here, about what is truly named "good" and "evil" in character and action. The questions of how near we can get to the truth, and of how universal any human truth may be, are further questions, but they are no less questions for epistemology than for ethics.

The Denaturing of Good

There is one other alleged side to the gap that is supposed to separate facts from values. This side holds moral criteria to be altogether in a class by themselves. They would not be knowable by ordinary means, not employable in the carrying out of ordinary inferential procedures, and not open to rational interrogation. The immurement of moral criteria is defended on the ground of the "nonnatural" character of these criteria. This extremely puzzling, not to say conversation-stopping, view of goodness has been abroad since G. E. Moore's landmark study, *Principia Ethica* (1903). In its own way *Principia Ethica* made moral experience as autonomous as formalism made aesthetic experience, opening possibilities of ethical anomie comparable to those that the postformalists have since opened up in aesthetics. (On this point see Mary Midgley, 1981, pp. 59, 64.)

Moore does not begin his program for the autonomy of ethics in the middle of the air, or riding on a crest of Edwardian *Zeitgeist*. Like any philosopher of substance, he works with his eye on individual predecessors. Some of Moore's key points are taken over from the illustrious nineteenth-century Cambridge Utilitarian Henry Sidgwick, to whom we ought now to turn briefly. In Sidgwick's *Methods of Ethics* (1874), it is argued that the good is not found in any natural structure, but in the strictly private sphere of pleasurable states of consciousness (pp. 395ff). Since all sorts of programs for self-development might result in such private states, Sidgwick determines that psychology lies outside the province of ethics (1874, pp. 91f, 179, 182–90, 374–79, 412). Since, further, motives of acts may have nothing to do with the hedonic states that result from them, philosophical ethics is again and yet again not to be concerned with motives (1874, pp. 205, 372, 394).

In truth, Sidgwick performed a great work of purification on ethics. Following from this work, the psyche is out of it. Culture is out of it. The ethically—or perhaps we should say spiritually—superior man or woman is most decidedly out of it (1874, pp. 138, 174). The human species is out of it. Nature is out of it. No spatio-temporal objects or living beings can be in it nor form intrinsic parts of it. By the time G. E. Moore was to come on the nearly bare stage, he would have little to do beyond insisting that the theme of ethics is after all not even subjective as Sidgwick thought, but "objective," its object being something strangely "nonnatural," "simple," and "indefinable." The consequences would be blazingly clear to a little child, but perhaps only to a little child. If goodness in Moore is not a part of nature and is no longer even a state of mind, as at least it was in Sidgwick, then it will come more and more to resemble a beautiful nullity, giving our moral judgments less warrant than the emperor's new clothes gave him.

Let us turn back to take a somewhat closer look at Sidgwick's part of the denaturing operation, since it left the deepest marks on subsequent philosophical work in ethics. It is in his account of the desirable subjective states that Sidgwick's ethics seems least happy, and indeed it is there that Moore himself finds fault with him. Pleasure, Sidgwick admits, is precisely what we seldom seek as such (1874, pp. 49, 53), what evolution would not have programmed us to seek in disregard of material results (p. 53), what gives us enjoyment only when we *don't* seek it directly (pp. 51f), and what—when it comes to fine-grained choices—we can't even rank, since rankings require direct comparison of pleasures, and these cannot "be felt together, precisely as they have been felt separately" (p. 146).

If Sidgwick meant pleasure to provide the standard by which to rectify our moral intelligence, it does not turn out to be very handy for that purpose. In fact, it vanishes in the hand. What is more, Sidgwick himself does not seem to use it much when he gets down to business. For practical purposes, he defines it as the feeling that intelligent beings prefer (1874, p. 127) and that is made available to them by the instruments of culture, power, wealth, and family (p. 135). In short, what "pleasure" comes down to is simply the state of consciousness consequent on the exercise of the most reasonable options available to favored members of a high culture.

This is all very well, but it is most imprecise, and also wobblingly relative. We are offered neither method nor criteria for determining which options accessible in our own cultures are *actually* (as opposed to socially) preferable on rational grounds. Nor have we any way of deciding *which cultures* offer the more reasonable options. Instead, where there is a clash between values, Sidgwick refers us to the utilitarian standard, the same that earlier vanished in the hand.

By taking the psyche, exemplary individuals, culture and history, our species and nature, *out* of ethics, Sidgwick has diverted our gaze from the real relations of dependency in which we stand and must make our important ethical judgments. By his complacent emphasis on "the phenomenal," we are discouraged from feeling the weight and taking the measure of our circumstances. In the real stories of our lives, it can happen that we will confront a choice of fragile goods, unpredictable sources of harm, differently impinging threats to reputation, self-esteem, and effectiveness, that there will not be many options, that the options will get fewer as they get better understood, that there will hardly be time to review our motives but they will need reviewing if we are not to be most expensively self-deceived.

I assume here that I am describing the sort of situation that ethical thinking may clarify "in a cool hour." What I notice about such thinking, whether it occurs in a cool or a heated hour, is that at no point does it find the ranking of disembodied pleasure phenomena *relevant*. Such ranking may be relevant when one is deciding whether or not to take an aspirin, or whether to bring on or send away the dancing girls (or boys). I cannot imagine that such rankings have anything at all to do with what concerns most people insofar as they are ethically constrained. For the latter kind of concern centers on how the story that they are living will turn out, and whether they will, as Bishop Butler puts it so simply and so well, "die the death of the righteous" (1751, vol. 2, Sermon VII, para. 16).

As we have said, Moore takes over from Sidgwick the autonomy of ethical criteria. But he takes the denaturing operation several steps beyond Sidgwick's. Sidgwick is a robust Victorian, concerned to help the reader decide hard cases in casuistry (albeit with the help of an admittedly porous utilitarian standard), whereas for Moore, practical problems are not the business of a treatise on ethics (1903, pp. 2ff, 20). Rather, its guiding questions must be strictly theoretical, to wit: "What kind of things ought to exist for their own sakes?" and "What kind of actions ought we to perform?" (1903, p. viii). For the second kind of question, a Sidgwickian calculus of results is the only thing applicable. And that turns on the answer to the first question, which will tell us what results are most nearly good.

Moore's first question is, however, disorienting, suggesting as it does that we command a cosmic vantage point, from which we can determine absolutely and for the whole world what ought to exist. If we made Moore's question into a real one, about the sorts of things that we, *from our standpoint,* ought reasonably to support, it might seem obvious to us that certain kinds of people are the primary things to support, endorse, and work toward becoming. (As for other living creatures, it would be hubristic for us to decide whether they "ought" or "ought not" to exist—except where they impinge on our well-being.) Since, by the same token, it might be apparent that kinds of chains of intentional acts are causally connected to the formation of cor-responding kinds of human character, Moore's separation of the study of action from the study of persons in his second question might seem equally unsatisfactory, from an ethical standpoint. In sum, if we began with a real question, instead of two false questions, ethics might forthwith return to its old place, as the central study of and for man.

Suppose, however, we follow Moore's line and try with him to separate goodness from persons and their life stories. Let us go along with Moore in assuming that what exists makes absolutely no dif-ference to the nature of goodness (1903, pp. 113, 124f, 127f). Let us agree with him that goodness is on the following grounds undefinable: (1) definition involves analysis into parts, while goodness is, self-evi-dently, simple; (2) definition involves translating the *definiendum* into other (and natural) terms, exposing the *definiens* to the open question, "But is *it* good, or isn't it?" (1903, pp. 15ff). And let us further assume, with Moore, that the actions we ought to perform are just those that conduce to "good effects," or the appearing in the world of instances of goodness. That is, character is not important. As Moore puts it, apart from my skill in making good's instances appear, "neither my various performances of . . . duty, nor my disposition to perform them, have the smallest intrinsic value" (1903, p. 176). Let us provisionally concede all this and see where it leads.

We draw together our eyebrows. We close our eyes. We try to see it, goodness, a small flicker on the mental screen. Now, can we get any clearer than *this* about it? Moore encourages us to believe that we can. We can look forward to lengthy and clarifying discussion, at least about what things in the world are instances of goodness (1903, pp. 9f). But I wonder where he gets the warrant for this assurance to the reader. How does he know when to call any particular set of instances "good"?

The autonomy of Moore's ethical criterion becomes most troublesome when we try to set up the connection between the alleged nonnatural quality of goodness and its alleged instances. Moore compares the quality of goodness to yellow, in that both are simple and therefore defined ostensively. But yellow, unlike goodness, is equally simple in its instances, as well as being incontrovertibly there or not there in any particular alleged instance. Again, Moore's goodness has sometimes (though not by Moore) been compared to Plato's Idea of the Good.[7] However, while Plato's Good is also non-phenomenal and also picked out by ostension, the ostension can only be done after the trainee has climbed up an educational ladder whose rungs are clearly specified. We are told in *The Republic* which aesthetic, affective, volitional, and intellectual qualities are to be renounced or progressively incorporated and surpassed as we get nearer the Good, and this is practical information. (Thus we learn from Plato that it is not good merely to lie around experiencing the flux of phenomena. Also, it is not good *enough* merely to have deductive knowledge, without putting its premises under dialectical review. And so forth.) Finally, we have, in Socrates, a detailed, animated illustration of a good man, shown going through all kinds of paces. By contrast, Moore's "Platonism," if that's what he has given us, is vastly less instructive. I don't claim that this is because Moore is less talented than Plato. I claim that it is so because Moore, unlike Plato, has a notion of goodness that is not extrapolated out of the human struggle for rational self-dominion. It is not enough to rest on Plato's laurels, after one has thrown away his ladders.

All we can do with Moore's goodness, really, is note how it *doesn't* relate to its instances. To this end, we can say that it is not the *superlative* case of its instances, as Dickens's Little Dorritt might be of filial piety. It is not the *smooth or ideal* case of its instances, as the concept of a straight line might be of the ruler-drawn line, or the concept of a frictionless moving ball might be of any real case of the law of inertia. It is not made *intelligible* in and through its instances, the way a rule of the propositional calculus is understood insofar as it gets used in proofs. It is not, like Kant's moral law, the *categorical* rule for delivering the instances, since Moore denies that the instances can be delivered by any universal principle of action (1903, pp. 146, 149; 1912, pp. 97–107).

How then does Moore pick out the instances? His "method of isolation" is to ask, about anything up for the asking, whether it would be "'a good thing'—that that state of affairs should exist, *even if nothing else were to exist besides*" (1912, p. 68). Like the opening question of *Principia Ethica* ("What kind of things ought to exist for their own sakes?"), the question is disorientingly cosmic. Surveying the whole world from an unspecified vantage point, Moore asks us to rank states of affairs that will benefit or harm no one, and rank them in terms of no specified criterion. How we could even perform Moore's thought experiment, except by imagining such states of affairs to be of potential benefit or harm to someone or something, Moore does not tell us. However, the proceeds of this thought experiment (that we doubt ever got conducted) are Moore's delivered instances of goodness. He calls these instances "organic wholes," although their parts have no functional relation to each other, or to any larger system. They are simply collections of qualities that are said more nearly to instantiate "goodness" together than apart. Typically they combine "the pleasures of human intercourse and the enjoyment of beautiful objects" (1903, p. 188). *Principia Ethica* ends with brief descriptions of the instances, which make clear that they are found in the friendship of physically attractive and erudite people, who would do well to aim at goods affecting themselves and realizable in the present, rather than goods affecting the wider polity, or even themselves over the long term (1903, pp. 166f).

A good deal could be said against such "organic wholes," in connection with the possibilities that they offer for social and personal irresponsibility. Some of what could be said has already been urged against Sidgwick's predecessor notion of desirable states of consciousness. But the main thing wrong with Moore's instances of good is the unreasonableness of the method of their selection. John Maynard Keynes has written a memoir of Moore's first devotees in the Bloomsbury circle, which is so sympathetic and yet so sharp, that he must be given room yet again to illustrate this point.

> How did we know what states of mind were good? This was a matter of direct inspection, of direct unanalysable intuition about which it was useless and impossible to argue. . . . In practice, victory was with those who could speak with the greatest appearance of clear, undoubting conviction and could best use the accents of infallibility. Moore at this time was a master of this method—greeting one's remarks with a gasp of incredulity— *Do* you *really* think *that*, an expression of face as if to hear such a thing said reduced him to a state of wonder verging on imbecility, with his mouth wide open and wagging his head in the negative so violently that his hair shook. Oh! he would say, goggling at you as if either you or he must be mad; and no reply was possible. (1949, pp. 243f)*

A final reflection on the unreasonableness of Moore's method seems due him. One of Moore's strongest reasons for rejecting ethical relativism was that it would convert ethical judgments into simple reports of what individuals or groups were actually feeling. Being true

---

*I am indebted to D. C. Stove for bringing Keynes's "My Early Beliefs" to my attention. Keynes's story and its point have been noted by Mary Midgley and others.

relative to the reporter, such reports couldn't be wrong, if the reporter were candid. Also, if two reporters disagreed, they wouldn't be found to be in mutual contradiction. Yet common sense tells us that people can make contradictory ethical judgments, and also that an ethical judgment can be wrong (1912, pp. 55, 59f). In holding out for the irreducibility of ethical disputes, Moore should, by his own lights, have been holding out for something more than what Keynes describes: the irreducibility of ethical posturing.[8]

In this chapter we have defined goodness in terms of ideal life stories and then drawn some of the relevant contrasts between actual efforts to live ideal stories and fictional efforts. We have shown that evaluation of intentional acts in terms of life stories is ordinarily presupposed, even where its possibility or usefulness is denied. To refuse (on any intelligible ground) to undertake such life evaluation (assuming one has enough relevant material to make the refusal count for something) already involves one in some such evaluation. Likewise, to shrug off proposed purposes is not to descend into a purposive void. It is still to react to them purposively.

The question, then, is not whether one should or should not refer to one's own version of one's life story, in evaluating and ranking one's purposes. One does that anyway. The question is, rather, how to make that life story as ideal as possible, or how to be good. And here the main question will be the correlative one: how does it go with one when one chooses against ideality, or chooses evil actively?

The intention that gives life stories their ideal cast is that of making rational approximations to self-knowledge. These approximations require continuous adjustments between memory and the purposed future. To live in such terms is to live more reasonably than to live in terms of economic reason, or platitudinous reason—and this fact is introspectively and practically confirmable. On our showing, then, this claim about good has universality and necessity. Like a law of logic, it is unreasonable to try to bypass it and, where it is denied outright, it is assumed in the very denial. That is, when one denies it, one does so for what purports to be a good reason, and a good reason contributes more to self-knowledge (the reason here having to do with how much I truly *can* know about myself) than an inferior reason would do. If, on the other hand, one does not take these refusals of good reasons case by case (where the refusals are always made on account of what purport to be *better* reasons), but instead rejects across the board the relevance of good reasons to one's course in life, then argument itself ceases. Argument ceases, and evil begins. We say evil begins (rather than error or ignorance) because there is no cessation of reasonableness that is—when carried through—sincere.

In the epistemic realm too there is nothing to say if one's interlocutor is simply *refusing* to be reasonable. There is of course an ancient question about how sincerely a commitment to reasonableness may be refused. It is easy to claim to refuse it. It is harder actually to refuse it. The sincere epistemological sceptic is a textbook animal. Any living, breathing ones must have rapidly become extinct. But the person who explicitly and deliberately *refuses* reasonableness in living out that theoretical thing called a life story, his own or that of another, is real enough and is embarked on the hard course of evil. The way sincerity and insincerity play flickeringly over that course is one of the characteristics of it, a characteristic that will be studied here. If what we have claimed about good is well founded, then the corresponding claim about evil can be assumed to be universal and necessary as well. But its appearance in practice is something we will look at more closely in Chapters Three through Seven.

Having pointed out how our own view is presupposed by some of the opponent views, we then considered two related philosophical objections: the claim that we invalidly reason from facts to values, and the claim that we commit the "naturalistic fallacy." Against the first objection, taking epistemic values to illustrate the general relations between facts and values, we showed that evaluative criteria already accompany factual evidences at every recognizable stage of cognition. Since no invalid leap from facts to epistemic criteria takes place in ordinary cognition, it follows that no invalid leap from facts to moral criteria need take place in ethical reasoning. The second objection holds moral criteria to be vastly different from other evaluative criteria, for instance, because they are simple, indefinable, or in some other sense drastically "nonnatural." This view, we showed, is vacuous.

The way is now cleared for a discussion of evil in motivational terms as the intentional thwarting of an ideal story. With this discussion we shall be occupied for the remainder of the book. In Chapters Three through Seven we shall give detailed consideration to three such broad types of evil: personal dissolution in Chapter Three, institutional corruption in Chapter Four, and genocide in Chapters Five, Six, and Seven. The first two broad types have been chosen because they are of perennial concern, and the types of genocide were chosen partly because they haunt moral consciousness in our era. The three broad types are intended to illustrate rather than to exhaust the possibilities for this method of analysis. Since each of the three types will be studied in sharp, individual focus, rather than broad outline, with ranked phases of the type calling for different individuations, an explanation will be needed of the method by which this individuation of types is secured. That explanation is offered in Chapter Two.

CHAPTER TWO

Pure Types

The Method Explained

FROM NOW ON, in tracing the course of evil through action and character, we will be methodically assuming the standpoint of pure types, or artificial characters. We will give each of these types an ideal story in potential. We will see how the thwarting, of his own story first of all, and of other people's in consequence, makes the life of this type an evil one. On this view, a bad man is a good man gone wrong. As Kant says in *Religion Within the Limits of Reason Alone:*

> Every bad action, when we inquire into its rational origin, must be viewed as if the man had fallen into it directly from the state of innocence. . . . He ought to have left it undone, . . . for by no cause in the world can he cease to be a freely acting being. (1792, p. 348)

On Kant's view, a person's freedom is his essential goodness or "innocence," and he never loses either. Though we do not take Kant's view that freedom is the same thing as goodness, we do here suppose that wrong choice is only *understandable* as a voluntary refusal to live some measure of one's ideal story, or a refusal to live one's innocence.[1] On our view, freedom is one's almost never-lost potentiality for voluntarily living or voluntarily debasing one's ideal story. If freedom were not the potentiality for either the good or the bad, there would hardly be a point to characterizing people in moral terms.

The first implicit task, then, is to combine the elements of the good man, who is the bad man's unlived contrasting moral possibility. The good man who *might have been* would have had a set of purposes that helped him make sense of his memories. By acculturation and reflection, he would have acquired a set of beliefs that informed these purposes. He would have been equipped with conditions, ecological, biological, temperamental, and cultural, that would do the utmost to facilitate his sense-making or good purposes. For the pure type (that is, the most legible case) of the *good* man in a given moral case, things would not be made so easy that he could put less than his best energies and talents into the accomplishment of his purposes. But neither should conditions be made so hard for the pure type who lives his ideal story that he would be overwhelmed and brought to confusion. We would not want to enrich or impoverish his situation in such a way as to call for additional talents and purposes, irrelevant to the ones we want to study here. We want, so far as the artificial or pure case makes possible, to *isolate* the purposes under study. Since, pedagogically, we would have had to do all this for the good man whose ideal story is the rejected possibility here, we will have to do no less for the bad man, who rejects his own story. For a given sort of rejection of ideality, we shall also want to see the pure type. In fact, purity in evil is what we want primarily to see here.

Let us construct him, the first such instance of our theory, in a preliminary and partial way, pending more complete development in Chapter Three. The first negatively pure type whose progress we shall want to follow in Chapter Three is *the rake*. What type of person should he be, for our purposes? Who is it that typically goes to the bad in this manner? What stages of dissolution serve to bring out the pure type? When, in human life around the globe, does the option present itself? Does it do so always? Or, more typically, when the human sense of story is under some kind of threat? In the latter case, a moral crisis would be one that superimposes itself on some other kind of important challenge. But it would be extremely hard to determine, for all human beings, the common element in challenges that precipitate moral crises. It would be more feasible to try first to define a moral crisis as such, leaving aside the hopeless question of what tends to precipitate them in humankind. A moral crisis, then, would be under way when *one stopped trying to make sense of one's story.* It would seem to occur at different turns of fortune's wheel for different persons. Whenever it does occur, for a few brief seconds perhaps, it is as if fortune's wheel were spinning without one. Of course, if we were correct in the argument of Chapter One that there is no interpretive void in human experience, then one never *actually* stops trying to interpret one's story. But, when one emerges on the vanquished end of a moral crisis, one settles for a rationale (for the particular happening or action that was challenging), which rationale gives deeper obscurity to one's remaining purposes. One is in the case where one doesn't try any longer, or one tries a little less hard, to get the whole story to hang together.

If no common psychic elements precipitate a moral crisis whenever they combine with common circumstances, and if no such constants determine who will *lose out morally* by such a crisis, then one is not able to equip the rake as a pure type with very many special features. His opportunities are constantly present, and to us all. He could begin going to the bad as a teacher, a corporate executive, a lawyer, a doctor, a printer, a dental technician, a street cleaner, a writer, a dancer, a polished dialectician, and so forth.

One might, however, consign the pure type to a high culture, so that the rake's progress can be allowed to go through many stages *without immediately becoming visible* to his fellows. A simple tribesman or yeoman farmer could not sit out more than two cooperative hunting expeditions or weeks at the plow without visibly suffering for it. One might also give the pure type an occupation specialized enough so that colleagues and friends will only get to see some of his many facets. So we shall not send him out on prolonged sailing expeditions where his mates can size up his mettle in typhoons. Neither shall we even set him going in a small town, where his reputation might precede him into any place where people gather. We don't want to settle him in an environment where people are hard put, with the passage of the years, to fool one another. What we mean by a "pure" type is a maximally intelligible type—one who will permit us to understand the purposes in question. For the sake of our study, we shall therefore want our rake to be as effective as he can be, in carrying out his obscure purposes. So we shall have him going to the bad in a big city (appropriately enough, according to folk wisdom).

Is the pure type of the rake a man or a woman? Obviously, anyone going to the bad could in fact be either. But to see what sexual dispositions and conventions will best serve the pure type, we shall have to follow him or her awhile, see what he or she wants to do and to whom, and consider whether all this could be more *effectively* carried out by a man or a woman. On that basis, the generic human "he or she" of our story can eventually get a sex. The assignment of sexual identity to the pure type will not involve an empirical judgment as to which sex has the greater number of bad characters. It will only require us to judge which sex can make a more canny botch of its ideal stories.

Before we go forward in the company of our rake—to do that in detail will be the task of Chapter Three—some additional remarks must be made here about the present method and its adequacy. There is an objection to the method, from the side of armchair anthropology, that might sound like this: "You pretend to consider the pure type in the case of going to the bad, without noticing what the study of non-Western cultures brings to light, that no exemplification of a moral problem in one culture will do for illustrating the same problem in a different culture. Furthermore, the culture-bound character of moral illustrations has two aspects: (1) the same action can have varied moral interpretations in two different cultures; (2) different cultures can visualize the very spectrum of moral possibilities (goodness and badness themselves) differently."

The armchair anthropologist's objection is partly confident of its ground because it has not yet touched on all the investigative difficulties opened up by the study of exotic cultures. The difficulty of getting the *correct* moral picture of a culture (of determining whether the culture exemplifies the same moral concepts differently, or actually has different moral concepts than ours), is vividly illustrated in the recent Mead–Freeman controversy over standards of sexual conduct in Samoa.

According to Mead in *Coming of Age in Samoa* (1928), Samoan girls have (or had in 1926) casual emotional ties (pp. 61, 105ff, 210), were noncompetitive and unambitious (pp. 33–38), attached no special value to virginity (p. 98), and either could not or would not characterize other people with any psychological acuteness (pp. 122f, 127f). One has the impression therefore that in Mead's Samoa the moral concepts are different from our own. There is an apparently easy-going, non-judgmental attitude toward life itself, and this attitude is apparently mirrored in relaxed sexual mores. If the human art of self-characterization arises out of the practice of assessment of character and personality *per se*, then the wherewithal for self-interpretation is minimal in Mead's Samoa, and the incentive for telling a coherent story about oneself is likewise low. So the good life as we have defined it would be hard to work out in Mead's Samoa, although by the same token the opportunities to thwart oneself or others would not arise so dramatically in that culture as in ours.

By contrast, Freeman's Samoa is a culture with moral concepts similar to ours, but rather differently illustrated. Thus in Freeman's *Margaret Mead and Samoa: The Making and Unmaking of an Anthropological Myth* (1983), Samoans have tragically ambivalent relations to their parents (pp. 209ff, 215f), are aggressively concerned with rank and status (pp. 150, 170f), desperately preoccupied with virginity (pp. 232f, 235ff), and were presumably capable of offering Freeman sharply etched reflections on their fellows. The culture Freeman found on "Mead's" Samoa has tensions and dramatic peaks similar to those we find in our own life stories; like our culture, it has a place for deep human and political intelligence; going beyond our culture, it has perhaps too much place for the experience of humiliation, and not enough clues as to how the individual may reasonably deal with that experience. In Freeman's Samoa, the chances to become evil are magnified, but so are the motives (if not necessarily the intellectual instruments) for living a good life in the sense *here* defined.

Aside from its making clear the difficulty of separating anthropological accounts of exotic cultures from the personal or theoretical biases of the anthropologist, what is the relevance of the Mead–Freeman controversy to our method of pure types? The analysis we conduct here is not a sociological or an anthropological one. Thus we are not required to find a high statistical incidence of our "pure types," whether in other cultures, or in our own culture. Nor need we find that our pure types exemplify some alleged generic possibilities for action and relation among human beings, whatever those might turn out to be.[2] Nor do we need to find that the moral conflicts of our pure types have crucially to do with the power conflicts within societies in general. We need only say that, given the following way of spoiling a story, such and such a social context and situation will be most serviceable for *bringing out* what was morally at stake in the story. Freeman's Samoa is more serviceable than Mead's if what we want to provide is illustrative material for a moral typology, but it is a matter of indifference for our analysis whether Freeman's or Mead's happens to be the real Samoa.

This leaves it open to the reader to suppose that other cultural and historical situations could give scope for life stories generating similar moral problems, but *not doing it so clearly* as in the case of the pure type delineated here. It is left open that there might be still other cultural and historical situations (if not in Mead's Samoa, then in some other possible world) where *the story might never occur* that would have precipitated the moral crisis for our pure type. (However, any anthropological account that seems to offer the reader the armchair "option" of explaining what does occur in terms markedly different from the reader's, without also making clear the material, psychological, and intellectual *costs* of the exotic way of telling the story, may simply be encouraging in the reader a loss of grip. Hunger is hunger all over the world. Fear is fear. The search for truth and the manipulative lie have features in common all over the world. Truly malevolent story thwarting is recognizable all over the world—and it is probably recognizable also across the species barrier.) There are societies that make it apparently costly to live reasonably as here defined, and apparently cheap not to. And there are morally better societies that make it rather more costly to live unreasonably than not to. But there are none, nor could there be any on the supposition of human freedom, that make it impossible to go to the bad. And that journey is the one we want to study, in whatever societal context will make it most visible to us.

Since no system of society could in principle foreclose the opportunity to choose wrongly, the social reformer's question as to what system might make people *less* likely to do so will not specifically concern us here. A few remarks about the social dependencies of moral thought and of the good life will, however, belong to these considerations of method. Two out of three of our pure types will be placed in democratic societies, which would provide equally to their citizens legal channels for redress against bodily assault, theft, fraud, slander, and arbitrary deprivations of access to social goods. This is because going to the bad and selling out are mild enough types of evil to be still obviously parasitic on the good life, and the good life is scarcely conceivable without the practical safeguards against predators that one finds in societies with commitments to the Enlightenment or to some non-Western equivalents of the Enlightenment. Repressive societies may have been the more usual ones in the long course of human history, but those that allowed men and women of self-corrective rationality to grow to adulthood must have modified their repressive tendencies, at least where those exceptionally gifted survivors were concerned. (In Chapters Five through Seven, where more extreme forms of evil will be studied, we shall see in the case of the genocide what the breakdown of safeguards against predation may mean to the person who helps bring it about.)

The connection between the good life and civil safeguards can now in principle be generalized. If there are universal moral rules, these would be linked to the civil conditions under which alone such rules could have application. It may be that the full set of such civil conditions are to be found nowhere in reality, but only in idealized hypostatizations, such as Plato's ideal city, Hobbes's social contract, Kant's rational system of nature, or Rawls's original position. Yet a reference to the full set of these correlative civil conditions is what makes the moral rules intelligible, even where in real life the rules may be inadequately instantiated.[3] In an analogous sense, we might say that failed or not-yet-attempted proofs in basic logic become intelligible only by reference to the full set of completed proofs, to which the rules of logic always in principle apply.

In the domain of human action there would be no moral law against stealing if there were not property; there would be no moral law against lying if there were not promising; there would be no moral law against murder if there were not living members of the community the killing of whom counts as murder; there would be no moral laws against slander, or usurpation of social goods, if there were not that mutual trust that must be assumed because it is required by the common interests.[4] The moral rules dictate the most reasonable ways of sorting out these common interests. They apply, therefore, *in virtue of* contingent conditions, and are right because they are the precondition for making further sense of our lives in existing conditions.

Does this mean that a creature totally different from ourselves, without analogous needs, fears, without spatial or temporal extension, for example, or without consciousness, would require a different ethics, or perhaps no ethics at all? Yes, that possibility is left open by the present method and view. But it is not a possibility that authorizes the ethical sceptic to exempt himself from the strictures that apply to our sort of world. The sceptic is not so authorized, if by that is meant that he can exempt himself *and still be reasonable.*

It is this last qualification that has moved some recent writers on ethics to suggest that, insofar as ethical claims would only be accepted by the reasonable, they lack generality. The fact that ethical claims won't be voluntarily put into practice by the thoughtless, by fanatics, by sociopaths, by nondeviant members of bloodthirsty exotic cultures, and the like, is taken to restrict the scope of the claims.

There is, here, a misunderstanding. The good life does not lose its exemplary significance because some people are not up to it. The point was a cliché among philosophers who belonged to the tradition of classical rationalism. Plato, Aristotle, Spinoza, Brentano, and Husserl would all have agreed that a person untrained to argument, untempered by the prolonged effort to discipline his impulses, and unrefined by constructive outside influences cannot be reliably good and cannot profit from the study of ethics.[*] Why these admissions, which ethical absolutists made freely, should in our time make it supposed that the good life has its very goodness only relative to its being *accepted* by every sort of person is not clear to me. But no doubt the reasoning is enthymematic. Taken at face value, it would lead us to the surprising conclusion that no one is (objectively) good—unless everyone is.

Virtues and Relativism

The present rejection of relativism might perhaps be better grasped after a contrast is drawn with some recent revivals of virtue

---

*Brentano writes: "It is in this sense that Aristotle observed that it is not every one who can study ethics. He who is to hear about law and morality must be already well conducted by dint of habit. In the case of others, he thinks, it is but a waste of pains" (1889, pp. 40f).

ethics, which do take a narrative view very much like the present one, but hedge it about with caveats as to the insurmountable pluralism and relativism of the valued goals that must give focus to the narratives that moral agents tell themselves. In his defense of virtue ethics Alasdair MacIntyre argues, in *After Virtue* (1981), that the so-called gap between fact and value that was felt by philosophers who wrote after the collapse of Aristotelian metaphysical teleology could not have been felt by philosophers who had worked in the earlier Aristotelian tradition, a tradition wherein the virtues were those recognized qualities that conduced to success in achieving aims eternally sanctioned by the system of nature. Under the Aristotelian system, it would no more have been a "value judgment," in the modern, free-floating sense, to say what constituted a good man than it would be today to say what constituted a good race horse. In both cases, the good horse and the good man, these would have been judgments of fact, with some room for moral deftness (moral evaluation) in pinning the judgment to the fact of experience. Because the classical virtues were thought to be innate (in the sense that linguists nowadays think the ability to speak grammatically may be), and their gradual appearance the natural culmination of a well-guided human development, an individual's life could be thought of as *the story* of that development—or of its failure to be realized (1981, p. 135). MacIntyre does not claim that Aristotle himself held the narrative view, rather, that the view flows from, and in the long term makes even more sense of, that classical view of the virtues.

MacIntyre argues that virtue ethics, and the related narrative view, can be lifted free of its original dependence on Aristotle's no-longer-defensible metaphysical teleology and attached instead to the institutionalized "practices" required by a working polity. If it is understood that the ground and support of the virtues is political, and that the requirements of the polity make the virtues sufficiently "natural" for us, though no longer cosmically natural in the original, fully Aristotelian sense, then the "de Sade objection" to self-realization or virtue ethics will collapse.

A word is due on the "de Sade objection," which can also be leveled against the view we have proposed. Aristotle held that the good for man is self-realization, achieved by the practice of the virtues (the intrinsic human excellences), rightly ordered. The "de Sade objection" is that the Marquis de Sade's fictional characters *also* claim that they want to realize themselves, and that they carry this out in vicious or predatory ways. Therefore, so runs the objection, self-realization ethics is compatible with viciousness. What MacIntyre makes clear is that within the complete, original Aristotelian system of physics and psychology ample instruments were available for the diagnosis of the Sadean antihero as a representation of a human being in a morbid and degenerate condition of body and soul. What MacIntyre has done to hold off the de Sade objection is (1) make it easier to see the historical context of the objection, that it depends on the collapse of background metaphysical assumptions that were made by Aristotle and were the most reasonable assumptions going prior to the modern scientific period, (2) argue plausibly that *objective constraints* on self-realization nevertheless remain, since the virtues are kept in place by the shared requirements of a reasonably conducted human community. (The latter point has been made also by other defenders of virtue ethics, for example by Philippa Foot.)

Up to this stage, MacIntyre has defended a view to which the present one is entirely sympathetic. His relativism, to which we do take exception, does not seem to us to follow logically from any of the above-mentioned points. The reservations about virtue ethics on the score of relativism are similar to those expressed by Stuart Hampshire, also a defender of virtue ethics and the narrative view, who writes that "Our moral intuitions . . . are irreducibly plural . . . for the same reason that the virtues and vices are plural; namely, that the ways of life men aspire to and admire and wish to enjoy are normally a balance between . . . disparate elements" (1983, p. 20). In MacIntyre's version of the problem the disparate elements governing moral choice are embedded in disparate and partially irreconcilable cultural and historical values. In Hampshire's account the disparities have more to do with the fact that, even within one individual, no *single criterion* does or can govern moral choice. In Hampshire's view, this indeterminacy of the moral criteria arises partly from the fact that the single individual is not wholly self-transparent when he comes to make moral choices, partly from the fact that he may have to choose between irreconcilably conflicting values, and partly from the fact that his assignment of priority to one value over another involves him in a choice between whole ways of life, or "between two possible types of person, each with his own set of virtues and defects, now incompatible sets" (1983, p. 33).

The latter kind of choice, most significant for relativists, between possible types of person, is however partly described as negotiable by a process Hampshire calls "brooding." One broods over a choice, precisely in those cases where what is to be chosen is linked to the kind of person one has already tried to become over the years. One broods to assess and get a feel for the degree of linkage. Hampshire's account of brooding reads like a close psychological and epistemic description of the kind of forward-and-backward-looking rationality that we have advocated here as instrumental to and reflective of a good human being. Since the initial nontransparency of the facts relevant to any particular choice would not prevent those factors from becoming *more* transparent to the agent over the course of the brooding years, what is left of Hampshire's relativism is also what is left of MacIntyre's, namely, that ways of life or self-told life narratives may be incompatible in the values assumed and in the concrete goals at which the different story tellers aim.

However, since the narrative view conceives the good life as a quest, a quest animated by self-curiosity, no fixed ranking of external goods or of the virtues is presupposed by it. The difficulty of reasonably assigning a fixed ranking in advance to the goods and the virtues does not present any *theoretical* obstacle to one's taking the narrative view, therefore. Equally good people can have somewhat different ranking preferences, for example, because their stories had different starting points, in different settings. Moreover, in practice, for most of us, the fact that there are conflicts between the values animating life stories is a problem that belongs to history, or a problem of intercultural relations. It is not so much the problem that besets our personal progress through our own stories. Or, if it does beset our personal progress, it does so only enough to make that progress difficult and interesting, not enough to stop it altogether. In practice, we do negotiate our way between conflicting values, which are often the sedimentary deposits of cultures once in conflict. For example, we make our way more or less between the Hellenic and the Biblical values. We do this aided at times by some of the great philosophers, who did it frontally and for the sake of their cultures in history (for example, Augustine or Philo), and we also do it improvisationally, amateurishly, all the time.

Hampshire seems to suggest that one gets committed to relativism simply by realizing that the factors influencing morally effortful choice can't be translated into such "prepared grids" of criteria as are constructed in "abstract moralities." But here again Hampshire's argument would not seem to apply to virtue or self-realization ethics so much as to those abstract moralities that are deontological. It is the latter that propose rules that are to be applied undeviatingly to concrete cases of practical reason, conformity to such rules being constitutive of a person's whole duty. The moralities attractive to Hampshire, such as those of Aristotle and Spinoza, are concerned with the development of a certain kind of person by the cultivation of the appropriate virtues. In Aristotle and Spinoza there is room for the kind of flexibility that goes with trying to be reasonable in real situations, involving real people, where questions of tact and feasibility have also to be faced.

However, to make the point come clearer, let us take a case where an imaginary group of people were all agreed on a single set of rules for correct behavior, and were all confined to the culture in which only those rules obtained—a sort of prelapsarian cultural condition. The point here is that the correct application of those agreed-upon rules would still involve careful consideration of the concrete cases, to see whether and how the rules fit them. A kind of moral good judgment would still be called for, for which the precise rules could not be specified, for which instead the general situation and way of life aimed at would have to be consulted. So, the very argument that is supposed partly to serve the cause of cultural relativism and pluralism of moral values—serve it by showing that no prepared grid of rules will suffice to inform actual moral choices—will also work even against a single culture with a simple, uniform moral code. It is not an argument against the universality of moral theory. It is really an argument against an abstractly deontological approach to moral theory.

In sum, what happens when the values of one culture come into conflict with those of another is not different in kind from what happens when rules and values are to be put into practice within a single culture, though it increases by many degrees the complexity of the relevant moral deliberations. As has been indicated, there is already a long train of precedent attempts in human history to negotiate such intercultural conflicts. Sometimes the negotiations are creative and constructive. Sometimes they are broken off, either because of bad intentions or genuine uncertainty as to how to go forward with them, while still preserving what is valuable in the negotiators' own background cultures. Historical impasses do certainly occur. At such times, for one reason or another, the negotiations must "wait." And, sometimes, the waiting has tragic consequences, not inevitable in principle, but psychologically unavoidable.

Given the fact that we *do* negotiate cultural conflicts, on the same dialectical basis that we negotiate subjective and interpersonal ones—negotiate them as well as we can at given junctions, or as badly—what is the real point of suggesting that it is impossible in principle to do what in fact we do do and have done? To put the question another way, what is the real basis for the current popularity of moral relativism?

If one were to play the Hegelian game of holistic cultural diagnostic, one might voice the suspicion that it arises out of a disguised tendency to stern and absolute self-condemnation—by the culture of the culture—in moral terms. What could have provoked such culturewide moral self-condemnation? Why would it take *this* covert form? Well, let us say briefly this: in the late-nineteenth and early-twentieth century, Western people believed in themselves. They believed, that is, that they were members of the most enlightened and progressive association of related cultures in the history of the world, and that they had both a right and a duty to bring their cultural light into the remotest corners of the inhabited world. Since that belief's heyday, members of Western cultures have seen World War I, the Armenian massacre, the Great Depression, the failure of the Versailles Treaty, the Hitler and Stalin eras, the nuclear arms race, the ecological threats to the habitability of the planet, and other catastrophes, almost all of them issuing out of or related to factors in Western culture. One possible psychological consequence for thinking members of Western culture is that they would feel that they have been bad, morally, and would feel that they probably are bad.

Since the self-condemnatory feeling is very uncomfortable, and since working out the precise significance to the human story of the catastrophes that occasioned the feeling would be an immensely difficult and challenging task, it is much more *relaxing* either to insist on certain Western values in a blinkered way and misname that parochial, blinkered insistence "moral absolutism," or to affirm that there is no good and no evil, none in the world and none in ourselves. The latter strategem of moral evasion seems to be the one that belongs to the cultural relativists. Nevertheless, the covert cultural self-condemnation implicit in much of current cultural relativism depends on a firm and universal morality, which, if it made itself explicit, would be seen to assign value to human life and to self-realization within the bounds of virtue.

The familiar repair of the relativists to twentieth-century anthropological reports from the field likewise contains its covert moral absolutism. First of all, some of the most philosophically influential of those reports implied that eugenicist racism ought to be rejected, rejected—that is—absolutely and universally, *whether it happened to have cultural support or not.* That is fine, but it cannot base itself on the claim that what is good and right is whatever a given culture approves. Second, cultural relativists often argued from the internal meaningfulness of other cultures, as described by anthropologists, to the wrongfulness of exploiting the members of such cultures economically while pretending to bring them the greater benefits of Western culture. In other words, when cultural relativists took this line, what they were doing was condemning exploitation and hypocrisy, condemning them generally and across the board, *whether culturally supported or not.* In the third place, besides the absolute moral condemnations of racism and hypocritical exploitation, anthropologically minded cultural relativists often had social reform in view. Insofar as feminists pointed to cultures where women were reported to have more political authority, or counterculturists to cultures where masculinity was less rigidly stereotyped, what was being advocated was this repatterning of our own culture after the pattern of another one, one that reportedly did things *better* than our own. This is certainly not relativism either, whatever it may choose to call itself. It is, rather, an appeal to ourselves to make dialectical use of the experience of other peoples in our own moral learning process. Where a real (and not merely culturally believed) moral learning process is conceded to be possible, cultural relativism is again being covertly rejected.

To allude to a moral learning process that might be culturewide is already to recognize that culture is not merely an incorrigible collection of habits that come to be acquired and approved by a process of stimulus-response conditioning. By the same token, moral preferences are not just the vocalizations of those alleged, conditioned approval and disapproval behaviors. Rather, cultures are collective interpretations of the real, worked out over generations in the context of a shared version of the past, common needs and, often, a common terrain. Cultures are, then, partly informal metaphysical systems, with implicit and explicit views of the best life and the model man or woman, that make sense only in terms of the hypotheses about reality to which these model lives have reference. Sometimes, cultures make use of professional metaphysicians. Often, as Hegel saw, the unfoldment of a culture is affected, directly or indirectly, by the work of such professionals, and by the separate scientific investigations of nature of which metaphysics would be the ideal synthesis.

Good and bad are therefore only culturally relative insofar as the metaphysical systems, within which ethical value terms make sense, may be produced initially to give a general explanation for a local condition, or to answer questions that would occur particularly at one time rather than another. Not every metaphysical system would be called for at every time and place. If we forget to look for the fit between the formal or informal system of metaphysics and the particular conditions that were the occasion for it, we may feel that, in reading the metaphysics, we are being loaded down with answers to a question that nobody we know has asked. In our own culture, knowledge of philosophical history therefore allows us to recover the uniting thread of genuine and live human curiosity ("wonder"), running from metaphysical system to system. The point of such knowledge would not be to underscore the incommensurability of systems, but to find those junctures where different systems are addressing and answering the same questions, rather than passing each other like ships in the night. At those juncture points, a common dialectical evaluation may be imposed on the competing systems, or on parts of them, and we may briefly be relieved of the temptation to construe the long human search for truth as historically relative in the privative sense of ultimately directionless.

All this is to say that metaphysical systems, including those produced informally by whole cultures, are open to confirmation and refutation. Of course, it may be—as metaphysical relativists have urged—that there are rival ways of describing the same world that are equally adequate evidentially, have the same explanatory and predictive power, and are equally consistent internally. In that case (a case for which we can presently find no two *cultures* with informal metaphysical systems to serve as illustrative), the rival metaphysical systems would indeed be equally well confirmed, although different. There would be then no rational way to explain a preference for the one over the other. But usually the cases cited as illustrative of metaphysical pluralism and relativism occur in certain details, or affect niceties of formulation, of the single, contemporary, Western system of nature. Putting aside the very fancy problems of scientific formulation that concern contemporary relativists, there is no one who would hold that *an equally good case* can be made for saying that the universe is like whatever current physics says it is like, and for saying that it is like green cheese. For practical purposes (and these are the purposes that would affect the ethical implications of metaphysical relativism), there is still in the West a broad consensus about what the real is like, a consensus to which Western thinkers—relativists and realists both—would adhere. When, in future, this consensus undergoes further revision, it will be on the basis of evidence that both relativists and realists will find compelling.

It follows that a culture can be wrong, in whole or in part, about what reality is like, wrong about what technology would be best able to deal with it, and hence wrong, in whole or in part, about what sort of life would be the best life for a man or a woman to lead. That is not to deny that the culture's view of the best life might have been perfectly reasonable *had its view of the real been the right view*. But, given that its metaphysical assumptions were off, its ethical recommendations were correspondingly skewed.

For example, in the crisis that affected Plains Indian culture during the latter part of the nineteenth century, a belief spread through that culture that the military, political, and economic defeats suffered at the hands of the whites would be reversed if members of the threatened culture wore special shirts conferring immunity to bullets and danced a special dance. As it happened, and as was discovered at Wounded Knee, the sacred shirts did not confer the promised immunity. In consequence, the Ghost Dance movement quickly subsided. Since sacred shirts don't cause bullets to rebound (i.e., since *reality is not like that*), it was intelligently seen that dancing the Ghost Dance in those shirts was not the best thing for a well-intentioned member of that unhappy culture to do. The relation between metaphysics and ethics can at times be as direct as that.

If one culture is less able than a rival culture to deliver on its promises and to confirm the metaphysical premises that are the warrant for the promises, then its own members will see that. It is for this reason that imperialist ventures have sometimes had striking successes where the invading party was heavily outnumbered, but the assaulted community could see at once that the technology of the invaders was and by inference would be vastly superior. To see that is immensely demoralizing for the members of a culture, cognitively and—for some—ethically. When they are forced into such moments of truth, members of the beleaguered culture will be likely either to become frankly demoralized, or to try to pull into retreat and isolation, or else to attempt to incorporate the improved views and techniques into their previous informal or formal metaphysical systems, with ethical recommendations revised accordingly. To do that most complex third thing is, for the long term, cultural success.

Delusional cultures can persist only until some forceful part of denied reality strikes. The great cultures have often shown an ability to adapt to harsh stresses, to incorporate alien metaphysical views and technical skills, and to stretch their own, all without losing some essential coherence. Which is to say that the great cultures have often held, in important respects, truer metaphysical views. We must hasten to say "in important respects," since it is obvious that advantage of ground, brute force, and sheer numbers can combine to crush and eliminate cultures whose members share more or less true views in fragile conditions. It must also be acknowledged that the members of great cultures were and are perfectly capable of perverting and squandering their initial advantages. In admitting that, however, we have left the standpoint of relativism, and opened the way to ongoing, corrigible moral assessments. To a consideration of some of the pure types whose moral assessment would be most transparent to ourselves, we may now therefore freely turn.

PART TWO

Evil Under Wraps

CHAPTER THREE

Going to the Bad

The Rake: The Pure Type

ONE CAN ALWAYS go to the bad. One has that option. Most of one's time is, or can become, one's own. One can put it to bad uses. Its reasonably self-corrective uses can be *let go,* one by one, into shapes and degrees of dissolution, private outlawry, defiant eccentricity, icy slippage, or bland and snowy incoherence. (We take it that to be prepared to say frequently to oneself or others, "I can't explain the things I do," "It had no justification," *is* an explanation, of the icy, bland, or snowy kind.)

We want to open for close inspection what is involved in the dissolute's going to the bad, in relation to the corresponding ideal story that is being rejected. With what sort of rake or dissolute shall we begin? With the gambler? The alcoholic? The drug taker? The power broker? The deliberate risk taker? Or with the seducer, who is the classic rake?

Well, why not the gambler? The gambler, by virtue of his typifying activity, has refused the part of his ideal story that would have tried to match *effort* with *appropriate compensation.* In his typifying activity, the gambler cannot deserve to win, and likewise he cannot deserve to lose. What he lets himself live out, therefore, is a particular sort of incuriosity about himself: he is incurious about what he deserves, or about what he would deserve if he set out to deserve something. Can this incuriosity be studied, for our purposes? Would we learn more about it if we tried to find *the psychological mechanism* of it, locating, for example, in his childhood the gambler's motivated distrust of earned rewards and chastisements? Possibly we would learn something more, but hardly something to the point at issue here. For our curiosity, even working overtime, cannot supply the defect of *his.* We cannot make good the slippage in *self*-investigation that gambling represents.

51

The gambler is the one who has let himself go. He has permitted the apparent scattering to the winds of what he was. As would-be psychologists, scavenging among the gambler's hints and refusals to find the fragments of an original coherence and to attach those fragments to the hidden mechanism that—by hypothesis—did the fragmenting, it remains a commonplace of the clinical psychologist's trade that we cannot make him whole again unless he "wants" to be. For our purposes, this means that he cannot measure himself against the hoped-for coherence that ideally he might have had, unless he is curious about the insights which that comparison would make accessible to him. And this self-curiosity is precisely what he cannot feel, insofar as he remains a gambler.

Would there be some other way to learn about him, despite his own typifying refusals of self-curiosity? We seem, in our would-be diagnostic earnestness, markedly less playful than he does. At least he seems playful when he is, so to speak, off duty. "It is the best life in the world," said a croupier to me when I asked him about the life. This was in "Paradise Island" in the Bahamas. "You play for a living. When you were a child, you played all the time." The disposition to play may be innate in our species, but there is no psychological mechanism forcing any individual to play in a particular way or time. One is not playing at all, unless one plays to that extent freely.

We have already noted that we cannot get the gambler to cooperate in self-disclosure while he remains what he is. And if we observe him without his cooperation, trying to discern the hidden springs of his activity, we may get the picture of him out of focus and blurred. *Insofar as he is really playing,* he is not and cannot be wholly determined by an antecedent mechanism. If we look for such a mechanism, we will lose him.

What, then, is he freely doing? Well, what does he *say* he is doing? (A free person should be taken at his own word about what he is doing, other things being equal. And if he is not at all free, then he is not an object for moral study.) He ordinarily says that he is "trying to win." With what sort of winnings would he like to walk away, from the green reflected light of the gaming tables? Against what sort of opponent is his struggle to win undertaken? It is tautologically true to say that what the gambler seeks are *chance* winnings. The gambler's real challenger is, then, chance, although he may also have to "read" those human challengers who resemble him, in that they too are merely trying to beat the odds. (Despite occasional grandiose claims to the contrary, he could hardly be "reading" the face of mankind, since that is more discernibly encountered exercising mutually legible skills and letting *varied* occasions for conversation arise.) In sum, gambling could be described as the activity of letting accidents happen to one, perhaps in the unsubstantiated hope that the accidents will be beneficial and that the flow of them will decide one's real mettle anyway, magically. The gambler, then, is a person who is self-committedly accident-prone. Since accidents will *typically* happen to him, we can by no means count on him steadily to disclose himself over time, even to the limit of a rake's capacities. Since we want to open the rake's progress to close inspection, the pure type, for our purposes, cannot be the gambler.*

Why not the alcoholic, or the drug taker, then? If any human activity that requires consciousness for its performance must sooner or later be accompanied by an interpretation, how does the alcoholic or drug taker tend to *interpret* his appropriation of addictive and deleterious substances that affect him pleasurably? There would seem to be only one indispensable reason to take into one's body a pleasurable substance that is otherwise potentially harmful, and that is that one *wants* it. Insofar as there is one characterizing belief that accompanies this desire, it must be the belief that one may (or even ought to) act on what one wants, in disregard of other considerations. By intensifying the desire, the addictive substance tends in turn to lend conviction to the belief that *present desire is a sufficient warrant* for action.

Note that the desires in question are precisely the kind to which hedonists give a good press. Such a desire has its calculable degrees of intensity. And it has no intrinsic relation to the objective states of affairs that produce it, or result from it. It is simply a feeling. Whether produced by something drunk, sniffed, injected, or chewed, what is wanted is some modification of a state of consciousness. The difference between these addictions and the more common ones, to other substances widely accessible in civilized life and known to be rather bad for the body (salt, sugar, caffeine, and so forth), is that the modifications of consciousness effected by the former are known to be drastic, cumulative, and irreversible. The difference, then, is one of degree. The former sort of addictions are *immoderate.*

---

*The addictive gambler should be distinguished from the professional gambler, and also from the assortment of people who may be grouped somewhere between on a spectrum. The professional has genuine inductive skills that correlate in a determinable way with his winnings. His mentality may therefore be closer to that of any businessman than it would be to that of the addictive gambler. The most salient difference between him and the majority of other businessmen might be that—like a cop who upholds established values, or like any bohemian—the professional gambler has a taste for life at the social margin. This taste would not of itself seem to be an occasion for moral judgment. On the professional gambler, see Custer and Milt (1985, pp. 171f).

When one is trying, as everyone does, to live out one's life and make a daily economic estimate of one's forces, these differences of degree are precisely what one has to bear in mind. So we can now qualify our characterization of the immoderate addict as follows: he takes in the harmful but pleasurable substance, (1) because he *wants the modification of consciousness* it affords; (2) because he *believes* that his *present desire is a sufficient warrant* for action; and (3) because he believes in the sufficiency of present desire as a warrant, *despite good evidence that* this desire, acted on, will have the result *of noticeably diminishing his control* over states and powers of his consciousness, and over the other circumstances of his life. In other words, by acting on this present desire, he will diminish the option of making anything else *but* this present desire a warrant for his actions. (From now on, his life choices will be shaped by this desire, and possibly by the later desire to be rescued from this present desire.)

One may say that the immoderate addict is the only egoistic hedonist who is absolutely and obviously sincere. To believe that pleasurable states of consciousness ought to be decisive objects for the agent is precisely to *disbelieve* in a detour for the calculation of effects. For the individual, long-term effects are never predictable. The individual may, after all, die tomorrow. Why not die happy and satiated, after a tremendous binge? Furthermore, ecstatic pleasures may outweigh, in their subjective desirability, the debasement of the individual's presence in the world that could be their price over the long term. To want to enjoy certain feelings above all is precisely to want to enjoy those feelings *now*. Feelings "convince" by being felt. If one is guided by something else (for example, by the painstaking computations of a Utilitarian), then one does not *sincerely* believe in the supreme decisiveness of one's feelings.

The immoderate addict is, then, in his early stages, the only demonstrably pure hedonist. Among the hedonists, he alone is ready to die for his beliefs. He prefers pleasurable states of consciousness to the other goods of life, and he has shown that he believes this preference to warrant his actions. (There is a point beyond which the addict becomes literally determined and compelled by forces over which he has entirely lost control. At that point, however, he still retains for a time a choice as to whether or not to get outside help for the addiction. Once the second point is past, and the brain is too damaged for help to reach the sufferer, the addict has passed out of eligibility for a moral evaluation.)

Certain puzzles about the will and agency should be noted at this point, although we will make no effort to deal with them in detail. Insofar as an action *is* one, rather than a mere response to stimuli, we would have to assign the decisive role in the action to *the belief* on which it is taken. Thus any agent who, like the addict, is guided, but not determined, by pleasurable stimuli, *believes himself to be warranted* in doing what he does. So free choice, even the choice of pleasure, seems to be accompanied by belief. But it is hard to know what starts the process. If one has a choice at all and is not simply exhibiting a reflex, then one chooses because of a belief. But one also holds a belief because one has, at least tacitly, chosen to hold it. Is that "tacit" choice itself belief-bound? Probably so, but here one would want to look to a whole network of mutually ratifying (or, sometimes, mutually reversing) choices and beliefs.

In this connection, we may recollect how Donald Davidson alludes to the interaction between belief and choice in his discussion of the "principle of continence." This principle requires that the agent "perform the action judged best on the basis of all relevant reasons," and it has as its negative counterpart the practice of the "incontinent" agent, who does not "let his better reason prevail." So, in Davidson's view, it appears that there is a *background choice,* operating behind the fact that we act on beliefs that are in turn governed by a hierarchy of reasons. It is the choice of continence or incontinence. In the *in*continent case, Davidson says that "the actor cannot understand himself; he recognizes in his own intentional behavior, something essentially surd" (1970, p. 42). It appears that Davidson has characterized the implicit background choice just as we have, self-referentially. The agent either chooses to know, or chooses not to know, all that he can about why he acts as he does. This we take to be the primary choice, which in turn governs the beliefs on which we act.

When we say that there is one fundamental choice, from which beliefs tend to flow, we do not claim to identify a chronologically "first" choice. But it has been our understanding that there is a logically first choice, which determines motivations and is not itself determined by them. This we have understood to be the choice for or against self-knowledge. One can scarcely go beyond or behind the desire to know what one is, will be, and has been all about. One can choose to honor the desire. Or one can choose to rationalize its repression in various ways. It has not appeared to us to be true to say that one has any third choice.

If the immoderate addict is the only demonstrably pure egoistic hedonist, how shall we characterize him in terms of the good? The human good, we recollect, is the choice of an ideal story, which makes maximal sense of the connection between one's past and one's future. In choosing the pleasurable modification of his consciousness at the expense of his long-term interpretive abilities, the immoderate addict has chosen *against the very possibility* of idealizing his story. At a progressively increasing risk of irreversibility, he has chosen what Davidson calls "incontinence." If, changing the metaphor, we say that the ideal story is something like an autobiography, then he has chosen to defy its syntax. If we say that the ideal story is something like a sequence of portraits, then he has, from here on, chosen to blur the faces.

This, then, is the ethical meaning of his choice, insofar as he comes to understand the effects of the addictive substance. Since these effects are neither a well-kept secret in the cultures of the modern world, nor slow to show themselves in the course of a single, solitary binge, it appears that the ethical component of the choice figures in it on a regular basis. (The self-help groups, with their twelve-step programs that appear to have the greatest success in rescuing addicts, partly function so as to bring that ethical component to the addict's attention, in beneficent and supportive circumstances.)

We come back to our question. Would the addict be a good subject for our further inquiry? He would not. He has not made himself so unintelligible as the gambler, since his field of adventure remains the expanse of his own subjectivity, rather than the realms of accident *per se*. The waters of subjectivity have many transparent currents, even when some currents are getting opaque or, as it were, oil-slicked. Even when the waters of subjectivity are pulled into a vortex, there is still, intrinsically, a lot to see. But the addict's subjectivity, though it remains visible, is *by his own initial choice* a partly adulterated subjectivity. As a matter of fact, that is the tragedy of it. However, what we have set ourselves to do here is to follow the rake over a course of rakish action, and to see him clear. *Prima facie*, the addict has made that project much harder in his own case. We pass on, therefore, to another candidate.

Why not the power broker, as the pure type of the rake? The power broker, with his special relation to the generally agreed-upon constraints on social life, has as his counterpart the person who "sells out" at his behest, agreeing to come in on the deals that he proposes. Their relations are the subject of sustained inquiry in the next chapter, "Selling Out." What places the power broker in a separate category, or identifies him as a different type, is the following fact of experience: the power broker is in a shrewdly insistent relation to the respectable and useful elements of society that form the background to his deals. By the nature of the deals he makes, the social order itself is compromised. As such, his adventurism is not the purely personal kind that typifies the rake whom we want to study here.

Why not the deliberate risk taker, then? Can he present to us the rake as a pure type? The risk seeker (as we should rather call him)

wants to storm the gates of significance, deliberately placing himself
in hazardous situations so as to force out of his body and psyche
resources accessible only in emergencies.

For our purposes, what is characteristic of the risk seeker is his
impatience. Since the emergencies that are his testing grounds are
avoidable, they must have occurred because he forebore to use *some*
of his practical intelligence. (Here we distinguish him from the so-
called accident-prone individual who, presumably, gets into trouble
because, for some reason, he lacks the capacity consciously to see
trouble coming. However, insofar as the person who is frequently involved in accidents is consciously complicitous in his misfortunes, he
may require a more differentiated characterization. That person must
consciously suppose that injuries are a genetically preprogrammed
or else morally merited part of his life story, and in any case belong there. He hopes to precipitate from others, or from his circumstances, telling responses to self-wrought emergencies. By losing
again and again he hopes, somewhat desperately, to find out *why* he
has been a loser. His role will be relatively despondent and passive.)
The risk seeker, on the other hand, wants to put to the test his own
capacities, intellectual and physical, real or believed, for avoiding
injury or surmounting injury's effects. For this purpose he has gotten
himself into the kind of trouble that, with a little forethought, he
could have avoided altogether. In this connection, he is likely to take
expert advice about how to cope with the trouble, but not to take
knowledgeable advice about how to miss altogether the encounter
with the trouble.

Let us regard the risk seeker in the best possible light, as someone who feels that he needs his emergency resources in order to
clarify his situation, his past, his concealed bent in life. Henceforth,
however, he will never know how he would have comported himself
had it not been for these voluntarily assumed risks. Without the
artificially precipitated emergency, he would have had to take the
longer way. He would have had to struggle to make sense of circumstances naturally obscure, against odds felt by him to be great,
and against his own greater impatience. Instead, he gets himself into
an emergency, or a series of them. But what he wants from the
emergency is, simply and suddenly, crisp clarifications.

It is a good thing to want them. However, these particular crisp
clarifications depend on a certain practical imprudence. Sustained over
the long term, imprudence requires its own compromises with one's
intelligence. In place of natural skill in avoiding needless trouble, one
acquires excrescent skills in the handling of self-induced emergencies.
To get into such an emergency, one has to be, as it were deliberately,

stupid. To get into them repeatedly, one has to be stupid repeatedly. Insofar as such a life involves this noticeable and self-induced stupidity, it puts in question the earnestness of one's efforts to make one's whole life intelligible.

Eventually, risk seeking does raise ethical questions. By putting the good life at unnecessary risk, it will at last put the goodness of such a life in doubt too. If it has become hard to suppose that the risk seeker is living an admirable life, neither has it been possible to suppose that the sort of risk seeker we have described is *per se* a bad man. If he does not add other elements to his life, he will eventually veer toward the bad. He will not steer toward the bad deliberately. If he goes there at all, that will be a by-product of his main pursuit: the *sudden* clarification of his life. As the pure type of the rake, therefore, he will not do.

We are left with the seducer. Unlike the gambler, he is not, so to speak, "accident-prone." Unlike the alcoholic or drug taker, he has not necessarily adulterated his subjectivity. Unlike the power broker, his journey is a personal and private one, taken without intrinsic reference to the institutions, official norms, or public face of his society. Since, unlike the risk seeker, he *must* get other people involved with him, we cannot make on his behalf the charitable supposition that we made about the risk seeker, namely, that he might merely be seeking a short-cut to *self*-awareness, by defective means. In sum, no consideration thus far advanced stands in the way of his turning out to be, as he is commonly supposed to be, the very type of the rake.

There is, however, one additional consideration, which threatens to make the seducer a mixed rather than a pure type, after all. This is that the seducer believes himself to be acting on desires that he cannot help having, because they are natural and instinctive, and *in this the seducer may be right.* In the seducer's own view of himself, he is not immoral but, as the saying goes, amoral, or pre-ethical. He is therefore innocent *qua* natural.

Illustratively, sociobiologist Donald Symons argues in *The Evolution of Human Sexuality* (1979) that the promiscuous male and the coy female are equally products of genetic imperatives. Among species where the female gestates and cares for the young, the male has virtually nothing to lose by fertilizing as many eggs as he can. Insofar as he has been evolutionarily selected because he acts so as to maximize the chances for his genes to be preserved and transmitted, he has everything to gain reproductively (that is, his genes have everything to gain) from his being as promiscuous as possible. The female, on the other hand, has much to lose in time and energy if, because she has imprudently mated with a noncompetitive male, she gives birth to an infant that is unfit. To put it more precisely in sociobiological terms, her genes have not been well served if she does so.

These genetic imperatives, Symons argues, have nothing to do with *cultural* biases in favor of the male sex. In those species, such as the pipefish and the sea horse, where the males invest more time and energy in caring for the young, it is the females who are larger and more aggressive, and their sex is the promiscuous one. Among birds, on the other hand, we find true monogamy, where male and female parents invest equally in the task of raising the young (1979, pp. 24f).

However, in most species that reproduce sexually, reproduction is more taxing to the female of the species. As a result, we usually find what might be called a natural "double standard," with male promiscuity and aggressive competition for females contrasted with female sexual passivity and fidelity. Thus, there is evidence that mammals of other species get sexually fatigued if they mate continuously with the same females (1979, pp. 208f). As to marital fidelity among human beings, Symons points to evidence of many kinds, all tending to show that a behavioral double standard can be found both in the United States and in primitive tribes (1979, pp. 218ff, 228ff) He takes note, too, of recent studies of sexual behavior in Western countries that conclude that, though the gap between frequency of intercourse in males and females is closing, the gap between *desire for variety* in partners among males and females is *not* closing. Males want variety. Females don't.

The news from outlying districts like Samoa is not good. Despite claims to the contrary from Margaret Mead and some other anthropologists, Symons believes that the preponderance of the evidence shows sexual jealousy—and resultant exercise of personal control over one's mate—to be markedly greater in men than in women, even in primitive cultures (1979, pp. 152f, 242f). Some feminists may refuse the point on doctrinal grounds, but I have yet to meet the wife having tea in Schrafft's who would raise her eyebrows over it. The apparent exceptions, Symons thinks, are cases where "paternity is uncertain" (1979, p. 242), and such cases are not all that common.

Because nature rewards adultery in men and penalizes it in women, culture tends to do so, too, Symons argues, giving prestige to the male adulterers and letting the female adulterers run the risk of dangerous reprisals or abandonment.

> The waning of lust for one's wife is adaptive both because it promotes a roving eye, and . . . because it reduces the likelihood of impregnating one's wife at times when an offspring cannot be reared. . . . A woman has noth-

ing to gain reproductively, and a very great deal to lose, by desiring sexual variety *per se*. (1979, p. 208)

As if in confirmation of the hypothetical reproductive purpose that Symons thinks probable, there is experimental evidence that men are more easily aroused sexually than women, and are even aroused by stimuli that seem to women to be without sexual content (1979, pp. 172–75). Orgasm is apparently less frequent in women than in men, no matter what their culture (pp. 83ff), and it is also less frequent in female primates (p. 81). Symons infers that if orgasm accompanied intercourse more frequently, females might be less easily impregnated, and become too promiscuous to be dependable nurturers of the young (p. 92).

Against claims that these differences are cultural rather than natural, Symons cites the widely varied cultures in which the differences are found, the persistence of these differences even in those Western countries where *other* sexual patterns are yielding to the influence of egalitarian reformers, and evidence that the same basic contrast, between promiscuity and sexual competition among males and monogamy among females, is also found among homosexuals (1979, pp. 293–99, 302f). This last item is particularly significant, if true, just because homosexuals have voluntarily dissociated themselves from prevailing cultural norms and have worked out a sexuality of personal preference instead. The sexual egalitarian might want to say here that homosexuals still show, *in this regard*, the influence of nurture over nature, but it begins to sound as if one were straining a point.

It is not my purpose here to subject to further evaluation the expertness of Symons as a synthesizer and interpreter of the sociological, anthropological, and ethological evidence. Nor can I go back and independently review the studies on which his interpretations are based. Whether he is right or wrong in his general contentions about the sexual character of our species, it is worth noting that his case can find support also in folk wisdom. Our grandmothers could have told you as much.

A point ethically akin to Symons's was put with less protoscientific embellishment by David Hume in *An Inquiry Concerning the Principles of Morals* (1751). Hume remarks there that the society of known seducers is enjoyed even by virtuous hostesses, while men known to be impotent excite mere derision in society. As Hume sees it, the reason is the same in both cases: people *naturally* value those who suggest to them the prospect of pleasure, and naturally disvalue those who fail to suggest to them that prospect (p. 70 and n.5).

In addition to the recent evidences of sociobiology and the older testimony of folk wisdom and of "Humean" common sense, there are other grounds on which to find Symons's overall view believable. One has only to recall the thundering condemnations of rampaging (and, on the initiating side, male) lust in those strata of Western culture that have opposed the double standard on theistic grounds, and to muse on the practical uncertainties generated by the recent, partial overthrow of that theistic moralism. That moralism tacitly acknowledged *the natural force* of what it opposed and urged that on irreconcilable nature a higher standard be imposed. To recall all that is to hear parts of Symons's theme again, in another register.

Where does this leave our seducer, as the pure type of someone *going to the bad?* Is he, on the many way stations of his journey, innocent or guilty? *Of what* is he innocent, of what guilty? Shall we say that the seducer is a man who is "guilty" only of violating social conventions, but innocent on the natural level, in his thoroughgoing submission to the genetic imperative? What sorts of judgments has the seducer blended in the composing of his natural innocence?

He has chosen to engage in an activity he believes to be warranted by the fact that he desires the activity. In the case of this activity, its performance will involve securing the cooperation of a second person. This cooperation is in turn secured by persuasively *leading away (seducere)* that second person from a path where, on better advice, her interest would have been seen to lie. So the seducer must believe, not only that he is warranted in acting on a desire, but that he is warranted in persuading another to act—not necessarily on that other's desire—but necessarily on the seducer's. What is the seducer's warrant for believing that he may justifiably exercise such persuasion? According to the point of view we have just been considering, the seducer has a warrant *in nature*. He is acting in a way that will bring advantage to his genes.

It is, however, quite obvious that what is to the advantage of our genes may not be to *our* advantage, as individuals or even members of a species. For example, as Peter Singer points out, we use birth control for our personal (or even specieswide) advantage, despite the alleged genetic imperative (1981, p. 131). On the same basis (that is, in consideration of personal or group advantage), cultures have traditionally imposed controls on what Symons describes as the genetic imperative.

The sorts of controls have depended on the manner of the genetic imperative's self-exhibition. In the hunting and gathering cultures, where the technology is most primitive and the human society is small enough to be an intimate one, the controls are, on Symons's own view, present in the form of threatened reprisals from husbands, fathers, brothers, or other male relatives. (See Symons, 1979, pp. 152f.) So jealousy itself necessitates open or tacit negotiations to stabilize claims to a confined erotic territory. It seems that even hunters and gatherers tend not to want to have sexual border disputes in their own families. By and large, they also tend to want to see to it that their children are raised in approved circumstances. The person or group that flouts these constraints has to be self-maintained in a kind of stupor with regard to the general and obvious reasons for the constraints. (Note that we are still here talking about hunter–gatherers. We are not yet talking of seducers in more complex societies, where there may be a larger pool of unprotected women, where physical reprisals against sexual predators may be illegal, where social reprisals are open to a more sophisticated challenge.)

In the simplest human societies, then, the philanderer may be serving some of his interests (e.g., the interest he has in satisfying one strong desire), but he is putting others in jeopardy. Human beings are not single-interest creatures. (It is rather hard to think of any single-interest species, but that is another matter.) But, even granting that his is not on the face of it a case of enlightened *self*-interest, is the primitive philanderer serving the interest of his genes? Of *his own* genes possibly, but he is not necessarily serving the interest of the fittest genes, if we suppose genetic fitness to comprise social intelligence. Likewise entire primitive societies, such as R. F. Fortune's Dobu (1932), which are alleged to function in defiance of social intelligence, are not interculturally fittest, from the competitive standpoint.

The above remarks do not apply to the behavior of primitive war parties, venturing into the territories of outsiders. The practice of rape by war parties, primitive or other, may provide evidence for the view that sexual predation is innate in human males and has merely to be released by any suspension of social controls. (See Symons, 1979, pp. 276–85.) In such cases, however, what requires preliminary analysis is the general situation of violence, on which rape depends. Since the use or threat of force comports different beliefs and intentions than seduction, it lies outside our present compass. Note however that the genetic defense of sexual predation has no better evidence on its side, and has roughly *the same sort* of evidence, than the genetic defense of violent aggression might muster. In the former case one refers to the naturalness of lust and the advantages it brings to the fittest; in the latter case one refers to the naturalness of aggression and the advantage *it* brings to the fittest. In the case of aggression, however, the personal damage that its untrammeled use will cause is so obvious, and the need-based ability that human beings have to bend aggression to social ends so frequently in evidence in daily life, that aggression's genetic claims are seldom pushed to the point of collision with normal self-interest.

Perhaps if genes could talk, they would push the claims of lust and aggression beyond that point. But even this is doubtful, since the genetic interest is also served by cooperativeness and group cohesion. (See Singer, 1981, ch. 1.) In any case, even the genes putatively responsible for lust and aggression cannot talk. Since they cannot, rape—in which untrammeled lust and untrammeled aggression combine—is open to any objection that can be leveled at untrammeled lust or untrammeled aggression, taken separately. The prudential objection to both is that both threaten the network of tacitly negotiated reciprocities on which the life of the individual in culture depends.

On the other hand, if either free-wheeling lust or aggression is taken outside the borders of the community, then it would not appear to threaten its own community directly. It can only threaten the community indirectly, by altering the affective and intellectual life of the perpetrators, and by drawing the community into a cycle of violent reprisals. (There is also the consideration that what the agent does to harm another he also is likely, semiconsciously, and by other means, to do to harm himself, but we shall reserve attention to this consideration for Chapter Five.) These are ways that people who are thoughtful, civilized, or both, have come only gradually over millennia to notice and to fear. That such acts provoke *fear*, as well as self-righteous disapproval, among civilians behind the perpetrators' lines is one important sign that they are felt to be in conflict with the self-interest of the perpetrators' community. At least they are so felt by the community's more reflective members, the ones eligible to live what we have heretofore denominated a good life.

If Symons's hunter–gatherer societies have *not* turned out to be societies where social, personal, or even unalloyed genetic advantage is in fact served by male promiscuity, what sort of human society would be best adapted to the purposes of aggressive competition for access to the greatest number of ova? It would seem that the society whose constraints conform most closely to Symons's genetic ones would be the one where the most competitive males could gain access to, provide for, and maintain a harem. The political requirements for the maintenance of a harem would seem to be: (1) a pool of subservient males to police it, and (2) a pool of docile females to supply it with ova.

It is not clear why any man should want to serve the interests of his own genes, which no more come into his direct experience than subatomic particles do. It is even less clear why an individual should want to serve the interest of another man's genes, or why a woman should want to subordinate personal to genetic interests. If we were to construct a hypothetical community conformed to genetic interests, we would have to postulate the disaffection of subservient males and females as a permanent likelihood within such a community. Those in commanding positions would have, therefore, to be adept in the use of force, shrewd in manipulating affections, on continuous alert for signs of disloyalty, and unashamed to crush it quickly, once disloyalty was found out.

Let us make our hypothetical community a bit less volatile. Let us place an insulating barrier of mystifying beliefs and sanctions between the subservient population and the dominant males. And let us redistribute benefits so that few of the subservient are absolutely deprived. However we cushion the blows, it remains the case that access to erotic benefits cannot be equalized in principle, without jeopardizing the system. It functions so as to maintain certain major inequalities, between dominant and subordinate males, and between all males and all females. Do away with these inequalities and the system would no longer conform to Symons's genetic imperative.

In such a system, then, two consequences follow: (1) most of the populace could lead more desirable lives under some other system; (2) the genes most likely to be passed on will belong to men and women of shrewd, manipulative, or violent dispositions. Of course, other genetic material might get passed along accidentally. Since such social structures would tend to be inherently unstable, the frequent political recombinations they would undergo could lead to genetic shake-ups as well. If, however, we endowed our hypothetical community with an *artificial stability,* then we could say that over the long term those genes that are conducive to shrewdness, manipulativeness, or violence will be the ones favored. (And indeed, even in politicogenetic shake-ups, those who would get on top would seem to be the shrewd, manipulative, or violent ones.) But even if such communities could draw on a sufficiently wide and varied population base to prevent particular genetic consequences of any kind following from their political structure, it is still doubtful that *the culture* would foster the exploration of any but the despotic talents. Other talents there might be, but they would get only the most limited opportunities to know themselves.

In sum, unless we want to favor genes for the despotic talents only, at the expense of other genetic material, there will be no strong *genetic* case for this society. And, if the desires of individuals, the welfare of communities, and long-term benefits to the species are also to be considered, there would seem to be a persuasive case against it.

We have found that the seducer does not have a warrant in nature for what he does. Whatever else he may enjoy, he cannot savor the "natural innocence" of himself. Nature does not demand him, as a type. Nature does not reward him, as a type. So far as nature is concerned, he is on his own. By the same token, it becomes possible to discuss seduction entirely in voluntary terms, provided only that we distinguish the desire (which may indeed be more incessant in males) from the practice. It is also possible at length to distinguish the practice of seduction from the infringement of common but arbitrary conventions. (Since seduction is not *per se* natural, the critical investigation of it is not *per se* conventional.) What the seducer must do, minimally, is persuade another to become intimately involved with him, in a manner necessarily conformed to his own desires and perceived interests, but not necessarily conformed to the desires and interests of that other. The seducer is, therefore, *not innocent.* He is at least guilty of a willingness to be less than fair in a personal relation. The understanding of this guilt belongs to the ethical analysis of personal relations. It cannot be secured by an analysis of the conventions alone.

The objection from nature having been laid to rest, it appears that the seducer will probably do, as our pure type of the rake. We can now place the seducer within the framework envisaged earlier for the rake (see above, pp. 34–35, 37ff). We discover him in a nondespotic culture, where the object of his attentions will be free to reject them, and where he would have been equally free not to go to the bad. Since the good life that remains open to him requires rational instruments of many kinds and allows the individual flexibility in the use of them, we will locate our pure type in a technologically complex culture, whose members have tasks that are not merely inherited but chosen; and they are at least fairly adept at reasoning. Within such a culture, the seducer will live in a city, where the reputation he has gained in previous encounters cannot easily precede him, or handicap him for future encounters. Only one question remains: is our pure type a man or a woman?

The fact that a woman, as well as a man, *can* be a seducer, is one more incidental nail in the coffin of the "genetic" case for the seducer. The point here is not that women too can be promiscuous or coquettish, which fact Symons treats as a genetic accident, but that being a genetically delivered human male is neither a necessary nor a sufficient cause of *the seducer as an agent in culture.* The erotic predations of the Marquise de Merteuil in Choderlos de Laclos's *Les Liaisons dangereuses* are no less unfair than those of her male coconspirator, the Vicomte de Valmont. If the eventual downfall of them both is unequally weighted against her, that does not signify that she was, in her prime, any less a seducer.

It is not inconceivable that a seduction could succeed without any physical desire being gratified thereby. So Kierkegaard writes in his *Diary of the Seducer:*

> One learns too from the Diary, that it was sometimes something altogether arbitrary that he sought, a mere greeting for example, and under no circumstances would he accept more, because this was the most beautiful thing about the person concerned. By the aid of his intellectual endowments he had known how to tempt a young girl and attract her to himself, without really caring to possess her. I can imagine that he knew how to excite a girl to the highest pitch, so that he was certain that she was ready to sacrifice everything. When the affair reached this point, he broke it off without himself having made the slightest advances and without having let fall a single word of love, let alone a declaration, a promise. And still it had happened, and the consciousness of it was doubly bitter for the unhappy girl because there was not the slightest thing to which she could appeal. . . . (1843, pp. 302f)

If Kierkegaard does here take note of a possible style of seduction, a style without sexual consummation, then we cannot explain seduction in Humean terms as the realization of natural and common pleasures, for which the seducer has simply a more unabashed affinity than other people. Seduction is not *per se* a case of acting on naturally stronger male desires, whether traced to the genes or to a strictly carnal pleasure principle. It needs only a single refuting instance, of a female seducer for the former claim, of a nonconsummating seducer for the latter claim, to drive home the point in each case.

There is, then, no intrinsic reason to make our seducer a man. We will make him a man only because men are more likely to come away socially unscathed from their seductions. We need to study a type about whom it will be believable to say at the end, as Henry James says of Morris Townsend in *Washington Square:*

> He had made himself comfortable; and he had never been caught. (1880, ch. 35)

The reader is made uncomfortable by the fact that Townsend *is* comfortable, and wishes that he had instead been caught. What fate, or summons, has he escaped? How can one spell out the seducer's privative relation to the good in the domain of personal life?

As the pure type of the rake, the seducer must persuade another to enter a personal relation, on the terms that she bracket or prematurely arrest her natural abilities to fathom the motives of the person by whom she is being persuaded. She is to be persuaded to suppress these abilities precisely because they would reveal to her a disparity between what she brings to the personal relation, and the views, hopes, and investments that her seducer brings. The seducer, insofar as he conforms to the concept of a seducer, knows about the disparity, is prepared to go forward with the relation on that basis, and is prepared to use the disparity in furthering his separate aims. These separate aims will be primarily *aims affecting the personal relation*, which remains in any case a shared experience, although that joint relation may in turn be useful in the furthering of additional private projects aimed at by the seducer.

What, precisely, is so wrong with all this, provided that one has made oneself comfortable and has not been caught? How can we be sure that the pure type is, in fact, going *to the bad*, rather than to the theatre-in-the-round of social life? What sort of choice has the seducer inescapably made, and how consequential is that choice, ethically?

We are talking about the seducer's involving another person in an intimacy on the basis of a willfully maintained informational disparity. This is not a provisional disparity, maintained out of tact, which would be closed in proportion as the other were seen to be interested in and capable of sustaining closer ties. It is, rather, to be maintained *because that is the kind of personal relation the seducer chooses to have.*

One necessary consequence of such a choice is that, thenceforth, one cannot know whether the intimate personal relation could have been sustained if the informational disparity had been corrected. The seducer has placed himself in a position not to know the answer to that question. Thus, insofar as he remains a seducer, some of his personal relations will be such that their boundary conditions are willfully self-obscured. He will, then, know that much less about personal relations.

How much does this matter, for *his* living of the good life? (Since the thread of *non*complicity in the victim will be hard to lift out, for the present it will be simpler to concentrate on the seductive intention *per se*.) Recall that, although a seduction involves bringing about, by deceptive means, an intimate personal relation, it does not necessarily end in a sexual consummation. By the same token, personal intimacy does not need to be bodily intimacy. Our question, then, must be whether intimate personal relations, taken in this inclusive sense, matter to the living of the good life, and, if so, how much they matter.

The good life summons one to a continuous and progressively more informed curiosity about what one was really up to all along, with a view to the living of a story about oneself that is as reasonable as one can make it. If this story fails to retain its reasonable character by dint of constant revision and self-correction, then by degrees it loses touch with ideality.

Our question is, then, how has the seducer failed to live reasonably and failed thereby to retain the ideality of his story? We should not say that his is merely a failure to see the trade-offs. It may be that, on the long view and in general, it is not "reasonable" (that is to say, not prudent) to deceive others about one's intentions in personal relations, because others may reciprocate or they may pull out of such relations altogether, leaving one personally inconvenienced and—in the long run—lonelier. On the other hand, we may without contradiction suppose that these sad consequences sometimes do not occur. In any case, we have not cared to suppose that the pure type of the seducer *suffers* acutely from these deficits. The one we have picked out for study has made himself comfortable and he has never been caught. He is charming enough to go on being admired, for his looks, skills, eloquence, daring, or whatever. He has perhaps won the secret admiration of those whose lusts are tempered by timidity, or the favor of David Hume's hostesses or of Kierkegaard's aesthetical youth. He is doing all right. In what sense, then, has *his* life failed to make sense?

The seducer will have stopped going toward the good and started going to the bad only if it's impossible for him to get all the correctives on his story from sources other than the one of intimate personal relations. I believe that seducers often claim to be based mainly outside of personal relations and *therefore* to suffer no personal ill effects from the harm they may regretfully do to others in personal relations. They are not, or so they often claim, starved of the corrective insights that freshen life and make it worth going on with. They get that corrective insight from creative work, from their sensitive responses to art, to nature, to theoretical sources, to sport. So the question of whether one *can* be mainly based outside of personal relations while still living the good life as here defined is the one that has to be addressed now.

As to creative work, aesthetic responsiveness to art, nature, or sport, none of these can by themselves fully answer the earliest questions of our lives, the ones that arose in lengthy struggle of a personal kind with the persons who first took care of us. Those first questions were, necessarily, questions about personal relations. So, to throw oneself in adulthood into questions and answers that are entirely extrapersonal is not to go on with the business of making sense of one's *entire* story. One can take temporary leaves of absence from the immediacies of personal life and get therefrom refreshment and ratification of one's enjoyment of skill or talent, intellectual, aesthetic, technical, mystical, or other. Such temporary leaves of absence may prepare one to go on with one's story; they may anchor or energize the effort of going on. It belongs to such extrapersonal efforts to have their own momentum. They can seem magically to keep a person going, as if something outside the person were pushing him or her along. But if one is not permanently *prepared* to go back to the arena of personal life for insights about one's own, then one is—albeit at the very highest levels—just muddling through.

Psychological theories about the opacity of the decision-making process, in particular where it affects personal life, are intelligible in their consequences for the good life only if they afford it greater clarity about how to *correct for* such alleged innate tendencies toward self-misunderstanding. If, however, an educated seducer wants to argue (on behalf of his innocence) that he cannot help misinforming others about the intimate relations into which he enters with them—cannot help doing so because (psychological theories assure him that) the ego is by nature misinformed in its intimate self-relation—it follows that, insofar as he makes this argument in excuse for some particular manipulative act against another, he is *not* entirely self-deceived. He is at minimum a co-conspirator against the norm of equal candor in intimate relations. Such candor cannot be a simple achievement. Nevertheless, the seducer has no warrant from psychology (Freudian, cognitive, or other) to conspire against its achievement.

Intimate relations are, then, indispensable to the living of the good life. Willfully to act so that, in consequences of one's act, one will know less than one otherwise would have known about intimate personal relations is to lose touch with reality. It is to go to the bad. The seducer is, phenomenologically, the pure type of the individual who chooses evil and not good in personal relations. Let us now set him in motion.

The Rake's Progress

We remove from him at a stroke the extrinsic gains that may be, and often are, by-products of his situation: sexual pleasure, a young woman's fortune, classified government documents, prestige in the eyes of other males, and so forth. For there are other (nonseductive) means of gaining all these things. And one can qualify as a seducer without gaining any of them.

To be a seducer, one *must*, however, enter into a personal relation with the intent of giving another false leads about the overlapping chapter in two life stories that one will (metaphorically) read aloud with that other. One will deliberately misinterpret one's own story to another in such a way as to get that other inadvertently to misinterpret in turn her own story. A seduction is a kind of deliberately contagious falsification of shared autobiography.

Again, let us leave out cases where tact or some undisclosable secret leads an individual reluctantly but intentionally to skew the informational content of an intimate personal relation. It may even be that in *all* such cases the withholder of information is misguided. The distinguishing point about such a withholder is that he or she is misguiding another for extrinsic reasons, whether sensible or foolish, and not just for the sake of doing so. However, the seducer, in the pure type, misguides another for the sake of misguiding another.

Styles of seduction change with changes in culture. They vary with differences in social level and personal expectation. Every seducer cannot have his way with every candidate. Nevertheless, an effective seducer can have his way with a great many types of candidates, whose social and personal expectations appear otherwise to vary greatly. Evidently, to have his way, the seducer must charm something in his candidates, or charm something away. One may suppose that this charm, of the seducer to his candidates, would be dimmed if the character of his initiative were quite visible to them.

How can so many be fooled? What does it mean *not* to be fooled? Are they all simply fools, simply "silly"? Is the seducer himself just a charming fool? Some people profess to think so. What is going on here? In the aftermath of an effective seducer, so many apparent passions are given the lie. Much of the victim's somber self-contempt seems to be dismissed by the generality of people with smiling malice or (what is almost as bad) brisk healthy-mindedness. In the aftermath of an effective seducer, one sees, or believes oneself to have seen, some sort of miragelike virginal hope, that formerly distinguished the victim, now abandoned by her as the counterpart of her own abandonment by the seducer. What has he touched *in her*, that she now shrinks from? One does not shrink from money, because one has once been defrauded of some. Nor avoid food, because one has once been upset by some. *This* seems to be different.

What about the seducer? If he is touching another in a particularly vulnerable moment, is he not touched at all? If he is touched, how can he go on like that? What is the charm of the event, to him? How does he get into it? How does he, at the same time, keep *himself* out of it? What becomes of him?

Let us, for the sake of the further analysis, distinguish three species of man: the *conventional*, the *original*, and the *seductive*. (There are not actually three species of man. These are options, between which all of us can move. If these options are clarified, one can retrace one's trajectory between them more self-correctively.) Each such species of man takes a different approach to the clarification of desire in his own life.

Conventional is the man who has become aware that the clarification of native desire is a more difficult, long-range business than the gratification of compensatory desires. Since one's culture must offer gratifications of some kind in exchange for socially and legally mandated behavior, the latter sort of behavior will generally elicit predictable and palpable benefits. Not everyone who does what is approved as right has his heart in it, of course. But many of those who do right habitually feel that the heart cannot wait forever for its satisfactions, as it might have to do if it insisted on satisfying its first desires, in their first strength and purity. To satisfy native and original desires is, as we have seen (Chapter One, pp. 7–10) to clarify them so that they reach the point where they become satisfiable: one finds the deed that answers to the heart's desire. If one does not set forth after these clarifications, one must have some satisfactions nonetheless. If the satisfactions do not come to meet one along one's native grain, then one must reshape oneself to fit the channels where they do run. And one will do well to do that in such a case. For one must have some satisfactions, and the man of conventional rectitude has *some*. If one's desires have remained vague, one will meet the schedules of normality without especially wanting to, feeling oneself safer there and no more expressly available elsewhere. So the meandering pursuit of the self generally winds up looking like "normal" behavior, where desires are deliberately vague and expressions of desire deliberately derivative, deliberately typical.

It might be objected that most people fall outside this discussion, since they pursue the self neither directly nor in a winding way. Most people, runs the objection, have concrete pursuits by which they make their living and find their recreation. Perhaps, the objection continues, what we have been calling the storylike clarification of the self is a wayward or idle interiorization of concrete pursuits. But, on the contrary, it is concrete pursuits that give information about or distraction from one's real desires, and therefore give information about or distraction from one's longer story. If these concrete pursuits seem over the long pull to be *shared* and *typical* pursuits, that one has neither made one's own nor rejected on one's own, then the information gained merely lends to the vagueness of the self an external or excrescent clarity. One does not wish to be glib about this excrescent clarity, which lends to society much of its necessary competence. Often, the conquest of frivolity and anxiety that was needed to produce the person of excrescent clarity was and is sufficiently engrossing to produce a person of hidden but profound pathos. But what is clarified in the process is still an excrescence. What was rendered pathetic, passive, and mute were the more native tendencies.

Original is the clarified desirer. And it is no part of the present argument to claim that the clarified desirer is translated into a dimension wholly incommensurate with his culture and his culture's satisfactions. The original man is not a mythical person. His satisfactions are not unique, and there is virtually nothing available to him that is not likewise available to another. How indeed could it be otherwise, since we are dealing here with the clarification of conscious expressions and overt pursuits, which must belong to shared expressive systems? The original man has stayed in touch with what he originally wanted. If one originally wanted to be someone whose closest approximation in practice would be a human being with this athletic or mechanical or therapeutic competence, then acquiring the competence becomes directly instrumental to the clarification of what one wanted. Each repetition of the skilled practice will bring one into further contact with the underlying desire. Each progressive refinement of one's competence will give information about the ramifications of one's original desire, and about the obstacles that it must confront from one's present place in culture and history. It is not an accident that among the skilled members of a culture are originals, who remain commensurate with the rest through their skill, which they simply seem to have more of. They are recognizable cultural types, but they are not the imitations. They are themselves. So they will be at least strong enough to bear the advancement they may bring to their fields of competence. They know they have more where that came from.

Seductive is the desirer who does not continue to want what he wanted in the first place. It is not necessarily the case that the seducers want what they first wanted more feebly than the originals. What they fail to do, however, is *hold on* to the original desire, through the arduously self-corrective training one undergoes for its attainment. (If they did hold on to that original desire, the project of seduction would not interest them, since, as we have seen, that project is inimical to the exploratory personal relations that are inseparable from the good life, and its rational self-curiosity.)

On the other hand, it is plausible to assume that the seducer has not wholly lost sight of his original intentions, since they are a part of what he misrepresents. The seducer cannot deliberately give a false picture of himself, unless he has some part of the true picture in view. (No one can deliberately lie, except insofar as he knows some part of the truth about which he lies.) The conventional man can, of course, lie too, but he cannot lie effectively about his underlying life story, since he's lost his identifying hold on it. If the conventional man wants to become a seducer, he must revive at least enough self-curiosity to make possible a lie about what he has therein discovered. Otherwise he cannot be what the seducer can be, at least to his immediate victims, namely, "an interesting man."

The seducer interests his immediate victims, and sometimes a wider public, in the kind of man he is, and is able to do so because, contagiously, he is at least *somewhat* interested in himself. The starved man of probity, on the other hand, has been faithful to a derivative vision of himself, in which he can have at most only the mildest, bemused sort of interest. His real desires have remained vague, or unrefined. His ranked choices match the generally accepted ethical priorities *because* the latter can be coordinated with the most available schedules for personal conduct in the culture. The norms are there and the self is not. The conventional man will take the norms, therefore.

It is true, if not very informative, to say that the instrument of seduction is the seducer's charm, or ability to be "an interesting man." We have additionally noted that the victim of seduction will become, eventually, disillusioned not just with him, but—almost violently—with something about herself. And we have noted that this toxin of self-disillusionment is not drained by those robust, sports-minded folk who urge the victim to get on with the "game" of her life, since it's not whether you win or lose, but how you play the game. Now we have to put a finer point on it. What exactly *is* interesting in the seducer? What exactly is no-longer-interesting-to-herself in the person who has been seduced? What, if anything, is the connection between the victim's initial interest in another and her subsequent loss of interest in herself? And, within the same general set of questions, why does the seducer lose interest in his victim, and how is *he* able to sustain interest in future victims and continue to seem interesting to them? How does he avoid catching a bad case of the demoralization that he spreads like a contagion?

A seducer is a man who seems to have, or suggests that he has, a *vision* of where he has been, or where he is going, or both. To have such a vision is already to have given oneself some importance. One becomes, by implication, a beginning of something. One is not bor-

rowed entirely from the beliefs and practices of others. One cannot
have a plan until one has some insight. One cannot light one's own
way unless one can first at least imagine that one sees it, in the
neighborly, breathing, human mists that surround one. With a vision,
an image, a path of one's own, fancied or understood, between the
separate ways that others travel, one begins to see oneself as something else than the shadow of what they do.

At minimum, the seducer has his own such inarticulate vision, or
fragmentary articulation of connections between his own real and
possible experiences. He could scarcely evoke some answering trust
or acquiescence in others without having on his side *some* powers. He
has some, and he has had to put in some work to develop them. He
has learned a thing or two. So has the conventional man, but the
motives were different in his case. The conventional man has learned
what he has learned so as to be like others. The seducer has learned
what he has learned so as to feel himself in greater accord with his
self-initiated possibilities, or not-fully-worked-out personal vision. He
has in some measure responded to an original urge—an urge at least
to be original.

There are, of course, degrees of articulateness achieved here. At
minimum, the seducer is likely to have a good, poetic hold on the
concrete, to know how to call up an image metaphorically suggestive
of himself and his original intentions. At maximum, seducers can be
highly articulate. But their articulateness *per se* does not make them
seductive. The articulateness of the book-learned seducer, like the
earthy poetry of the unlettered seducer, required effort, the effort of
matching this achieved expressiveness with an unformed vision of the
self. A bone-lazy seducer could not get far. So the seducer has had to
work at something and then work harder to connect that something
to his primal vision. He is trading on that work. His efforts have not
been commensurate with the efforts of the conventional man. He has
different and—partly—more desirable aims.

The candidate for his seduction is the woman who shares or
wishes to abet some of those aims. Insofar as women hope to convert
men into their supporters or particular protectors by putting forward
a shimmering psychic-somatic vision of the pinnacle that they already
occupy—rather than expressing their ongoing effort to make more
sense of their existence—women must be, at the start of their erotic
careers, seducers by default. To *understand* herself in other than seductive terms, a woman must considerably outgrow herself, at least if
her acculturation has been a fairly traditional one. (Almost any cultural tradition one can think of will support this point, at least in part.
Of course, a woman who is still entirely subservient to the wishes of

her guardians is not a candidate for direct and personal seduction, though she may still be regarded as passively seductive, and therefore eligible for a brokered seduction, in which she implicitly plays the correspondingly compliant part. However, it is the complicity of the relatively free modern woman that allows the typically male seductive operation to emerge as a dissolute phase of personal life.)

Personal relations between modern men and women are still set in the historical framework of an unequal contest. The male side of the contest still has immeasurable authority. It is an authority on which some women have written some fairly reliable, partial commentaries. It is an authority that many women can bend to a degree, even wield for a season, if they know how to respect its sense and momentum, but that women as such have nowhere superseded. Where there is real authority left in the world, theoretical, practical, or police authority, it is male-originated. That does not mean that all men share it, as if they were members of the same exclusive country club. But it probably means that most men share some aspects of the prestige of it, and some fragments of the overall force of it.

What this means, from the standpoint of our analysis, is that, when she sets off in pursuit of such self as she might in principle call her own, the woman in the story *begins* with less authority. She is not more readily made evil. But *she is more readily kept conventional,* beyond her narrow orbit of intuitive freshness. So, if she resists her seducer, it must generally be out of conventional considerations. And if her seducer wants to make headway, he is more likely to make it if he works in part against those conventional considerations. Insofar as she remains herself mired in her situation, she will be seductive by default, hence moved by the seducer as someone with whom she can identify, whose burdens are not unlike her own. She is seductive by default and wants, in a muffled or conscious way, not to have to be. He is seductive by design and may well pretend not to want to be. She is conventional by default and wants, in a muffled or conscious way, to be original. He is anticonventional out of aborted originality, originality without follow-through. (We speak of originality of attained self—not of other expressive attainments.)

Where then does the deception begin? What precisely is the false something that the seducer is furnishing, in leading her to a consummation of some kind? Why cannot the man and woman, struggling mutually against their respective conventionality and seductiveness, be friends?

We have said that the vision of himself that the seducer entertains has gaps in it, and has not been brought into the maximally attainable focus. All of us who strike out in pursuit of our clarified selves begin this way, with the course uncharted. The seducer has an image, a hankering, a tune. Nobody begins with very much more. If one would measure the distance between one's two- or three-year-old self and the distant, winking image one carries of one's achieved self, one must begin to take certain steps, go toward the middle, answer the assailing voices, try, in short, to handle what's out there. From such efforts, one gains a more advanced point of departure. One can begin again, to measure the distance between here and the still-more-realized eventual self. So one takes on the hard but promising burdens of self-education.

The seducer has likewise transformed himself somewhat. Enough to have kept some intuitive hold on his original vision or desire. Unlike the conventional man, he has not let his original vision sink out of sight. But he has not gone very far to clarify his vision. He is certainly not bone-lazy. But he is peculiarly lazy. He lets his vision go and returns to it intermittently, as if he himself were his own seduced and abandoned victim. He tricks himself out of the vision and tricks himself, just as suddenly, back into focus. His vision (of self, or life story) is not progressively getting clarified. So he can offer no sustained and faithful help to a fellow pilgrim.

He is not in a position to help others, since—in this most important matter—he does not help himself. So he asks the woman in the case, who certainly will need help in clarifying her own desires, to give that help to him. He cannot sustain his vision. So the burden of sustaining a fading, flickering vision is transferred to her as soon as possible. Meanwhile, *she* needs help in sustaining her own, historically feebler, and more tenuous vision of self. She reasons, plausibly enough, that by sustaining his, she can learn at the same time more about what it means to sustain her own.

Her reasoning is not unlike that of a teacher, who gives help to others precisely in the field in which she in turn would like to improve her command, and often learns from the very helping operation in which she is engaged and from the very people she helps. One may suppose that many people in helping professions have similar experiences. My point is that the woman who is vulnerable to a seducer is not, *in respect of her susceptibility*, necessarily a fool or a sufferer from erotomania. One may object that, in the professional analogy, the "help" operates within well-defined constraints, whereas in the unfortunate case of seducer and well-intentioned victim, it does not. This is true. But it is no simple matter to draw the moral.

The moral would seem to be that, in working out one's life, one can only *get* "help" within well-defined constraints, so that one sort of help is applicable to one sort of problem and can't be stretched to cover another sort. The lines connecting problems and purposes, one to another, have precisely to be drawn in by each person, individually, insofar as she commits herself to a good life. One wrongly supposes—perhaps because one has heard of the global promises voiced in religious traditions, or felt the holistic hopes held out by human love—that one can help another become himself, or be helped by another to become oneself, even if neither party is otherwise trying very hard. One wrongly supposes that one party's good intentions or intelligent purposefulness can be grafted onto the other party. One wrongly supposes that emotional support is transformative of human lives, magically. And one is all the more inclined to suppose this, in proportion as one is less experienced in working out one's own meaningful independence.

Since the latter process seems, while one is engaged in it, inordinately lonely and doubt-filled, the woman in our case will want, along her way, to do some good—to another creature of flesh and blood—and thereby earn the right to think better of herself. For all these reasons, she hears the seducer's half-audible plea for help and proffered companionship as occasions for her own constructive initiatives. Finally, such profferings come the more frequently *because* she looks, as the saying goes, "naive." That is, she looks as though all these considerations were passing through her mind.

In sum: a seducer is (in our pure type) a man who deploys before a (for historical reasons peculiarly vulnerable) woman his distant (that is, fragmentary) idealization of himself, *and then bluntly effaces that vision.* The woman in our pure case finds that she has been seduced by the vision, there being in him no actualizable desire-to-become-himself toward which she could learn to orient.

Our seducer was a dissolute character at the outset. By the time we meet him, he has dropped his original desire. That is, he has dropped it practically and effectively. There is not much he will do to serve it. There is not much, of cognitive moment, that he will risk to keep it alive. He may take other risks. He probably will, to keep the interest in himself alive. But there is not much he will undertake *for the purpose of learning more* about the original desire. But, if he has dropped it practically and pedagogically, he hasn't severed connections with it aesthetically. He still enjoys many of the sights and the sounds that remind him of the original desire. He can still artfully allude to it—the man he wants to be or the ideal he lives up to—incessantly in conversation. To himself and his companions he still tenders the original desire, as a promise to himself that he will betray, as his only pure love, as the love he will predictably abandon. He will tease himself and others with his original desire, or vision of the ideal story, as if it were his artifact and not his summons.

It is this kind of teasing, in the first instance a self-teasing, that he will share with the many candidates for his seductions. That there will be *many* such candidates is one overt sign of the self-betrayal that precedes and dictates each involvement. The seducer, whose end-point is *sexual*, is sometimes admired for having overcome "inhibitions" and given himself permission to act on his sexual desires inside the maze of social life. The seducer has, however, his own "inhibitions." He cannot stand intimacy that's gone stale.

Intimacy will, but not because one has lived through it with the same person for some length of time. It goes stale when one stagnates at some point along one's own trajectory. Familiarity itself breeds neither contempt nor self-contempt, but to be known in the directest way *while one is evading the sense-making summons* is hardly flattering. Intimacy is also hard to stand when one or the other party to it has temporarily outdistanced the other, whether in living his ideal story or in some other more specialized activity. To be possessively or enviously stifled at close range is neither pleasant nor easy.

Nevertheless, the person we have called *original* is used to having difficulties of this kind. He is his own close-up and familiar adversary, so that intimacy does not make his life significantly harder. He has the means of dominating his own envy, since he has so painstakingly intimate an acquaintance with his own nature that he cannot long be turned from its pursuits. It is hard to stifle him absolutely, since he cannot easily forget how far he has already come, nor where he was headed. He will not long be stalled through the fault of another. If he is occasionally stalemated, it will only be for as long as it takes him to find his way around the deadlock. His close-up with another may be provisional for one reason or another, but the nonimitative person does not have all that much to fear from being well known. He cannot be well known. In his fascinated self-pursuit, his own terms keep undergoing revision and adjustment. By candidly sticking to his original point, he so arranges his days that he does not empty himself out. The seducer is not like that. He needs a new candidate for his attentions, at just the point where the fact that he has—once again—emptied himself out might come under sustained, intolerably shared, recognition.

We have seen how the effective seducer keeps himself "interesting" and keeps *himself* out of it. We have seen why those who see through him are not necessarily in every respect wiser than those whom he fools. What we have still to study, for our purposes, are the charm of the practice to him and what becomes of him.

More than in any single intimate relation and its course, the character of the seducer becomes apparent in his almost tireless capacity for reentanglement. The charm of the practice to him? Recall that the vision of one's self as living an ideal story is sometimes miragelike, and more often so when one doesn't work at making the vision actualized. In such a case, it is fun, it is charming, it is rejuvenating, to turn willfully back toward one's mirage-vision and invite an attractive party to share it. It is pleasant and psychologically natural to identify with what is attractive in others, and to project upon them one's own mirage-vision of self, as painters used allegorical figures of "piety" and "chastity" to give body to their mirage-visions of the virtues.

Our visions of ideality take natural shape as attractive human beings whom we picture. To sully one's relations with an attractive human being, as the seducer eventually will, is to take from her her initial belief that she is in a position to produce truly constructive initiatives within the scope of personal relations. Although she may, with hard trying, recoup some understanding of herself as "naive," learn to read other people's motives with more expertness, try to outgrow the picture of herself as also a seducer, all that recovery, if it takes place, will take time. Meanwhile, what her seducer sees is her erasure as an ideal shape, as someone who can represent a vision. Thus she lives out, for him, his own relation to himself. In being false to her, the seducer allows himself meanwhile to imagine that he is being true to his vision, since *that* crumpled expression, *those* shrunken resources and deprecated flesh, bear small resemblance to the unspoiled story that he originally wanted.

Far from exhausting him, the new entanglement and the one that follows, and the one that follows that, reveal to his involved senses that he still enjoys the favor of his muse. The fact that he can be as thoughtful, as sympathetic, as unstudied with the new one as with all the previous ones shows him that he still has it: the gift, the grace, the self-delight. Certainly he is sincere! Certainly he can go on! He owes it to himself to go on!

What becomes of him? There is what one might call an ascetic way out. A vaguely unflattering sense of himself might prompt him to yield his energies to a discipline or a danger that comes to him from without as a kind of summons.

"If it had been otherwise"; Carton's hand was again watchfully and softly stealing down, "I never should have used the longer opportunity. If it had been otherwise"; the hand was at the prisoner's face; "I should but have had so much the more to answer for. If it had been otherwise—" Carton looked at the pen and saw it was trailing off into unintelligible signs. (Dickens, 1859, ch. 13)

If Sydney Carton has been, in his personal relations, a seducer, Victorian reticence has kept Dickens from clarifying that point. He is anyway a "dissolute" man, with a private vision of himself as something better, and that vision is given fictional definiteness to him in the figure of a pure-minded double who is "the prisoner" for whom he has "come to lay down his life," by making good the tally of those scheduled for the guillotine that day. It's a good story. We all know it.

The story is illustrative of our point that there is, for the seducer, the hope of an ascetic way out. Carton is summoned by an extraordinary emergency to stop disappointing people, to step into the magic looking glass, literally the cravat of Darnay, and become his private vision of himself as something better. It is the extrinsic character of the summons that permits him to make himself accountable to it. "If it had been otherwise . . . I never should have used the longer opportunity." True enough. But why not?

The actions of which he has previously been the author and ground were not compatible with the vague purity of his private vision. The sum of them has left him with a different face, body, and past than the ones belonging to his private vision. If the dream man deserved his secret, homesick veneration, then the sorry figure that he has become must not deserve to be the dream man's brother ego. (Of course he could make the dream man something less vague than a dream, and his relation to him something more actionable than secret, homesick veneration. But then he would have embarked on a life of realistic self-correction, of real clarification of desire, in which case he would have left the seducer and the fate of the seducer behind him. He might then, by degrees, become truly harmless. All power to such a reformation, but it is with the mentality of the seducer and *his* fate that we are concerned here.)

The seducer who responds to an extrinsic summons does not re-form his life, bit by bit, intelligently. He repents of it, and makes expiation for it, wholesale. If he wins glory on some—to him exotic—field, his victims will not find in *that* much balm for their wounds. To them, it might seem rather that, having first "had his way" with them, he is now "having his way" with mankind generally, and with God. Nevertheless, we must admit that the ascetic way is a way out of sorts, for the seducer. It will be extremely hard for him, with the memories he has, to become truly good. It will be much easier for him to offer definite help to someone, or some enterprise, and especially if the offer is for him somewhat attention-getting, or flamboyant. And his former victims will just have to live with their private misgivings.

It is also possible that the ascetic and the seductive projects can be used to keep each other going. If the seducer knows how to moderate his enterprises, so that the seductions can be played against his sacrifices for the common weal, or played against his explorations of a private talent, and if he knows how to be helpful to others from time to time, and pleasant to most, most of the time, and to do his duty when solemnly required to do so, he can live and die a seducer. The seducer of moderate habits can leave this earth late in life, with only the most moderate regrets. He will have made himself comfortable, and never been caught. He will have known how to sound authentic.

What about the downfall of the seducer? In a moment. First we must—patiently—entertain in imagination the seducer who is "saved by a good woman." This is the seducer who finds that one of his potential victims forestalls her victimization and transforms it into a constructive initiative. This is not an entirely gratifying picture, from the moral standpoint.

Why is one "good woman" more effective with her salvage efforts than the—let us say equally serious and well-intentioned—sisters who preceded *her* but were incapable of handling *him?* What is different about her? What has changed in him? Nothing obvious on either hand. Through no special merit of his own, he has charmed one more woman. Like many another, she has tried to be good, and good for him. But this time, unaccountably, these efforts *work.* She really does save him from himself.

It seems particularly unfair. He doles out about the same kind of charm that gave him detrimental influence on other women. The effect of his charm will be to cut short the process of his guilt and condemnation more surely than an ascetic retreat from carnal pleasure would have done—but to do all that without much shrinking his matrix of pleasures. Nerved by her influence, he may now *use* some of those "longer opportunities" of which Sydney Carton took his ascetic leave. The seducer has used about the same incomplete and unsatisfactory talents that he used every time before, and used them in about the same style. Because he happened to meet by their means a woman who could represent to him *das ewig Weibliche*, his own self-salvage, he has been brought home to himself a changed man.

The woman in the case may be entitled to feel that it is a particularly creditable victory.

Onlookers are known to applaud these occasional reversals of cynical expectation, even while onlookers may put them to the further trial of private malice or additional, furtive temptation. Still, the public stays relatively sympathetic to this sort of resolution of a bad man's difficulties. A "good woman" is one of a society's more readily relied upon and credible products. The usefulness of this product to society is confirmed in its usefulness to a troubled individual. The woman who repairs a dissolute man is knitting up the frayed sleeve of her part of society.

The implication is that we (that is to say, we members of our own society) *may* trust to our own socially given devices, since in the end we do repair ourselves. God Himself cannot do more. Indeed, He cannot do this kind of job at all, of readmission to the body politic. Only a good woman can do it, for a bad man. (Or, as is sometimes also said, a good man can do it, for a bad woman.)

What is piquant in these modern reformations is precisely their abandonment of any modern claims to be original, and the replacement of such claims with an enthusiastic imitativeness. It is almost as if there may be many ways of going to the bad, and many garlanded charms that hang about each way, but "strait is the gate," . . . etc. More than that, it is as if the *whole* charm of going to the bad is that one may, if God so wills that odd form of chastisement and reward, be saved by a good woman.

> Oh thou in whom my hopes securely dwell
> And who, to bring my soul to Paradise,
> Didst leave the imprint of they steps in Hell. . . .
> (Dante, 1321, 31, 79)

Eroticized redemption thus appears to be the unacknowledged prize for crime. And one merely collapses the pieces of this puzzle when one asserts that women are "attracted" to hurtful men for "masochistic" or "sadistic" reasons, whatever such peculiar reasons might add up to. What women are "attracted" to is necessarily the exercise of their full feminine vocation. It belongs to that vocation to get people who are in one's world to act in such a way as to protect the physical frailty and general vulnerability of oneself as a woman. The reasons have nothing to do with being spoiled or coddled, in the world. What one wants, Dr. Freud, is—thus protected—just to *get on* with the further adventures that belong to the recovery of one's projected self. One wants to mind one's own business. Taming a bad man is rather the long way round to that, but that is and was what one originally wanted.

To redeem one bad man is to redeem a part of "the world" with which a good woman must deal every day, a world in which her vulnerability may be augmented by the callous treatment it calls forth from men who lack self-discipline—and from others because first of all from such men.

It is therefore in all women's generic interest to redeem, that is, reform, bad men, if they can get away with it. If women do not do this interesting work more often, it is because they fear, and with reason, that they cannot get away with it. They fear the man will not become a trophy of the feminine vocation. The woman, rather, will become a trophy of his further dissolution, indistinguishable as such from many other trophies. *La femme qui a un passé n'a pas d'avenir,* as the French would say—with what truth we have tried here to show. They fear he will convert her into a sediment of his story-dissolving past.

In sum, the risk is very great, for her. So the occasional successes of "the good woman" are proportionately dramatic and interesting. They are no less interesting for having occasioned more literary than ethical or philosophic study. They are no less interesting for being quite possibly as mysterious to the good woman in her rare success as they were to her equally good predecessors in their commoner downfall. We do not dispose of these events in their significance for us by dubbing them fictitious or illusory.

What experiences have been recombined to make the fiction? What components have gone into the illusion? What is really going on here?

What is going on here is perhaps a little less impressive, or more modestly impressive, than what meets the eye. "Dissolution" is, of course, a metaphor. What the metaphor stands for is the fleshly face, or the experiential look and feel, of broken promises, whether the promises were made to oneself silently or to others, overtly or by implication. If that dissolution is to be repaired, whatever bland abjurings of the promises we've given to ourselves and others must be in turn repudiated. What we wanted to do, that needed to be done if life was to make sense, must still be done. The broken promises have to be kept, if we are to regain a sense of self as living its continued life-adventure from its own front lines. Terms like "redemption," "reform," "grace" either have mystification and political control in view, or else they may express the deliverance to experience of its own native outlines, its further coming home, its recovered originality.

A true reform would have to give us something more appealing and less punished-seeming than the burnt child who dreads the fire and stays home where it can't touch him any longer. But a good woman—can she effect in a dissolute man a true reform of that kind?

No. Evidently not. No more than a teacher can, in a wayward student. Or a parent can, in a willful child. No more and no less. No one "reforms" another, strictly speaking. The form of the self, or the self in form, is not a rigid mold into which we can pour ourselves mechanically, or anyone else mechanically. The moving mold of the self can be repaired perhaps, if it is torn, frayed, unreliable. One does this when one turns, belatedly, to keep one's broken promises. But the shape of the self, its outlines, its crisp edge, cannot be determined in advance of what it has to shape. There is an interaction here, between the crisp edge of the self—what it does in making itself felt—and the turbulent, fine-spun interior of feelings and long-term purposes. And only "time" or "higher purposes than ours" can give the precise formula of this compound. Indeed, to overcome discrepancies between the stamp one leaves upon the world and one's intentions is what it means to *gain* a self, show the form of one's intentions, and to "stay in shape," historically. We can suppose that the task of a good woman in a bad man's life would be this holding up the mirror (super-tactfully) to ethical discrepancies, in those patches of experience where she has overcome the said discrepancies and he has not. (Needless to say, two people who are intimate will have to do this for each other, at some points of their companionship. It can't all go one way. This discussion has to bracket the extraneous complexities, however.)

The "good woman," on this model, appears to be older than the man she has to reform, older in density of memory and thought at least, if not in years. Were the good woman not "older" in this life-story sense, she would be merely holding up to her more dissolute male counterpart the mirror of established values, and her own simplistic need to be protected by a general adherence to them. This kind of woman can be younger than the man, in thought-about experience, while yet being a good woman and good for him. But what she does for him that is so good is simply stop his progress toward decay. He'll pay some of the debts he owes himself, by learning loyalty at least, and by adhering to the established values that will give added protection to the woman to whom he is being loyal. He'll sacrifice the further treacheries he could enjoy and, in renouncing them, take somber satisfaction when they pass him by.

But he may also be renouncing that voyage on uncharted seas of which his former life was an imitation—however deceptive a one—and the tribute therefore that the vice in him paid to unencumbered virtue. In the eyes of the good woman, he has found himself worth more than what a rake's progress would be worth. But he has also found himself worth less than new solutions would have demanded of him, and out of shape for them. He has effectively retired from the lists.

In intimate affection, on these or any terms, there must be recognition of one's partner's hopes, and of his terms. If one has to, one can go on for a spell alone, conferring on oneself the monologic recognition for one's unsung efforts to become oneself inside the world. But one feels it is a bit like walking under water. One waits for the chance to exhale and breathe again the clean air of human recognition. In such recognition one finds heart for going on.

So there is recognition of a sort in this redemption-by-retirement to a good woman's confines. For example, there is recognition that the story-bearing self of the reformed seducer is just not in shape for further ventures. So it had best consolidate its gains and cut its losses. For no one quite brings off even so modest a reform as this without the close rewards of constant recognition. There is the sad fact that this sort of mild redemption "protects" one from what might be a more profound redemption. The person who needs to be saved is "punished" by the very terms of the salvage operation, viz., that there are loyalties exacted, and limitations on his further ventures, if he's to get the reliable incentive of incessant recognition.

He is "punished"—in one sense—beyond the punishment of monkish exile from a woman's constant recognition. For at least in monkish exile the romantic hope, of recognized self-unfolding, lives on intact, unrealized but unimpaired.

No one gets everything. We did not pity overmuch the person in ascetic self-exile, since he still had all his hopes, even if he had to take them to the scaffold. And we need not feel too much exasperation when a bad man is redeemed on a good woman's tender but confining terms, since he has not the means of realizing all his hopes and since he has—poor fellow—his reward.

But what about the bad man who is rescued from his heavy charge of debts, or from compounding the debts at least, by a good woman who does not confine him to conventionality? Is such a rescue possible?

Yes. It is possible, if its beneficiary wants nothing better and continues—despite the provocations to self-esteem inherent in close contact with a distinctly better human example—to want nothing better.

Shall we feel exasperated envy at the sight of such an undeserving fellow, rewarded so immoderately? It's hard to say. The sight is not, in fact, quite a familiar one. Undeserving men are not usually inclined to seek rewards of this demanding kind, nor to hold fast to them when they are proffered. If one is overly encumbered by one's debts, one cannot hope to form the plans or to assemble energies for further ventures. It is not a question of leaving anyone unfairly out in the dissemination of romantic hopes or expectations. No one is left out, although there is a point at which one does become practically insolvent. That point may vary with each man's resources and the way he will behave if he is given credit. Nevertheless, and despite these careful, qualifying remarks and due allowances, our final case, of the dissolute fellow who is released to his own further adventure by the good woman who knows how to hold up to him its convex, shining mirror, is perhaps a "classroom example." It is, in other words, the sort of thing that does not really happen. It is the romantic postulate of moral experience, as Aristotle's prime matter was the never-to-be-encountered postulate of physical experience. That we can at least postulate it, without contradiction, is a great relief. It suggests no one is "in principle" exempt from life's profounder rewards and compensations. But it also suggests that real rewards are not a magical replacement for an education. In other words, it is not easier to gain that difficult ascent because the way is known to someone closely able to inspect the distances traversed and those that lie ahead. A sheer face of rock to which one has just gained a hardy alpine guide has not become less difficult to climb because the climbing of it now is possible. There is nothing harder to climb. And it is harder still because it is just possible.

Now for the downfall of the seducer. Or is there such a thing?—apart from the comeuppance visited on the seducer by the sorts of redemption we have just outlined. Supposing him to have successfully evaded redemption of the ascetic or erotic kind, either because he doesn't see the need for it, or else because his naive capacities to enter into an enjoyed redemption have been jaded, what then will happen to him? "Redemption" has become for him the vanishing, trumped-up autobiography he held out and still means to hold out to his victims. If "redemption" in the valid sense is the hope of self-collection, on the self-given promises that have been and still will be kept, then "redemption" is precisely what he promised and betrayed, in others, in himself. His whole constitution and his way of life depend upon his going on as if *nothing* had happened and as if no special reckoning were on the way.

The blithe insouciance he displays as he apparently does this is rivaled only by the considerateness that he shows to children, pets, to needy strangers, worthy causes, and many other things that seem to show the face of suffering humankind.

He does not even seem ashamed of acting virtuous. It is discomfiting to us, the way he has the gall to carry on with life, the zest for living that he shows. At least *good* deeds ought to make him feel uncomfortable, we feel. But this is not a feeling that he shares. He will do the right thing too, and with impunity, and thereby give the lie to what we claim about him. (When *we* do the right thing, we must find out what it cost and often pay the price long afterward. But he seems to move through rights and wrongs, exempt from the accountant. He will also do the wrong thing, when it suits him, with what looks like careless grace.)

If, by any chance, he meets some accidental doom, he will be credited with careless grace, and some defiance of the laws of ethical gravitation. His whole life, its rakish progress and its end, will not be seen around the town as a seducer's downfall. (Except inside the pages of the kind of books that don't get written any longer.) One would have to go back to scriptural paradigms to see as clearly as we see today how "the unrighteous flourish." Or do we see it clearly, since we do not frame their flourishing in any sort of vision of their personal exhaustion or their ultimate entrapment?

How might we picture such a thing as the seducer's downfall? Why should we try to do so? Kierkegaard has pictured the seducer in his frustrating *endlessness*. What are we trying to bring off when we bring him—in imagination—to his end?

The seducer's downfall is not—how thoroughly we know this now—an external one. On the contrary. The seducer is the man who cannot fail, because he makes no serious efforts to succeed at the long-term life adventure. Since he cannot fail, nobody can exult in his occasional reversals. He never sought the cumulative payoff for persistent, purposeful activity of the reasonable kind. On the other hand, no one can register heartfelt surprise at his abilities, to sail through tight places or to right himself when his craft is upset. He has many sincere detractors, perhaps, but no tragic or unifying weakness to which his detractors can gain access.

It will be the detractors, rather, who will look spiteful, left-behind, out of phase with the authentic muddle through which the seducer carries on with life and gropes his way.

Those who are neither seducers nor detractors will look on and say that at least the seducer "takes life as it is," without imputing to real life any fictional finality. The seducer is for real, they will say. He has faced the mudflats and the quirky, tidal ebb and flow of actual events. He has "really lived," and how can anyone who's really lived experience a downfall? Even if he falls, that too is "really living," on his own terms. Who are we to ask another human being to justify the terms in which he puts his efforts to himself?

The point is that we *always* ask a serious and nonseductive person to be capable of justifying what he says and does. We ask that of him, since he asks it of himself. No matter how tactfully, discretely, indirectly, the reciprocal demand is put, each one asks of others the questions that he asks of himself, and makes on others the sorts of demands that he makes on himself. "Judge not, that ye be not judged" is, it seems to me, an unfulfillable demand. The fulfillable demand is: judge others on the same terms that you yourself consent to be judged. Each one overlooks in others what he pardons, by evasion, in himself. The seducer justifies the so-called neutral onlooker in each betrayal of a serious intention that the onlooker has also entertained. The man of determinedly serious intentions undermines the neutral onlooker in every motion of complacent self-distraction that belongs to the onlooker's more derivative way of conducting himself.

If we confront the seducer with a determined opponent, of serious intentions, we confront him—not with his nemesis (he has none)—but with the downfall that he has projected for all serious intentions, for his own, for anybody else's, but a "downfall" that refuses to fall down. The serious opponent cannot bring the seducer home to his doom, because the seducer will not cooperate. He doesn't feel a natural affinity with his own well-deserved doom. So they are simply and forever locked in an embrace of violence, the serious man or woman proving his or her persistent purpose in the face of opposition-by-dissolving-mimicry, the seducer discounting the solidity and the effectiveness of a life story, by every one of his attempts to make the other's enterprise look silly, out of line, beside the point—whatever the point was—outside the scheme of ordinary purposes, and finally destructible. They hate each other with a symbiotic hatred, whereby each may lead the other to get tripped up accidentally, but each still fails entirely to bring on the conversion of the other one's *intention*. Their relations convey and depend on an inbuilt and possibly eternal frustration.

The practical environment of the seducer is made up of people like himself, of more conventional onlookers, and of ordinary victims. He moves, that is, among the very dreams he conjures up, dreams of sincere, long-lived purposes, dreams he himself forbears to dream, dreams borne up in the minds of dreamers who will be—instead of him—the bearers of his self-deceiving promises. He conjures up the dreams. That is, he promises, overtly or by implication, and then snatches away what he has promised, again and yet again, without tiring appreciably, and without intrinsic downfall of any kind.

The activity itself is the seducer's sole undying downfall. It is Dante-esque; at least it recalls the suicides turned into pain-filled trees in the Inferno's seventh circle. They have lost a stable human form because they attacked the form they once had, in its bodily stability. In his own way, the seducer daily forfeits his salvation, daily sees that forfeiture confirmed by those who have come to accept his default, and daily loses hope of that reunion with oneself that gives to life its sense of closure, its familiar reassuring ring, its renewed hope of recognition.

Is there a charm in this inferno? Why, yes. The seducer has not carried to their term some sober succession of reasonable and self-correcting purposes. He is always the man who has "the world" before him. Having made good on nothing, he is still the man who could do everything.

This is his charm for "neutral" onlookers, who can never do a great deal, or not a great deal *that belongs to them*. This is his charm for victims who can suffer nearly everything, and for whom the world has its cracked mirror in the scars they will have earned. There is already *too much world* behind the victims. They must unlearn some things, if they are to get back to the starting place. And this is the charm of the seducer for the serious and nonseductive man or woman.

In any seductive and lifelong detractor, the serious and achieved contender for a story tends to hear a reminder of the claims that he or she has put on life. If one is serious, one has a world to gain, purpose by purpose, and one could gain it all. One has it all to lose, if one is serious, lost purpose by lost purpose, and one could lose it all. It is heartbreaking, heart to heart, this strange fraternity, between the person of serious intent who is undone at every turn by his or her unserious detractors, and the person of seductive and deceiving purpose, who is recalled at every turn to all that he has lost—and recalled to all that by his lifelong and serious opponent.

There *is* a charm in this fraternity, or would be, were it not so deadly. There is the charm of human intercourse. It portends recognition and suggests—that all our *real friends* are human, all our real opponents human too. So there is no archfiend, at the heart of things good and evil. No overarching bliss. All things of significance for us will find their places in a human conversation.

.

CHAPTER FOUR

Selling Out

The Sellout: The Pure Type

S ELLING OUT IS something that happens relative to a set of circumstances in which there is generally room for reasonable people to differ about what course of action would be the best one to take. What identifies itself as selling out to one person might look more like institutional or personal devotion to someone else. For example, the writer who laces his narrative with pornographic episodes may, from the onlooker's standpoint, seem to be pandering to a low public taste and selling his talent cheap. But the writer, meanwhile, may believe himself to be breaking down barriers of convention and clearing a path in his mind for original work. Again it may happen that the same agent may take the flattering view of his motives at an earlier stage of his life and take the unflattering view later, when he is older and more soberly cognizant of the consequences of a facile choice. What looks like the best one can do at an earlier point in one's life may look later on like an instance of one's having sold out, inadvertently, but still culpably. The eating of crow is, in sum, a moveable feast. Viewed from one side, the life story of a good man or woman is a succession of settings for this feast of crow. That being the broad context for this discussion, the pure type of the sellout has to be distinguished from the striving, fallible mass of humankind rather carefully.

In its concept, selling out would seem to include the following elements: (1) the betrayal of an ideal or trust that is recognized as such by the agent, (2) an unworthy motive for the betrayal, such as (*a*) social acceptance, (*b*) peer approval, (*c*) money, or (*d*) repose.* For

---

*I am indebted to Milton J. Schubin for this definition, and for extensive, clarifying discussion of the concept.

91

the purposes of orderly consideration, we shall further stipulate that the ideal or trust should not only be privately recognized, but also acknowledged actually or acknowledgeable in principle, within a given community of reasonable moral agents. Without this further stipulation, we might find ourselves having to deal again with the type of trust that is establishable only in an intimate context, ground we have already covered in the previous chapter.

This is not to deny that people do speak, broadly and casually, of "selling out" the trust implied by personal relations. Ordinarily they do so where a further unfolding of the personal relation is misleadingly promised, and the promiser fails to deliver, deliberately, and for *ulterior reasons*. The ulterior reasons usually have to do with the cool friend's outside investments, as when we say that so-and-so has no time to be a friend, because he is buying his way into social or professional prominence. So the understanding of what the seller-out of a personal relation is up to would have, in the long run, to center in his extrapersonal concerns anyway. It is therefore more useful to us, in the context of this inquiry, to give the expression "selling out" its more usual and limited meaning, of prostitution of a trust that is or ought to be an established trust, within a publicly recognized or institutional setting.

To reiterate the contrasting concerns of the previous chapter: if the failure to carry out the implicit promises of an intimate relation is deliberately *pitched to that relation* and has no ulterior motive beyond *its* betrayal, then it would be a case of personal dissolution of the pure type dealt with in Chapter Three, the section entitled "The Rake's Progress." If the default is on a trust that is more nearly *self*-assigned, as when I give myself a serious long-term task to pursue and then break it off incontinently, then it would be a case of personal dissolution, but one of the less "pure" or legible types of what we have called here going to the bad, such as was canvassed in Chapter Three, in "The Rake: The Pure Type."

In the pure case of the sellout, by contrast, there ought to be an identifiable, communally established consensus about what the agent should properly have done. In this chapter we will be dealing with the individual in a social context of mutually assigned expectations and tasks. Since the present context for viewing the individual has been widened, the individual's scope for self-invention will accordingly be seen to be more qualified.

In order to trace precisely the boundaries of our inquiry in this chapter, we ought first to confront two difficulties with regard to actions about which there is an actual consensus on the relevant norms. (1) The agent can be sincerely mistaken about how the consensus applies to the particulars of his situation. (2) The consensus itself might be considered, from some more enlightened standpoint, biased or even hopelessly wrongheaded.

Let us suppose, as in (1), that the agent sincerely believes that he has displayed institutional loyalty or appropriate creative adventuresomeness, in a given context of action. But in reality, which is to say, in the demonstrably reasonable and widely acknowledged view of others in the same community, he has betrayed a discernible public trust or discipline of his craft. Since the mistake is a sincere one, how do we place such an agent, with regard to the concept of selling out? Let us include among the "sincere" mistakes those that are honestly self-deceived, whether the deceiver is some feature of the agent's unconscious, or a break-away factor inside his conscious experience. If the unconscious motive has to do with a repressed sexual or aggressive drive (which may have helped our hunter-gatherer forebears to survive, but damages trust within our network of public institutions), then the agent who fools himself may be said to do so for an "unworthy" motive (see motive *d*, p. 91). But even that agent is, at least in the moment of action, sincerely fooled. Mistakes will happen, no matter how they are brought about. It is not open to us to undo the consequences of all past mistakes, nor to forestall all future ones. How do we classify the agent who acts under a mistaken belief?

The answer depends entirely on what he does after the mistake has been called to his attention. It *will* be brought to his attention, if the mistake contravenes an established consensus and he doesn't die or become a hermit immediately after making it, and he isn't crazy. What then? If he is a good man, he will move to correct it and to pay the price of those moves. If he does that, then he has *not* sold out. His goodness, at least, is safe. It is safe, even if the most calamitous consequences follow from what he has done, beginning with the loss of his peace of mind ever after. (Of such a type, Joseph Conrad wrote in the Author's Note to *Lord Jim* [1917], "One sunny morning in the commonplace surroundings of an Eastern roadside, I saw his form pass by . . . —under a cloud—perfectly silent. Which is as it should be. It was for me . . . to seek fit words for his meaning. He was 'one of us.'") Here we don't ask after his tranquility, only his goodness. If his loss of reputation is irremediable, we don't ask after his social consequence, only his moral worth. If property or innocent lives were lost, we don't ask here what others had to pay for his story, only whether he himself held back from selling it.

As to the question of whether Kantians or Utilitarians are correct, there is no absolute preference being expressed here for an ethic of intention over an ethic of result. These pedantic boundaries are not marked by surveyor's stakes within human experience. The point has been covered in Chapter One. The introspective reading of our intentions never gives them to us with fixity, transparently. We learn more about our opaque intentions from our actions, and particularly by seeing how we cope with the consequences of what we have done, consequences that are often partly unexpected. The only fundamental intention that can be discerned over time is the one of this kind of clarifying of what we intended, or the intention to explore our stories. (Cf. pp. 7–13.) If we have not got this intention, then other intentions we may choose to isolate for notice will hang in a peculiarly suspect, explanatory void. And, to repeat the point, *this* intention will be lost irrecoverably, if we do not hold ourselves accountable on the score of consequences.

Aristotle's moral analysis of the voluntary and the involuntary still seems to withstand the depth-charges from the unconscious. If an act is done without adequate prior understanding of its instruments and consequences, then the act that is done is not the one that was deliberately intended. As such, and however it happened to get done, it is an involuntary act. But the agent is not therefore exempted from retroactive accountability. If he becomes aware of the mistake but fails subsequently to make the reparation, he ratifies his act as, in retrospect, something closer to voluntary (Aristotle, *Nicomachean Ethics* 1110^b15–25).

We have deliberately situated difficulty (1) within a consensus about the proprieties of action that would quickly inform the agent of his error. We have done so because most actions undertaken by individuals have that context, and they must incessantly come to terms with the surrounding consensus. Some of the friends of the unconscious may, however, want to claim that the agent is able to interpret the consensus so as to bend it into line with his unconscious motivations, and thereby to persist in the error *unawares*. If this condition were held to persist absolutely, so that no gleams of awareness ever penetrated the mind of the self-deceived agent, then selling out (and all other types of evil) would be imaginary, or perhaps inconceivable, acts. We would all be adrift in the amoral seas, unable to say what we have seen there. The real situation is more taxing.

While a great deal of psychic information processing takes place unconsciously, and some of it involves a skewing of the evidence in line with innate biases, the very fact that experimental and depth-psychology "knows" this reflects a more fundamental feature of our cognition: it is fallible, it is corrigible, *and we know that*. Our cognitive activities have therefore a demanding character. They summon us to keep on the alert, to correct for our mistakes, and to keep on doing so. It does not take a philosopher of mind to hear this summons. The most primitive hunter, the hardiest sailor, hears it within his sphere of activity. So does the gardener. So does the cook, or the hostess. The main reason that most philosophers, and ordinary people, tend to reject extreme scepticism is that it is incorrigible and tends therefore to soften us up mentally. What could support or refute the claim that a *malin génie* deceives us? It is the sort of claim that takes us off the hook, cognitively, and gives more imaginative scope for laziness or irresponsibility than our real lives will allow. A mistaken belief is one that is out of line with reality. In small ways and in large, piecemeal or in crashing epiphanies, that fact will obtrude itself into our experience. What then shall we say of the agent who persists in his error "unawares," *because* he keeps redefining the consensus, and redefining the act, so that the latter will fit under the former?

If one takes successive and persistent measures to redefine the corrective, chastening experiences that have reminded one that one was out of line, then those measures belong to the ensemble of one's act. One can then ask about each such measure: was it deliberate, or was it mistaken? By the energy and ingenuity with which one dissuades oneself from correcting what obviously needs to be corrected, one can take stock of the deliberateness of one's default. At some point along a graduated incline, a rationale becomes a rationalization, and a default becomes culpable. If one wants to maintain that this never happens, or that it never happens *discernibly*, one must be prepared to wear the iron vests of hard determinism in morals (probably underlying the cloak of "soft" determinism anyway), and of extreme scepticism in epistemology. In this chapter we shall attempt to analyze a case where the selling out of a norm or standard with which one has been communally entrusted not only happens discernibly, but happens with exemplary legibility. The method of pure types thus makes accessible a point of comparison for deciphering in a rough-and-ready way the cases that may be less legible. So much for the first difficulty, where the agent is mistaken about the nature of the established trust.

Let us turn now to difficulty (2). Here the agent's persistence in error unawares is more understandable, because the consensus itself supports the same error. How do we classify the agent who acts to betray a public trust that would be *in principle* discernible, but acts under a mistaken belief that happens to be the most reputable one to entertain at that time inside his community?

Where an agent has defaulted on a public responsibility, to treat others fairly or perform some skilled task in the right way, the nature and degree of the default has to be calculated partly by taking stock of the cognitive sophistication of the community within which the rules for action have been laid down. We don't know what the agent has culpably neglected to do until we know what he could in principle have known.

Some rules preventing mutual predation are indispensable for all human communities that function well enough to perform their common tasks. Communities that are devoid of all such rules are in process of disintegration, and probably will not survive as such. If, further, there are some basic rules against predation, but these rules are not sufficiently grounded in a corrigible reasoning process to be in any sense "realistic," then the rules too, or the style of thinking behind them, will subvert the group's survival capacities over the long term. We can, however, imagine a community giving reasons for its rules of conduct that are so fanciful and weird that acceptance of these reasons gradually undermines the reasoning abilities of the group's members—but still the imaginary community survives by sheer grit and luck for some hundreds of years. In such a community injunctions to predation against subgroups defined as degraded or outcast, and injunctions to mutual help and kindness between upgraded members, are alike given on flimsy and unreasonable grounds. In that situation the agent who breaks a promise to the degraded members of the community, or who fails to meet such needs of theirs as he can meet, does what the rules have positively instructed him to do. He is not reprobated for this moral default, but widely approved for it. Nor can he be said to "know better," nor to have the means of getting to know better. Under a wrongheaded consensus, he persists in error unawares. What then is his moral status?

The example suffers from the weakness of textbook examples. It forgets that there are ways for people to know that they have transgressed against their neighbors, ways that are not available to the subjects of thought-experiments. So, in real life, such invidiously divided application of the moral rules would not, in *clear* conscience, be possible in a constitutional democracy. The repudiated members would rise, in voting strength, in brute strength, or at least in a crescendo of surly mutterings, to protest, if not absolutely to prevent, such invidious distinctions and the smiling complacency of them. Invidious distinctions might still continue to be drawn. But not in good faith, nor with clear conscience. As to residual and *ad hoc* inequalities, within a democracy devices of mutual rationalization are required so as to secure some semblance of mutual consent, even to the *ad hoc* inequalities. These devices for securing mutual consent must at least pay lip service to an ideal of equality under the moral rules, just as we say vice pays to virtue the tribute of hypocrisy. Because the devices of rationalization will tend in post-Enlightenment constitutional democracies to make explicit some ideal of equality, they will give an ambiguous and uneasy consciousness to those who commit or consent to acts of predation inside such a democracy.

So the situation that makes possible a wrongheaded consensus about the moral rules in which no one is *or can be* the wiser, the situation of complete cognitive unawareness coupled with a clear conscience is not to be found in ordinary Western-style democracies. For a changed cognitive situation, the requisite social changes must realistically be presupposed too. Our imaginary community might possibly be a theocratic caste society, or a totalitarian police state. What sort of moral accountability people might have in such a changed social and cognitive situation is discussed in Part Three. Here we need merely note that the situation of people in mental and physical bondage is so drastically altered, that those who live in it will require to have the moral categories more fine tuned to *their* possibilities. Insofar as difficulty (2) bears on the ordinary concept of selling out, then, it must be traced within a cognitive situation recognizably like our own. The betrayal of a public trust, human or technical, under a blanket of cognitive unawareness, with a clear conscience about that in perpetuity, is not called selling out, and is not found in a cognitive situation like our own.

In trying to discern the presuppositions of difficulty (2), we have moved closer to defining the pure type of the seller-out. He has his place amidst the cognitive resources and pitfalls of political freedom, however partial and conditional that freedom might be in particular instances. Political freedom supplies the motive and energy for members of a given community to recognize the equality of all under those moral rules that safeguard themselves from predation and permit them to live their own stories.

(It is true that the jurisprudential support for equality under the law might develop even in political conditions that tolerated slavery. The Stoic legal philosophy was a case in point. We may assume that the bondage conditions of Roman society were modified sufficiently to afford cognitive scope to some of those who were themselves in bondage, like, say, Epictetus, and also to some of those who held slaves or profited from a slave economy. The political freedom of enlightened ancient societies was evidently partial, but it must have been sufficient to enable some of their membership to conceive and picture freedom's extension into and imaginative completion in the ideal realm of moral and legal theory. Had the restrictions on personal freedom for the thinker been greater, it is unlikely that even this theoretical development could have taken place in ancient Rome, or had its influence on the course of European law and institutions.[1] This said, the investigative difficulties of separating the cognitive conditions of actual freedom from those of formal bondage, and vice versa, within a constitutional framework that has scope for both would have to be very great, even for the biographer of an historical figure like Epictetus, or Thomas Jefferson. Did Thomas Jefferson "sell out" the public trust by holding slaves? The answer is that Jefferson *suspected* he did. He wavered in his own mind. But he wasn't sure. And here the public consensus for bondage must have played a part in dimming his lights. So we will still get the most legible *reading* of the seller-out in his cognitive context, the reading that is freest of *ad hoc* opacities, if we situate our pure type in a universal democracy. The pure type of the sellout will have to know what he does.)

Insofar as difficulty (2) bears on the present search for a pure type, we look then for a case of wrongheaded consensus within a relatively free society, one where the agent has the means of knowing better. The agent in difficulty (2) does not violate the wrongheaded consensus, but shares it. How shall we assess the degrees of his possible culpability? Suppose that, sharing the wrongheaded consensus, he has made what is merely a *technical* mistake. Say that in the obstetrical wards of the previous century he has failed to wash his hands, or that in our century he has given a "pass" mark to a nuclear reactor that met widely but mistakenly accepted safety standards? Is this an immoral act? No, of course not. It is an act that raises moral questions only once the mistake begins to be suspected, opened for investigation, and finally discovered. At that point, the conduct of the individual comes under moral scrutiny. If he takes the hint, follows through investigative leads, takes on the burden of bringing his colleagues round and changing the consensus, then he is, like Semmelweis in the obstetrical wards of the last century, a good man. If he resists that burden, for reasons such as those in *a* through *d* of our definition of selling out (p. 91), then he *has* sold out.

So in the case of a technical error, consensual but rectifiable, difficulty (2) does not present us with special or new problems of classification. To reverse the discredited technical procedures and repair the damages wrought by them is an operation not different from the one discussed under difficulty (1), where the consensus was already in place for reversing the mistake. A good man's goodness is just as safe, in that second case, where the consensus had still to be built. And a seller-out is not hard for the ordinarily conscientious person to identify, in the technical case.

I said to my wife, "This guy is a bad actor. This guy is going to get me in trouble if I don't start documenting and protecting myself." This was colossal arrogance, callous indifference toward the safety of people. It bothered me even if only one person should die or be disfigured because of something I was responsible for.*

The difficulty presented to moral analysis by the wrongheaded consensus gets more complex where the individual member of an otherwise free society is tempted to draw or consent to the drawing of an invidious social distinction between full-status members of his society and those who have been irresponsibly classified as degraded members. Here—in order to get on with any sort of skilled contribution that the individual may want to make to his society—he is expected to treat *those people* less respectfully than he must treat insiders. Those being the social rules, what is the agent's degree of culpability, in that case? Some examples drawn partly from novels may help to clarify the question.

George Eliot's fictional Daniel Deronda finds out as a young boy that there may be some question about his legitimacy, or at any rate his birth. At that junction of discovery, Deronda could take the path of willfully despising his guardian, Sir Hugo Mallinger, either for (as he suspects) siring him out of wedlock or, at minimum, for keeping the circumstances of his birth a secret from him. But Sir Hugo has been very kind. He may have had his reasons for keeping the secret. It is in any case brutal and unfilial to demand the truth.

In sum, Deronda does not choose to treat himself as a "case," someone whose nasty and ungrateful lashing out is "caused" by conditions external to himself. He has his dignity, which would not seem to be improvable in its own kind by our psychologies. It would seem that, in the working out of his own story, Deronda knows how to be delicate, perspicuous, and persistent. Because he wants to remain sensible of the realities of his situation, which happen here to include his guardian's fatherly solicitude, he confirms in himself the deeper tendency to self-curiosity that we have called a good man's fundamental intention.

In Deronda this sensitive tendency expands as an aversion to fashionably snobbish denigration of others, by which full-status members of his otherwise relatively democratic English society separate

---

*Myron Glazer, "Ten Whistleblowers and How They Fared" (1983, p. 37). This is the case of a design engineer who suspects a dangerous flaw in the design of the cars produced by his company but cannot convince his manager, who fears a reduction in bonuses, to authorize the appropriate barrier crash tests.

themselves from those who count as its degraded members. Since the cognitive conditions are those of a democracy, Deronda is able to allow himself to entertain in private the sympathetic curiosity about himself and others that he has not stifled. His curiosity about a girl he rescues leads him to find clues about his birth, clues that conduct to the eventual discovery that he is a Jew, which is to say, a degraded member of the community in which he has been formed and educated.

The discovery "I am one of them" is, in a sturdy individual, morally the sharp suspicion and eventual discovery that the invidious distinction between "us" and "them" is a wrongheaded one. This is not to say that Eliot has realistically depicted Deronda's transit from "us" to "them," or that any such transit in real life could be cost-free. It is merely to say that, if one is otherwise good, one can work one's way free of the *wrongheaded consensus* that degrades some members of a free society. Or is Deronda's self-emancipation, like Huck Finn's unwillingness to see his runaway friend Jim as the lost property that is all that respectable slave-owners would see of him, *an accident?* The accident of moral insight would be caused in both cases by the overriding reasons that Huck Finn and Deronda have to take the outcast's point of view?[2] (In Huck's case, there is the wicked and brutal father. In Deronda's case, there is the mystery about his birth.)

Where the consensus to draw distinctions invidious to the equal dignity of persons is a wrongheaded consensus, it would seem to be a moral advantage to have suffered some sort of wounding ejection from the community and its consensus. Perhaps Deronda and Huck Finn deserve no greater moral commendation from us than their more conforming peers do, since it was not their doing but their moral good luck to have felt or been partly ejected from a wrongheaded society. (See Nagel, 1979.) George Eliot offers us the contrasting situation of the socially advantaged but morally disadvantaged Gwendolyn Harleth, who is the moral counterweight to Daniel Deronda. There is no question about Gwendolyn's birth that could have given her Deronda's uneasy consciousness of life, or a saving self-curiosity. Nothing therefore leads her to question the snob values that degrade some while upgrading others on the partly irrelevant ground that they enjoy social acceptance, peer approval, money, or that they will not disturb one's repose. Gwendolyn, who is portrayed by Eliot as selfish in myriad trivial ways, has accordingly never acquired the habits of mind that go with a rigorous self-concern. She doesn't have her own history, her own backward-and-forward-looking train of trials and errors. Instead, she has consistently regarded herself in the mirror of other people's reactions and mistaken the power of a pretty woman to influence those for some native force.

Mistaken in supposing herself to have native force, she is still more mistaken in supposing that believed occult force to be capable of triumphing over women's inferior legal position in marriage, and women's inferiority of culture and marketable skills. In the hour when she has to choose between a loss of social status consequent upon sudden family poverty and a socially advantageous marriage to someone she has good reason to distrust, she finds no stuff within herself able to resist the temptation. Entering the marriage upon these terms, she is unprepared for her first discovery within it: her prior knowledge of her husband's past will not just form a small cloud on her domestic horizon. Rather, given her husband's unswerving will to crush her, it will precipitate a great falling away of her self-respect.

What Gwendolyn has not understood is that she too was, from the very beginning, a degraded member of the high-status English community whose witty, airy, too-rapid-to-be-serious deprecations of others it flattered her to affect. Women were degraded members, too. But high-status women, like Gwendolyn, had this extra disadvantage: the fact of their degradation, its real consequences, its theoretical rationale, were all partly concealed from them. Had Gwendolyn had the saving moral intention of self-curiosity (an intention, by all the signs, far more developed in George Eliot), she could possibly have penetrated these secrets of her degraded status in time to save herself.

Can we imagine a Gwendolyn gifted with timely self-curiosity, one who has seized some portion of her story? She would be found among pursuits a bit less trivial at the outset, in which she could not be so *shallowly* self-absorbed. But she would be sufficiently interested in survival, and considerate of her relations, to have learned the aesthetic arts of social membership within a society comprising both high-status and degraded members. She would, then, have learned to swim gracefully at the aqueous surface of social life, sharing or at least not reproving its little, disdainful postures of exclusion. Somewhere in the middle of these exercises she would, however, begin to wonder how she might plant her feet on some rock that belonged to her, and from there commence to live her own life, as opposed to other people's.

At this point, her degraded status would necessarily begin to exact its cost. She would have had no training or practical experience (so we suppose) in finding or exploring a serious talent. The most enlightened opinion could advance all sorts of reasons, self-regarding and other-regarding, against it: ruin of her personal prospects, morbid effect on her health, subtraction from her family of emotional consolations she herself desires for them, loss of the good opinion of those who *have* been allowed to train their talents, and so on and on. So instead of a potentially bottomless dive toward a bedrock she has neither training nor practice in finding, she might instinctively settle for a half-dive into psychic or physical invalidism.

According to her recent biographer, Jean Strouse (1980, ch. 6), this was the situation of Alice James, whose brothers included the philosopher William James and the novelist Henry James. An exceptional home had fed intellectual and aesthetic curiosity in Alice James. The most enlightened medical opinion of the day, and the peculiar emotional economy of the James household, alike discouraged ambition in a woman. The biographer infers that lifelong, hysterically induced invalidism, which she was acknowledged to suffer from, was Alice James's involuntary settlement of that conflict. If we put a more self-curious or "good" Gwendolyn Harleth in that midway place smoothed out by partial invalidism, she could enjoy a self-curiosity that is partial because not fully actionable, and a corresponding sympathy for outcasts that would be likewise partial, because not much could come of it. If our redrafted Gwendolyn does not go the whole way into invalidism, she might go part of that course, into archness, a narrowly *mannered* style of life, a self-ironical, self-deprecatory conventionalism, a life that identifies itself—to others and itself—as not wholly real.

If one has a merely intuitive apprehension that the social consensus is wrongheaded, but those who are better trained and more obviously effective in society support that consensus, and if the consensus tends precisely to degrade oneself—partly by depriving one of an educated vantage point—then one's situation is not just profoundly pathetic. It is perfectly horrible. That fact that feminists have spotlighted the pathos for us, and made it the ground of a political program, takes nothing away from the horrors of self-subversion that such a life must confront.

> When the fancy took me of a morning at school to *study* my lessons . . . instead of shirking . . . the most impossible sensations of upheaval, violent revolt in my head overtook me so that I had to "abandon" my brain, as it were. So it has always been, anything that sticks of itself is free to do so, but conscious and continuous cerebration is an impossible exercise. . . . So, with the rest, you abandon the pit of your stomach, the palms of your hands, the soles of your feet, and refuse to keep them sane when you find in turn one moral impression after another producing despair in the one, terror in the other, anxiety in the third and so on until life becomes one long flight from remote suggestion and complicated eluding of the multifold traps set for your undoing. (Strouse, 1980, p. 118)

A woman who, like Alice James here recollecting her first breakdown at the age of nineteen, *consents*—on the best information she can get—to a wrongheaded consensus degrading her and other women is not morally culpable. She is doing the best she can in that cognitive context. It is certainly not for women onlookers of our day (whose spheres of action may have widened somewhat, but who can still find sufficiently many points of contact) to regard her with condescension. Given what she had to work with, the place on the moral map of a hypothetical Gwendolyn Harleth who, like Alice James, would be partially self-curious and partially invalided, seems no more marginal than that of the fictional Daniel Deronda.

Suppose our Gwendolyn had *profited* from this kind of wrongheaded consensus, instead of suffering from it? What would her moral condition be in that eventuality? We can suppose a third Gwendolyn Harleth who has made a more fortunate marriage and not had to struggle free to goodness by repairing some consequences of her degradation. This Gwendolyn's life is complacently frivolous, because a wrongheaded consensus has made any other sort of life too hard to be attempted. She treats others with superciliousness, or flattery, because all the members of her milieu do the same. She finds content in small social triumphs and is not too much disturbed by small defeats. Has she sold out?

One tends to suspect so, simply because the freemasonry of women exists under much the same conditions of partial social degradation all over the world, whatever the trappings. One tends to suspect she remembers the small gestures that crowded her childhood, pulling her down from ambition, from work, from effectiveness, warning her not to be overly serious. One tends to suspect she knows what it feels like to be ever-so-gently degraded, and that she ought therefore to show a becoming reluctance to degrade other people in her turn. But of course the freemasonry of women does not hold convocations, elect officers, or issue newsletters. It is hard to be sure what the colonel's lady, or Judy O'Grady, really knows about her situation, sisters under the skin though they may be.

In the case of women, there is a lurking suspicion that the most supercilious of them know more than they let on about the wrongness of getting on with their skilled contributions to the world by first profiting from invidious social distinctions. The suspicion may be unfounded. But I for one cannot shake myself free of it. It leads me to be, at one and the same time, more indignant at female callousness (because women would presumably know better) and less decisive in my condemnations of it (because women may be presumed to be in something of the condition of hostages). Let us therefore invent a *man* whose position in life is in every way improved by the drawing of invidious social distinctions. He is proud toward his inferiors, deferential toward his betters. He endorses Edmund Burke's rationale, on the view that his private discourtesies will, over the long term, help to support a society that encourages human superiority to flourish.

> To be bred in a place of estimation; to see nothing low or sordid from one's infancy; to be taught to respect one's self, to be habituated to the censorial inspection of the public eye; . . . to stand upon such elevated ground as to be enabled to take a large view of the widespread and infinitely diversified combinations of men and affairs in a large society; . . . to be enabled to draw the court and attention of the wise and learned, wherever they are to be found;—to be habituated in armies to command and to obey; . . . to be led to a guarded and regulated conduct, from a sense that you are considered as an instructor of your fellow-citizens in their highest concerns, and that you act as a reconciler between God and man . . . these are the circumstances of men, that form what I should call a *natural* aristocracy, without which there is no nation. . . . To give therefore no more importance, in the social order, to such descriptions of men, than that of so many units, is a horrible usurpation.[3]

What is wrongheaded about this consensus it that it flatters and encourages mindless and gratuitous personal arrogance, and also that, while it may betimes prevent natural inferiority from leveling down the top, it no doubt discourages or prevents even more natural superiority from rising out of the bottom. There are also covert, sly takings of advantage for which this sort of rationale provides a cover.

What degree of culpability does the man have who accepts a wrongheaded consensus to draw invidious social distinctions, believes the rationale behind that consensus, and meanwhile profits from it personally, to get on faster and further with his particular work in the world? If he does not mindlessly believe the rationale, we can still suppose that he believes that a social whole in which many achievements and virtues are to be found, and with which his affections and loyalties are interthreaded, would come partly unraveled if he started making a row about an ideal of perfect equality. There is something to be said for not beclouding people's dinner parties, or other small festive occasions, by refusing to smile at their ethnic or other somewhat mean little jokes. What is there of selling out in this? *Must* one either sell out, or be a boor?

If it is the achievements and virtues, the human superiorities themselves, that one wants to preserve, then one is accepting the Burkean rationale, or a watered-down version of it, on its own terms. In that case, one will want to be sensitive to the possibilities for superiority in others, and not want to be guilty of blocking any deserving person's rise, or of spoiling his or her innocent social enjoyments. In other words, however misguided one's Burkean views might be, they would give one a corresponding sense of *noblesse oblige* that would prevent social or practical usurpations, where the latter depended on one's own initiative. The rude or slyly usurping member of a privileged class who meanwhile professes a Burkean conservatism is insincere. As insincere, he is culpable.

What about the "sincere" member of a privileged class who laughs with secret misgivings at the denigrating jokes his hosts direct at the less privileged, laughs so as not to seem a boor? Or, if he does not laugh, he at least affects to weight the denigrating jokes more lightly than he really does. How culpable is he? He has shown a certain moral weakness. His excuse may well be that he *does not know* how to make his own position clear, without straying over the aesthetic line into social boorishness. He wants to play by what he thinks the rules should be, even if others seem to be playing oddly fast and oddly loose with the same rules. So his real deficit is perhaps a practical one, rather than one of appropriate intentions. It is after all *also* unwise to rebuff one's hosts, or to make fellow guests uncomfortable wantonly. If what is lacking is not good intentions, but social technique, one does not acquire a new technique except by the requisite thought and practice. The proof of one's real intentions lies, as we have noted, in one's course of conduct over the longer term. If there is a sincere good intention, then some approximation of the requisite social technique (which combines tact with a clear refusal to engage in morally compromising banter) will eventually be learned. The skill consists in a certain clean-edged minding of one's own business, hard to learn and necessarily self-taught.

We can sum up. The first preliminary difficulty obscuring our search for the pure type of seller-out was that a person who fails to carry out a trust about which there was a clear-cut and reasonable social consensus can simply have been mistaken about how that consensus was supposed to be applied to the decision he had to make. In that case of an innocent mistake, he has not sold out if he retrospectively seeks to repair the damage—even if not all the damage to the objective situation, or to his reputation, or to his sense of personal serenity, *can* be repaired. We are trying here to define selling out as a rather precise human operation. We are not trying to find out how many ways a person can be a loser in the race for high self-esteem or deference from his peers. Obviously there are many ways to become a loser in those races.

The second preliminary difficulty was that a person may conform to a clear-cut consensus which, from a more far-seeing standpoint, is nonetheless wrong. We determined in the second case that the category of selling out is most appropriately applied in cognitive situations like our own, where the means of discovering and righting a wrongheaded consensus are, in different degrees, near at hand or readily available. The moral alternatives, of selling out or not selling out, arise where such discoveries (about how and why the consensus was wrong) have begun or are in progress. The blurred outlines of the pure type of the seller-out come into sharper focus the more persistently such discoveries and their consequences are *dodged* by him or her. This is the case whether the consensus was wrongheaded about some technical matter, or about what would be a fair distribution of the basic goods or the niceties of social life. However, because as we have seen, the second kind of selling out, involving unfair discrimination, is a much more complex thing to analyze, we will here take our pure type of sellout to be more crisply revealed in the selling out of a consensus on a technical matter. (Nevertheless, in real life it often happens that the two kinds of selling out are interthreaded, making the task of precise moral analysis an extremely complex one.)

From our review of difficulties (1) and (2), certain incidental proceeds can now be gathered. It is not the case that selling out is typified by some outstanding, singular act, having the character of irreversibility and spreading over the agent something like an indelible stain. We confuse the moral situation, for ourselves and for others, by reading a case of having sold out on an analogy with the loss of sexual honor in a virgin. Loss of virginity is a physical, irreversible event in the life of a woman. It is not coincident with the loss of her character, however much she may have been taught to think so. Likewise, the inexplicable bargain by which, as we learn from some texts, a Judas, say, or a Faust sells his salvation for some worldly inducement by which he is horribly fascinated is not in fact an irreparable bargain—from the standpoint of his salvation. If it were that, we should all be lost.* It only seems so, in a fictional setting.

What has to be looked for, then, is the pace, the structure, the secrets of a historical development in personal life to which the description "selling out" belongs. No single act or instant in the life of an agent will serve to bring out the notion that we want.

What the story of one's sellout has that merely personal or psychological betrayal lacks is a public or objective component. (In the

---

*Cf. Søren Kierkegaard's journal meditations (1834–54), on Faust and the Christian "night of betrayal," with their underlying expectation that these situations repeat themselves over and over and are, for that very reason, reparable over and over. See *The Journals*, paras. 109, 115, 306, 1342, and 1345. I am also indebted to John Bacon for clarifying discussion of these points.

cases that haunt Christian imagination, of Judas or Faust, their stories depend on salvation's being open to public inspection and shared enjoyment by a community of readers or seekers. The point is contestable, since each man dies alone, and is saved or lost alone. Yet the good that in him is saved or lost is a common good, which belongs to humankind. On any other reading, Faust and company would not belong in this chapter. But it is at least European folk wisdom that they do belong here.) The public trust defaulted on will continue to be connected, directly or indirectly, to the skilled, rule-bound performances in the public arena that define the agent to himself as a responsible, talented, and reasonable individual.

There is therefore a language of shared responsibility that he must continue to understand and to speak in order to get on in the projects of his self-realization. Thus the failed whistle-blower who neglects to report that the airplane his factory is building will be unsafe must live with the evidences that it won't fly—evidences that will continue to pile up. The surgeon whose techniques are not adequate to the demands made on them must live with the evidences of that, evidences not all of which lie a-moldering in the ground on which he walks. The opportunistic academic who throws his support behind an underqualified superior in order to help secure a promotion or tenure must live with innumerable repercussions in the daily application of his craft.

If the whistle-blower lives the major-key chords of a public reprisal, the person who dropped the whistle ordinarily lives the minor-key notes, muffled and repeated, of protracted consequences. There are unforeseen layoffs and unpredictable realignments of whatever in himself is still fit—and whatever has become progressively less fit—to get his work done in the world. This minor-key medley of notes, many of them hardly audible to the public, is what we want to listen for now.

The Sellout Sold

To sell out is to wander into an adjacent set of rooms that are nonfunctional, in the apartments of the soul. The shape and function of the whole house (that is to say, the character of the public trust in question) is incidental to that wandering. The decor, the protocol, the instruments for this operation will of course vary, depending on whether it is an airplane factory whose maladministration one decides to play along with, or an academic department. But they are not important to the study of the pure type. Whatever the setting, the essential gestures look very much the same, and they play the same kind of part in the script.

First would come the moment of temptation, when something like a bribe or a threat (usually both) is offered recognizably to the potential sellout. The initial resistance, if the potential sellout produced that, would ordinarily have to be verbal. One could also be called upon to walk past a physical barrier, or over some visible line of demarcation, in which case the way one walked would signal one's resistance or surrender. (One pictures a strikebreaker, for example.) Sometimes a slight tightening of the mouth and raising of the chin, as opposed to a nod and the turning out of the palms, would signal that one has either refused to make, or else has made, the decision to sell out. The human repertoire of gestures is limited.[4] There are not a million ways to show that one has seen which way the wind is blowing. However, even where the responses to the crucial offer seem to be mere physical acts, those physical acts have their verbal equivalents.

They mean either "Sorry, my friend, I'm not that kind," or "I'm very glad you've broached that needlessly touchy subject, and I'm also glad that we have this opportunity to get to know each other better at last."

Let us say that one has, by words or gestures, made the second kind of response. What sort of thing has happened to one in that case? One has dropped and thereupon lost the connecting thread to one's antecedent projects, insofar as these made sense to one. The antecedent projects made sense to one on at least two levels.

First, they made sense on a deep level. To the question "What am I really all about, taking me from remembered beginnings and going forward from there?" the choices one made of kinds of *training for action* provided some parts of the answer. It took some training to get into a position to fulfill an established trust. One has rather systematically chosen to perform in one sort of skilled way in the world, and that choice among skilled performances has told one something about oneself. After giving in to the threat or the bribe, one finds the connection cut between that choice and what—up till now—it has told one about one's self viewed historically. The underlying choice has nothing further to tell one. It henceforth ceases to be "telling," and becomes mute.

Second, they made sense on a surface level. At the time when the threat or bribe was offered, one had to one's credit a pattern of behavior that was, and was intended to be, subservient to the skill or function one had acquired. The threat or bribe led one to shrug off in midair one's silent obeisance to the skill. The skill one had acquired said that after *a*, one would necessarily do *b*, *c*, *d*, and *e*. But after *a* came the threat or bribe. As a consequence, *b*, *c*, *d*, and *e* didn't get done, or got done the wrong way from the point of view of the skill. Let us start by looking at this second, or surface aspect, of one's loss of connection to antecedent projects.

In the second case, the motive for breaking off the skilled operation is not to be found within the process whereby one acquired and perfected the skill. The motive is adventitious to that process and makes no further use of it. It functions, rather, like a call to stop work. This is so even where one is induced by threat or bribe to call off what seems to one to be a justified work stoppage. The outward form of that invitation may include a promise of a quicker return to work than any other course of action would allow. But then one returns to work under substandard working conditions, or conditions that remove the element of voluntariness from the work contract, or on the sole condition that one violate some principle in terms of which the job had dignity in one's own eyes. If no such considerations were to be weighed in the balance against the threat or the bribe, then the offer before one would not be, in one's own eyes, an offer to sell out. One *wanted* to continue to do the job, but not just to do it like an automaton. Automata cannot sell out. One wanted to do it, but not first to have to grovel for it. If one is told that one can get to do it forthwith, but only on the groveling condition, what is then held out to one is the breaking off of the skilled behavior *that one had had in mind before,* and the disruption of that skilled behavior for no craftsmanly reason.

The main point, in the second case, is that a craftsmanly decision was called for, and was not made. So what? One can, in the very next seconds, make ten craftsmanly decisions—and be in an even better, more influential, position to make them. Why is this one so important? There are dozens of ways to break the connection between *a*, *b*, *c*, *d*, and *e*, modes of forgetfulness, modes of distraction. What is so special about this passage from *a* to *b*, et cetera? Perhaps one could get there in some other order. But, as it happens, this time one has not forgotten the order. Neither has one been distracted. Nor is it particularly clear that one will live long enough to become, with one's ill-gotten gains, a powerful philanthropic influence. One might become that. One might some day feel urgently desirous of becoming that. But all that development belongs to the fog-blanketed future. One has, in this moment, only this moment to be lived through.

There is no good craftsmanly reason not to go straight from *a* to *b*. One has been pulled off course by a threat or a bribe. What does that mean for me, just in case it is my situation? Does it mean that

I wanted something else more than I wanted to get to b? Or does it rather mean that I feared if I didn't bow to the threat or take the bribe I would never see b again, even in altered circumstances? It is unlikely that I wanted something else more than b unambivalently. If I had wanted x (for instance, money, power, or sex) more than b unambivalently, I would have set about to get x more directly ere now. I wouldn't have got tied up working in this airplane factory, or Ph.D. factory. I would have gone directly into crime, or perhaps learned the *techné* of making big profits legally, or gone into prostitution *per se*, or perhaps wardroom politics. There are in fact many walks of life where selling out as defined here is unknown. I could have gone into one of those. I would not have acquired these fancy, irrelevant skills. So I didn't, in any simple and robust sense of wanting, want power or money more than I wanted to get to b. No, no. I wanted to be around b. I loved b. And its mates, c, d, and e.

What then? The truth is I feared I would never see b again. Or never see it again with myself in good repair, well oiled and well heeled enough to enjoy it, unless I sold it out just this one time. Or sold it repeatedly on just this one long installment plan. Or on these several installment plans. By definition, I cannot sell something out unless it has some sort of public value, even to me. I cannot, with knowledge, induce someone else to sell out unless one part of my motive is to find justification for my having done so myself on some previous round, or for my doing so on this round. "You see," I may say to a new inductee into the sellout's life, "we all have to do it. Therefore, I too had to do it. We are just human. This is a fellowship of compassion. We all have our price, unfortunately. But one must forgive oneself, and forgive one's fellows. Unless of course they do something that I myself wouldn't do. For reasons of nature or nurture. Reasons for which I am not responsible." So, offerers of threats and bribes can be notably sensitive in regard to their honor. The whole offer may finally *have to do* with their honor, in a funny, inverted way.

So I get from a to b via the detour of selling b out, because I'm afraid if I don't sell it out that I'll never see b again. Is that so wrong? Isn't it, at the very worst, an error of judgment—if it is that? Every human activity has its cost. Why should I think I can get straight from a to b without paying the cost? Better to pay the cost than never to see b again.

Here calculation suddenly fails. What is going on here is not only a process of induction and deduction. One has come to the end of that process, probably taken the weighing of means and ends just about as far as the weighing will go. Many such sales of the public trust would look justified, put in a calculus of this kind. Something else also is at stake here—as we dimly discern.

One's story has another dimension. There is some larger, ideal agreement that one has with the public, being a part of that public oneself. If this agreement depended on incessant surveillance and enforcement, it would not hold. Insofar as it really works, on a day-to-day basis, it is supported by one's own confidence, and other people's, that it will be supported. In other words, its real foundation is trust, in a fairly literal sense. One is trusted—by an unseen mass of people—and one trusts them. One must trust, even to mail a letter, or to place a stamp, or to write a check. What is unnoticeably incessant is trust, like a background noise. What is sporadic and noticeable is surveillance and enforcement. All projects, whether craftsmanly or creative, presuppose that cushion of trust on which they rest, as an airplane rests in the air. It has nothing to do with liking people. One must trust other people, whether or not one likes them.

In not getting from *a* to *b* by the straightest path, but instead by a route that partly betrays the trust of the public, one has taken a step that does not merit one's own confidence, insofar as one helps to make up the public. If the domain of action enjoying the public trust is pictured spatially, one has stepped over its borders. One is just where the public trusts that one will not be. And one is there, in the pure case, not by inadvertence, but knowingly.

The concept of *the* public trust is not in itself vague. Rather, it is incomplete and inconsistent. I know, without any vagueness about it, that I trust the postal clerk to put a valid stamp on my letter. I do not know how exactly the systematic elaboration of the basic rules safeguarding against predation and allowing maximal human good would look. I have read several such theories and am aware that the ones I have read are considered controversial philosophically. That may give me a slightly more precise vision of the public trust completely articulated ("I promise this insofar as you promise that, and so on, to the end of that line . . .") than have members of the public unfamiliar with these particular philosophic classics. But the difference is one of degree, mainly. Nobody has in his pocket the complete manual on the public trust. Nor could one have it, even if all the philosophic controversies could be settled. The exchanges of promises that actual individuals, embedded in their economies, their cultures, and carried on the stream of history, are willing to make differ in all sorts of ways from what would ideally be fair. Texts like Hobbes's *Leviathan* or Plato's *Republic* make a case for the promises that people ought to be able to make to each other were unfair impediments removed. They don't handle the touchier questions of how people might fairly be got into a state of ideal willingness to make these fair concessions on all hands.

Nevertheless, this philosophic and specieswide confusion does not excuse the postal clerk who says to me, "I forgot to stamp your letter, though I remembered to take your money, which I kept for myself. So you'll have to pay again." Suppose he went on to say, in extenuation, "the philosophic articulation of whatever is involved in the public trust has yet to be completed. That's why I did this to you. Come back when you have a winning theory." I would not think he had thereby exempted himself from the requirements of the public trust. (In this case they coincide with his job requirements. But he has tenure. And I am not willing to take the time to bring a complaint.) Where he and I stood, the concept of the public trust was rather specific. He had no business to appeal to the ambiguities at its border.

It is the same in the case where I did not get straight from a to b, because I was under the influence of a bribe or a threat. I violated that most literal and particular part of the public trust that was clearest to me. I didn't just—by some merely unexpected or bohemian way of conducting myself—overstep its ambiguous borders. Now I can't trust myself. But I *am* a part of a public network of trust, clear in the middle as we have seen, even though ambiguous at the borders. There are agreements ("I will do x if you will do y") into which I must enter all the time. Indeed, I would be hard put to locate a part of myself that is not at least by implication a part of the public too. No place is outside of Athens. This is the Socratic insight (*Crito* 53 A-E). So, what I now feel is that other agreements into which I will enter ought also to be under surveillance. Where my good faith is concerned, I have the best of reasons to keep myself under suspicion, until I am proven innocent.

This is rather a heavy burden to carry, in respect of what might after all be considered merely a failure of craftsmanly follow-through. I will meet it by explaining to myself, in more situations than ordinary, why I am to be trusted. A breach in my future has opened up. It has to be healed, by incessant applications of the ointment of explanation. Yet each explanation I make to myself has this inconsistency about it: it wants not to be heard in full since, if heard by myself in its full context, each explanation would include, within silent parentheses, *a confession*. If I became sensitive to the confession and inclined for once to accept the fact that I am its author, then a repair of the reparable damage would be called for and would have to follow, and the explanation of my trustworthiness in the other connections would no longer be needed. My sellout of the public trust would have been repaid. However, in the pure case of the sellout, the case under study, that repayment has been postponed indefinitely.

Without it, my explanation of my trustworthiness for the new agreement, although addressed to myself as a member of the public on equal terms with other members, is only half-heard. Thus I insert into my consciousness the habit of partial inattention. The thing that I do not want to hear is my confession.

Is this unheard, unlistened-for confession merely my expectation of punishment internalized? Was it my Freudian "superego" that I did not heed in the first instance and that I will not heed in the psychic aftermath? No. A breach of faith is a breach of faith, whether or not it is punished. Punishment that is *not* deserved could still be feared, but the fear would command a different part of one's attention than does fear of a punishment that is deserved. Sometimes indeed people go out of their way to seek punishment, which they have no practical reason to expect, but which will address the part of themselves that is attentive to the fact that they have deserved it. The feeling of guilt that is said to drive them is sometimes altogether appropriate. Let us leave Nietzschean or Freudian postulates aside. They are not proved, they are not provable, and they are not relevant to this part of the inquiry. The reason I inwardly "confess" a breach of faith is that it happened, and I remember it, and I myself require good faith in my future dealings with myself and others. I might for the same sort of reason "confess" to myself that a certain stepping-stone that I wanted to use to cross a brook has in the past been covered with wet moss and may therefore be expected to be slippery in the future. If I am such a stepping-stone, metaphorically speaking, then so much the worse for me. I will still have my reasons of prudence to bear my own slipperiness in mind.

We are talking here about inattention. I have constantly to explain to myself how it happens that I am such a reliable fellow, since my good faith is no longer to be taken for granted, *and* I will have to pay only partial attention to my own explanations, lest I notice among them the unvoiced confession that has occasioned them. How this habit of inattention affects my account of myself in general, and in all the disparate things that I do that involve the public trust, was the subject of the first, or deep-level, question about my antecedent projects insofar as they cast light on my story. We haven't dealt with that deep-level question yet. At this point we want merely to see how the habit of inattention affects my getting from *a* to *b*, the next time I have to get there.

I come back to *b*, explaining to myself all the while that I was a good fellow. But I don't believe it. There is nobody but me in this room of the soul. And I don't believe me. I can't stay here alone. If I stay here alone with myself, I will have to bring disciplinary measures to bear. I can't just stay alone in a room with a miscreant. There is work to be done. The miscreant is assigned to the same task that I've been assigned. She must therefore own up, pay up, and get back into line. Else the task won't get done. And I've made a commitment to do it. If I walk away and go into a new walk of life, take up a new craft, then sooner or later I must face the same sort of decision again. If I keep walking away every time the decision to sell out or not comes my way, then I soon will be craftless. I'll be some sort of drifter or dissolute, having placed myself outside the pale of the public trust. That is one way to stop selling out and also to cease to come under consideration here. The dissolute has been dealt with in a previous chapter. He has his own evil.

No, there is nothing to do but get on with the task. But how? There is only one answer. I must never again be alone in a room with her. I must bring my colleagues into the room. I must team up with them. I must get my work interthreaded with theirs. If I am an academic, for example, I must read all their articles, write little responses, take up their concerns, show up at colloquia, whether or not their concerns are mine at all. My concern will not be with *what* they are saying, its truth, its explanatory power, or the light it may shed on the projects I entertained antecedently. I am concerned because *they* are saying it, whatever it is. It could be arrant nonsense. It could be chillingly out of touch with something I cherish. No matter. They are saying it. And I need them. I need the discipline by which their behavior is roughly circumscribed. It will keep me *relatively* honest. I will still be and be taken to be a member of the guild.

And so on. At heart, it is a sort of bluntly boring failure to be what one *is* objectively, viz., a committed practitioner of one's *techné*. Forthwith, one must be something else, for example, a glitterer.

The sellout is oneself, taken to the nth power. It is nothing to write home about. It is rather pathetic. Only, the public good suffers. And one is bored. So one suffers oneself.

What about the deep-level question, the one concerning my story? Selling out put me out of touch with my story insofar as my choice of a craft was a way of finding out what my long-term intentions were as a person. What will I put in the place of the craft as a source of that kind of intelligence? There is lots to put there. Somebody's psychology. Somebody's causal theory of general human—and by implication my personal—history. I will put "science fiction," of some personal-hybrid kind, in the place of my story. Or I will put fiction pure and simple. I will put art and books there. A case can be made for misjudgments. One can get through. There is *nothing* to worry about.

PART THREE

Evil in the Daylight

CHAPTER FIVE

The Types of Genocide

The Impulsive Type

W E HAVE CONTENDED that evildoing is in itself the deliberate thwarting or spoiling of another's life story. Evil is not yet in the picture where the harm done to another is strictly impulsive, or mindlessly antisocial. It comes into the picture where the victim's life story is in a measure *discerned*.

We have been talking all along about character, not methods and measures for social control. Thus the question of whether society metes out punishment for the sake of its deterrent effect, or retributively, is differently answered according to the *character* of the criminal being sentenced. One can hardly treat a man as deserving punishment if he has, by a succession of strictly impulsive acts beginning in infancy, exempted *himself* from any consideration of deserts. One cannot, simply because one cannot in actual fact impose on another person better treatment than he will consent to endure. The better treatment will not get through. He will get round it somehow. So the violent criminal self-exempted from any deliberate and reasoned consideration of his merits will have to be reached on the level of deterrence, and punishment, if it does in fact quickly and predictably follow the crime, will help him to build up an association of ideas between illegal, harmful, antisocial acts, and his own discomfort. That is, it will do so *if* the punishment in fact makes him uncomfortable. If his tolerance for punishment is high, punishment will fail even to have a deterrent effect. At best, then, it will keep him out of our way for a while.

In sum, while the impulsive harm-doer cannot be a good person or live a good life, in the sense here defined, he cannot be evil either. He is not sufficiently reflective for that. He knows not what he does. Society must take protective measures against him. It may even, where possible, try to protect him from himself. But, with regard to full-fledged moral capacities, he is, for good or evil, a child. He can of course be "bad." He can also be disciplined from without, by society. It takes more than that to be evil. Perhaps he can grow into it, if he sits in on psychology, philosophy, and literature seminars while he is in prison.

If it requires a certain portion of intellectual self-command to be evil, it may require a larger than usual portion to be both genocidal *and* *evil*. The evil genocide would be a person whose deliberate project it is to thwart the life stories not merely of individuals but of whole peoples, and of individuals just insofar as they attach their life stories to the stories of their peoples. Like the criminal described above, the genocide can move to divest his victims of social safeguards impulsively and without a conscious design. Or he can have a somewhat plausible view of history, a somewhat plausible view of the role of his target people in history, and he can move to wipe that people out with a fairly sophisticated sense of what he has undertaken. That kind of genocide is more truly evil, we shall contend.

But how can the necessary discernment of a life story, which attends an evil character using his discernment for destructive ends, become the *discernment* of the life story of a *genos?*

> The practice of extermination of nations and ethnic groups as carried out by the invaders is called by the author "genocide," a term deriving from the Greek word *genos* (tribe, race) and the Latin *cide* (by way of analogy, see homicide, fratricide) . . . . Genocide is effected through a synchronized attack on different aspects of the life of the captive peoples . . . [viz.] institutions of self-government . . . intelligentsia. . . . (Lemkin, 1944, p. xi)

Included in Raphael Lemkin's definition are a people's economic and reproductive base; also instruments of culture such as language, and of high culture, such as study or productive work in the humanities; also a people's domains of religious expression; also, and crucially, its instruments for moral self-regulation.

It would seem that the genocide who is in a position to carry through the assignment Lemkin has outlined would almost certainly be in an extreme situation where—because of a falling away of electoral or legal accountability to an informed public—he could not discern *anything* very well. Hence he could not be evil in our sense at all.

> I recall [Field Marshal Wilhelm] Keitel's reaction to the atrocities, particularly vividly in connection with the atrocities films. And when I saw him in a cell later he said, "Those dirty SS swine. If I had known what

they were up to, I would have told my son, 'I'll shoot you rather than let you join the SS.'" He was of course at the same time trying to indicate that it was not the army that had committed these horrible atrocities. But he did react emotionally and with great shock.*

Let us sum up the problem thus far. It would seem that greater discernment is required to be an evil genocide than to be an evil dissolute or an evil sellout. If that greater discernment is less accessible in the very conditions that favor genocide, how is the possibility of a pure type to be explained? To put the paradox face up, how can the genocide become *good enough* to become truly evil?

It seems that we have conceded that one can plan or participate in genocide *without* being, so far as one's character goes, truly evil, and that this would be the case even where one's *results* could match up against the results of the worst. This particular paradox should not disturb us unduly. Once we admit character into moral assessment, we must notice that terrible conflagrations can from time to time be ignited innocently. Here we don't deal with innocence, of course, but we are descending a slope between badness and evil. The same slope can be found inside the confines of civil society. What we must do now is discover it on the terrain of history.

Let us begin by supposing, in line with our general concepts of good and evil, that the impulsive genocide must be a "better" man than the deliberate and carefully self-crafted genocide, "better" since he has not quite discerned the story he is spoiling. At the top of the slope, then, let us find the impulsive genocide.

If impulsive, then reactive to stimuli. To the impulsive genocide belongs a reactiveness that must signify that he does not intend *any* outcome fixedly. By the same token, since he must react incessantly to surrounding forces, identifying with some, stamping out others, he cannot shut information out of consciousness by any mechanism that would be too elaborate. The conceptual shield must be rather thin. About Talaat Bey, for example (leader of the Committee of Union and Progress that ruled Turkey at the period of the Armenian massacres), U.S. Ambassador to Constantinople Henry Morgenthau wrote, "I would find him fierce and unyielding one day, and uproariously good-natured and accommodating the next" (Morgenthau, 1918, p. 332). Once, after Talaat had set forth his reasons for the Turkish murder project against the Armenians, and Morgenthau had candidly and more reasonably still refuted each successive pretext, Talaat

---

*Testimony of Professor Gustave M. Gilbert, military psychologist assigned to the major defendants at Nuremberg, in the Eichmann Trial, 55th Session.

concluded, "'No Armenian . . . can be our friend after what we have done to them'" (pp. 336–39).

When Morgenthau, thinking to flatter the steelier, would-be Napoleonic Minister of War Enver, who was another leader of the ruling committee, suggested to Enver that full responsibility for the horror might lie with subordinates, "Enver straightened up at once. I saw that my remarks, far from smoothing the way . . . had greatly offended him. . . . 'You are greatly mistaken,' he said. 'We have this country absolutely under our control'" (1918, pp. 351f).

With Turkey's entry into the war on the side of Germany and the Allies' subsequent defeat at Gallipoli, it became clear that the Turkish government would enjoy a long respite from international surveillance. The mass deportation of subject populations was already being explicitly promoted by the Pan-German ideology which, according to Morgenthau, was at that period a Turkish import from Germany, along with Germany military training, German materiel, and German naval personnel.* If Greeks were only deported to Greece, while Armenians were "deported" to uninhabitable Mesopotamian deserts, to be pillaged, enslaved, and slaughtered en route, the absence of an Armenian government would have been what made the real difference to the Turkish tormentors. Among the nations of the world, Armenia strikingly had no military power, no effective representation (Morgenthau, 1918, p. 325).

The Turkish representatives, or strong men, spoke to Morgenthau of a national struggle for survival and victory, targeting alien peoples and, against these peoples, calling for the indiscriminate use of harsh methods. On the whole, however, they did not impute to the Armenians traits of character or negative talents of which they themselves would have been ashamed had they owned them. The whole thing does not appear to have been put on the plane of deserts at all. Let the German naval captains and the Kaiser depart, let the Allies return to place the Turkish government under international restraints of some kind, and the "struggle for survival," if that's what it was, would have to take some other route. But even without massive political rearrangements, let the fresh breeze of some benign humor play over the impulsive genocide, and the clenched fist would relax.

> One day [Morgenthau] found [Talaat] sitting at the usual place, his
> massive shoulders drawn up, his eyes glowering, his wrists planted on

---

*Morgenthau (1918, p. 47). On mass deportation as an element of the late-nineteenth-century Pan-German ideology, see Stern (1963, pp. 67ff); see also Stern, pp. 282f, on the Darwinian struggle for survival between peoples, another article of faith for the Pan-German movement.

the desk. I always anticipated trouble whenever I found him in this attitude. As I made request after request, Talaat, between his puffs at the cigarette, would answer "No!" "No!" "No!"

I slipped around to his side of the desk.

"I think those wrists are making all the trouble, Your Excellency," I said. "Won't you please take them off the table?"

Talaat's ogre-like face began to crinkle, he threw up his arms, leaned back, and gave a roar of terrific laughter. He enjoyed this method of treating him so much that he granted every request that I made. (1918, p. 22)

The trouble was in the wrists, then. And the wrists were moveable. On the whole, it would take heavy ammunition to move them, but occasionally, exceptionally, it could be done even with a little bit of street smarts, or martial arts of the psyche. Lean on a highly reactive person in an unexpected place and the very surprise of it may delight him. If Morgenthau, who for two years represented the conscience of the world in Constantinople, is to be believed, this was a case of brute malevolence, evolving on the scene, indifferent to the fate of Armenians who were not directly under the Ottoman aegis, and not even visualizing the whole train of events too precisely.

> At first the Government showed some inclination to protect these departing throngs. . . . The gendarmes, whom the Government had sent, supposedly to protect the exiles, in a very few hours became their tormentors. . . . Thus every caravan had a continuous battle for existence with several classes of enemies—their accompanying gendarmes, the Turkish peasants and villagers, the Kurdish tribes and bands of *Chétés* or brigands. And we must always keep in mind that the men who might have defended these wayfarers had nearly all been killed or forced into the army as workmen, and that the exiles themselves had been systematically deprived of all weapons before the journey began. (1918, pp. 313f.)

The official mood seems to be one of hubris and fright, awaiting external restraints and attempting to steal a march on them.

> If two hundred Turks could overturn the Government, then a few hundred bright, educated Armenians could do the same thing. We have therefore deliberately adopted the plan of scattering them so that they can do us no harm. (Enver to Morgenthau, 1918, p. 347)

Evidently the Turkish officials with whom Morgenthau vainly pleaded had decided very early, long before they met Morgenthau, to be guided overridingly by the considerations that Hobbes calls reasonable *if* one is in that abstract, never-met-with condition Hobbes calls the "state of nature," but *only* if one is in that condition. Out of the profuse experiential resources of a natal environment, Talaat and his men had come somehow to abstract the element of force and to focus on it exclusively. We don't know why or how. Perhaps because the soldiers, the police chiefs, the ex-telegraph operators had found most of the preferred places preempted by the sons of more privileged families, when they were growing up. Talaat had been a letter carrier and a telegraph operator, "and of these humble beginnings he was extremely proud" (1918, p. 21). They may have thought that a man should not merely bend to such circumstances. Rather, a man should excel, should outdistance his contemporaries, should do something to make his mother proud of him. To have taken the more tenuous course, toward building a community whose practices would have permitted the virtues to flourish—that might have seemed powerfully abstract, even ludicrous, in the context.[1]

To be guided by the elements of force is to be reconstituting oneself, incessantly, as a blank slate. Internally, in *our* sense of story, there can be no story progression. One dodges force, or uses it, and gains in technical proficiency in its use, or tries to. Apart from that, one remains pretty much where one was. One awaits the impulses of one's nature. Against others, one "retaliates" in advance, fearing the retribution that one has either earned in advance, or will soon have earned.

> "You are very foolish to try to play such tricks on us," I [Morgenthau] said. "Don't you [Bedri Bey, Prefect of Police at Constantinople] know that I am going to write a book? If you go on behaving this way, I shall put you in as the villain."
>
> This plea produced an effect; Bedri consented to postpone execution of the order until we could get Talaat on the wire. (Morgenthau, 1918, p. 154)

Bedri's alarm is understandable. He has no autobiography of his own in reserve. Any journalist can scoop him up, pretty much in his entirety. If Morgenthau wants to put him in *his* memoir, Bedri will have to appear there, in full regalia, with no darkened corners omitted. Bedri's is not magical thinking. It is not merely childish. It shows psychological realism. If he seems unaccountably reckless, well, he has very little internalized sense of self to lose. If he seems as easily startled as a deer in the forest, and as moveable, well, he must stay on the *qui vive*.

We are trying to picture here an impulsive genocide, who is not insane and has not been driven insane by drugs. For the man we are trying to picture, genocide looks to be the most natural thing in the world—the thing in the world that most recalls Hobbes's state of nature.

What makes the sane but impulsive killer, even the impulsive *genos* killer, less implacable than his premeditating cousin is his relative truthfulness. Impulses truly do strongly move him—overridingly—impulses in the genre of early resentment, wild ambition, lust to command, and lust to destroy. He can be as hard to turn back as a tidal wave. But he can also be jerked on the strings of certain fears. He fears capture. He anticipates his end and fears it (1918, p. 24). He fears daylight. Hence he knows himself to be already on the run, always just a step ahead of the daylight. His crimes against the target *genos* multiply themselves, partly for "internal security" reasons—the need to get away from his best-informed witnesses, his victims. From the standpoint of an underdeveloped life narrative, and a Hobbesian frame of reference, one might call him a practical sort.

He is a better man to deal with than the premeditating killer of *genē*, because he can be moved. He will respond to whatever truly moves him. He has acted in a horribly bad way. He is accordingly, as we say, a horribly bad man. If he could begin fully to expiate his crimes, there would be almost no end to it. If we could begin fully and adequately to mourn his victims, there would be almost no end to it. But he is not a sufficiently *focused* man to be counted as evil. By the same token, he is not sufficiently legible to serve as our pure type.

Loot and Glory

If the coordinated stages of genocide can be carried through by people who are storyless because they are thoroughly impulsive, and if impulsive perpetrators stand at the very top of the slope of genocidal evil, so far as their character is concerned, on what moral stratum do the genocides stand who are prompted by their avid and fervent concern for loot?

> Drawing his sword [Francisco Pizarro] traced a line with it on the sand from east to west. Then, turning towards the south, "Friends and comrades!" he said, "on that side are toil, hunger, nakedness, the drenching storm, desertion, and death; on this side, ease and pleasure. There lies Peru with its riches; here, Panama and its poverty. Choose, each man, what best becomes a brave Castilian. For my part, I go to the south."*

---

*Prescott (1847, 1:260f). On Prescott's biases, see Slotkin (1985, pp. 174f). Allowing for biases, Prescott's Pizarro is richly documented, and morally plausible—an exotic version of ourselves, when we are set on similar adventures.

As Prescott tells the story, we will not have here a deliberate effort at wiping a people out. But we will have a succession of acts, leading in a sustained way toward the destruction of a culture, its contrivances for self-government, its religious order or system for negotiating the path between the human and the superhuman, its leadership, its technology, and its educational structure. In the rubble, we will find many massacres, the widespread occurrence of slavery, all in consequence of a project of plunder (Prescott, 1847, 1:406–13; 2:184f, 231). "Deliberate intent," which was ruled into the definition of genocide as part of the language of the U.N. Genocide Convention, could perhaps also be found, on cross-examination, if Pizarro and his band were required to submit to that.[2] "But you knew, or could have figured out, that slavery would destroy the social structure?" (One imagines representatives from the U.N. Commission on Human Rights, or the Inter-American Commission, cross-examining Pizarro.) "Yes, obviously," Pizarro answers. "And so what? Our men had to be paid, didn't they?" Yet Pizarro and his men seem to proceed along their southbound way with an *unconscious* thoroughness. What was originally wanted was loot; the rest followed, and belonged to the loot.

There is a curious, and perhaps not atypical, feature of Pizarro's progress south. He had a conviction that the right of way already belonged to him. Responding to a question about his intentions put by a Peruvian noble,

> The Spanish captain replied that he was the vassal of a great prince, the greatest and most powerful in the world, and that he had come to this country to assert his master's *lawful supremacy* over it. He had further come to rescue the inhabitants from the darkness of unbelief in which they were now wandering. (Prescott, 1847, 1:271)

Mingled with Pizarro's unashamed lust for gold, there is self-righteousness and ferocity. On the sixteenth of November, 1532, the Inca will be invited to spend the night at Pizarro's quarters in the city of Caxamalca. There he will be exhorted by Pizarro's chaplain to accept vassalage, spiritual to Jesus Christ and temporal to Charles V. On a sign of the Inca's disinclination, between two and ten thousand of his followers will be massacred, and the Inca captured. On what excuse, this violation of the implicit rules of fair play, call them laws of hospitality, rules of warfare, or what you will? The excuse given the royal prisoner will be "his hostile intentions towards the Spaniards and the insult he had offered to the sacred volume." The pretext for the later drumhead trial of the Inca will be "charges of paganism and inciting insurrection," the latter false, the former irrelevant surely. Whence the *ferocity* of his particular brand of self-righteousness?

Strewn behind Pizarro were a bastard's childhood, a swineherd's youth, the manhood of a man without family, and an array of implacable convictions about how rewards were parceled out, in this life and the next. In front of him lay a territory naively studded with gold, the "tears wept by the Sun," as the Incas were supposed to have put it, whose conquest meant glory. A pitiless climate around him, ignominy and defeat at his back, inside him a hard ambition. No obvious way out, for Pizarro. If this is Pizarro's story, he must be a humorless man.

> The most enlightened of the Spaniards, who first visited Peru, struck with the general appearance of plenty and prosperity, and with the astonishing order with which every thing throughout the country was regulated, are loud in their expressions of admiration. No better government, in their opinion could have been devised for the people. (Prescott, 1847, 1:173)

If Pizarro is not "the most enlightened of the Spaniards," he may still have to steel himself against humbling comparisons, as he and his men destroy the terraced fields of the Incas, watered by underground channels, their monumental buildings and public works, what Prescott describes as a benign religious system and cloisters, their elite schools, their traditional assignments and rewards to skilled craftsmen:

> the wretched natives were parcelled out like slaves, to toil for their conquerors in the mines; the flocks were scattered and wantonly destroyed; the granaries were dissipated; the beautiful contrivances for the more perfect culture of the soil were suffered to fall into decay; the paradise was converted into a desert. (1847, 2:184f)

But suppose Pizarro had dealt *fairly* with the Incas? We can scarcely conceive of such a thing. To deal fairly with a people who abide within the common framework of the human community (i.e., they are not a herd of crazed killers), is to leave them alone. Or, if one wants to make them an offer, to wait for what answering terms they will propose. Not even Prescott imagines such an outcome.

> Contented with their conditions, and free from vice, . . . the mild and docile character of the Peruvians would have well fitted them to receive the teachings of Christianity, had the love of conversion, instead of gold, animated the breasts of the Conquerors. (1847, 1:173)

What is packed into Pizarro is an inability to separate pillage and conversion. Conversion, or the plan of it, is what gives one the "right" to pillage. The spiritual superiority of one's culture (a superiority marked by its greater military capacity, know-how, and science, as much as by its creed) is what gives one the absolute right of way, which includes the "right" to break faith.

Suppose, however, being Pizarro, I left off the conversion and pillage project. If I am Pizarro, I have been treated roughly in my youth, when by instinct I would have wanted to be treated compassionately. I have been presumably disowned by my father, when in simple justice I would have wanted to be his acknowledged son and heir. I have been rolled to the bottom of the social ramp, with the scum and the desperadoes, in a society where those who are privileged shine like bright gold from afar. Very good. I am still Pizarro. I have made my way to the outskirts of the Inca's domain, with a force of men. But this time, our supposition goes, with a different, more ethical script. This time I want only to play the part of a visiting anthropologist and economic theorist—not a conquistadore. If it seems tactful to do so, I may yet leave the value-neutrality of the social sciences and proffer my faith to the Incas, or make them a fair offer with regard to their mineral rights. But only if there is some sign of genuine interest on their side. And they would have a permanent right to abrogate all such commitments unilaterally.

No. Imagination breaks down. With such relatively gentle motives, and so universal an optic, Pizarro would not be there. Not in the sixteenth century. And not coming from Spain. We don't picture the man working his way toward such motives, or such an optic. We don't see him laboring arduously to pick out his earliest memories, of childish ambition, suffering, and *blocked* childish ambition. We don't see him matching his present plans against those early events of which he is often reminded, so that the life he is living now undergoes continuous redrafting and becomes a more accurate way of responding to the bitterness of a past that only he owns. We don't see him going forward in order to gain retrospective vision of and contact with his past, or going backward retrospectively in order to be free for the forward push—which are the two essential circular movements of a life story. We don't see him doubting that whole masses of humanity are deprived of every opportunity to get at a good life (to be "saved")— a belief that is the very projection of bitterness. If there is in him any abstemious disinclination to "get even," we suppose that any gesture he makes along that line would be one he can well afford, surveying the territory. Either it would have a pacifying intent, or it would handsomely advertise "what best becomes a brave Castilian." Such a gesture would not be likely to follow from inward knowledge that getting even doesn't put balm on the original wound suffered by the original child, nor arrest its ongoing effects on the man or woman today. Nor would such abstemiousness, if it were to be found, show understanding that getting even as a life project ordinarily picks out the wrong guys, namely, the guys who got in one's way *later*. It is hard, excruciatingly hard, to picture Pizarro wanting to be accurate about himself. In sum, we can't picture him as a good man. The times and the places don't permit it.

For what, then, precisely is he to be faulted? All he wants is what the rest of us want: glory. He has certain handicaps, a certain *Weltanschauung*, peculiar talents, that fit him for one thing supremely: this enterprise. Who are we, with our own guilts and compensatory refusals, to condemn Pizarro? We too want Peru in the Western world, and it's too late to put her there in an ideal fashion. Too late, and—in our century—still too early. We haven't learned to do it right yet.

We notice that Pizarro comes with governmental permission and conditional support, at first from the governor of Panama, and finally from Charles V and Isabella at Toledo, who award him the "right of discovery and conquest . . . titles and rank of governor and Captain-General" of the province of Peru or New Castile, and suitable titles and emoluments to his two partners, and his men (Prescott, 1847, 1:301f). He may be in Peru to line his pockets, and perhaps he would not be there at all were there no loot in it, but he is fully authorized and enjoined by his culture to take, subdue, and rearrange the elements of Inca culture. In Lemkin's inclusive sense of the term, this is genocide. In what may have been a more civilized and measured way, the Incas did it to the forest tribes that bordered their expanding empire (Prescott, 1847, 1:72–87). All cultures do it, sooner or later, or get it done to them. History is a struggle for the soul and the body of man.

Where are we? Pizarro, the perfidious Pizarro, stained with Inca blood and his own greed, has emerged suddenly—an innocent. He was a poor, downtrodden Estremaduran boy, trying to gain respect and honor. If he ever heard that the love of money is the root of all evil, he might well have wondered who was financing his informant. In any case, whoever told him that was likely to have been a priest, a man marked as exceptional because he did not carry arms or enjoy the other passions. Priests were fine in their place, but Pizarro would not have been likely to suppose that their warnings applied to him especially. But even if their warnings did apply, the turning over of pagan lands to the ministrations of Catholic Spain was likely to count heavily in his favor with the priests and the priests' God. Perfidy and cruelty was inextricably bound up with the work of handing over Peru. A small band could hardly take over a great empire and bend its inhabitants to an alien will by fair dealing. A kind of "parental" high-handedness and imperviousness was needed to make children out of adults, or to remind adults that, as cultures go, theirs was a culture for children. We can imagine a very clever invader from outer space being "compelled" by circumstances to deal with us similarly.

Pizarro is innocent! We are all innocent—or all guilty—it comes down to the same thing. But can't we get hold of him at all, for a moral assessment? Does he wriggle out of our grasp altogether, leaving us with the usual headshakings—the heads being shaken to conceal their excessive emptiness?

Let us try morally to assess ourselves, if we can't do Pizarro as yet. Pizarro is not unusual in coming equipped with cultural sanctions for his brand of greed, sanctions that pretend to detoxify the greed and make it an instrument of historical progress. One cannot destroy the patterns of an entire culture, and keep them destroyed for future generations, without teachers, troops, priests, entrepreneurs—the major resources of one's own culture backing one. Without cultural supports, no individual would be equal to that task. If the supports and rationales supplied by our culture for genocide were not Pizarro's in every case precisely, well, we have managed to find other, equally persuasive ones.

One can, for example, consider the target culture simply as a negligible quantity, to be brushed away like a fly. Historical progress pushes forward, one helps the historical process along, and one need scarcely notice what has been crushed by progress. It is no longer necessary to descend on one's target *genos*, in Pizarro's way, with an embrace of violence. The devastation can be wrought without looking, from a comfortable distance. This is what happens when multinational corporations make use of their outside influence with federal governments to get around Indian treaty obligations. (See Halsell, 1973, pp. 42ff; Davis and Zannis, 1973, pp. 37f.) As a by-product of mineral extraction, hydroelectric projects, "forest cutting . . . tourism . . . water diversion" (Davis and Zannis, 1973, p. 60), the native lands that are supposed to be protected by treaties become unfit to support the culture and correspondingly unfit to support other species that form part of the interactive system of life there.

When genocide for loot is done at a distance, the rationale that is required is like any rationale for distantiation. It merely verbalizes the distantiation. The perpetrators require little more than the ability to look away mentally, to see the company's entitlements as the main thing, to regard Bureau of Indian Affairs and federal treaty safeguards as lawyerly challenges, Indian culture as a textbook item, and the ecosystem as something other than what it is—the fundament of every human culture.*

This is not hard. We no longer need the accompanying chaplains that sacralized Pizarro's forays, the romantic flowing locks and dashing horsemanship of General Custer, the whole paraphernalia of popular frenzy, or the mentality of the prospector.[3] The entire enterprise has become more than easy. In its present, bland incarnation, its *blinkered* character is mainly what identifies it as evil, in the sense here understood. If I am the agent of a multinational, I can certainly act to put across my company's project, overriding the interests of Indians whom I either do not see or with whom I do not feel in any way identified, and I can feel okay about it. But to do and feel that way, I must take a small jump, which lands me, lock, stock, and barrel, within a system of mutually reinforcing rationalizations such as a company may provide to its employees. I become then a function and a by-product of my company's manners, mores, and projects.

Such a *compression of identity* is compatible with compensatory good works, in my community, or my home, or both. We need not even say here that a "bad" human being is concealed behind a string of compulsive good works. It is not so simple as that to make out the moral feedback loops. Good works do rebound on their producer, making him in a measure "good," or at least "good-hearted." Eventually, one can become nerved by this rebound process to want to become good in a deep-going way, and even to confront the long-term effects of one's work in the world. (So a program of exercise can in turn make one want to quit smoking, by the same kind of rebound effect.) But many people stop short, along this continuum, out of a confusion that they do not absolutely care to unravel, and out of reluctance to step off the soothing grooves of routine. "Companies do bad *and* good works," these people may explain. "If one stays in the world, one does both unavoidably. I have a kid in college." To which the same people's internal riposte *should* be, "Yes, but right now, going down this particular groove, my company asks me to ruin these particular lives. If I investigate further, I will get a pretty exact picture of what I've been asked to do. At least I will see that someone doesn't want me to see the effects of my work, where those effects may be irreversible. At the point where I see the effects, or see that they don't want me to see them, I will have a decision to make." The

---

*I am indebted to David W. McMullen for detailed discussion of the irreversible damage done the Hopi and Navaho nations by uranium mining companies, and for his article, "Trouble in Turtle Island" (1981).

postponement reply that concerns us now goes: "Let me therefore *not get to that point* along the continuum of inquiry." By this small piece of footwork one rejects the good life. And it has ramifications, this small jump.

Let us now take a better look. If I rip out the foundations of a culture, yet pay that whole process no mind, I cannot be working out *my* life story. I can only know intimately what a "culture" is, by comparison with mine. I only know *what I am* by bringing up into my consciousness my continuous work of reinterpreting my own past and future, work that uses in a reflective way the self-interpretive tools that the culture supplies. If I have such an impact on the culture of an Innuit or a Hopi that that sort of life scripting for the purpose of self-definition is largely stripped of its *future* dimension for him, then I can know what I have done and *find it ominous* only if I continue attentively to work on the unfolding script of my own life. Otherwise, I will have nothing in me that can identify with the Hopi or Innuit.

This capacity to identify with the story-preserving motif in another is crucial. I cannot simply fall back on the golden rule or some variant of it. Almost any rule that purports to be universal will founder on the exceptions—the hard cases of conduct and motivation, or the grand rationales that cultures themselves provide. The golden rule is a hollow rule of conduct, therefore, unless there are significant barriers in me that prevent my doing damaging things to myself.

If the capacity to identify with another's effort to avoid damaging his story is a necessary condition of my freely desisting from this kind of genocide, is it a sufficient condition? No. To find the sufficient condition, I have to go back to the particulars of my own life story: the original reasons I had for joining my forces to those of the mining company. What was it I wanted to solve, over the course of my life, from the beginning? Some technical problem perhaps, as a means of exploring my talents, or addressing a human need? But surely I would not have chosen to realize *that ambition* by destroying a land, a people, and the culture of future generations, other things being equal? Well, then, what I will do now ought for the sake of my story to be a coherent response to the original reasons and deeper ambitions that have brought me thus far. Either there are safer and fairer ways to get oil or uranium out of the soil or, if there are not, other fuels must be looked for, and other means of disposing of toxic waste. Why are we in such a hurry, on behalf of the stockholders? A generation from now our hurry will have had widespread and lengthy consequences. Consequences that have *nothing to do* with my early ambitions. Despoiling the environment can hardly be termed a fiduciary obligation. In sum, it is only if I continue to be good in the sense here defined that

I can know intimately what it means to rip out the foundations of a life story in a culture, and be willing to stop myself from doing that. If this is cumbersome, goodness can be very cumbersome.

Let us now suppose that I've made the small jump instead. I will not continue to be good, in the sense here explained. How *evil* does that make me? I don't feel that I'm very evil. Actually, I'm in rather an awkward spot. I would be just as pleased if the uranium mill waste were found to be harmless, or if it proved more feasible to put hydroelectric projects on the moon than it is now to put them on Innuit lands. I don't have it in for the native peoples.* On the other hand, I want to be able to look upon them as "expendable."†

The most efficient psychological shortcut to achieving that view is to *treat them* as expendable and see if the treatment doesn't "take," at least on me. Coerced relocation, instruction in cultural self-contempt in their schools, reaching for the cotton to put in my ears when they protest—all these seem to belong to the project of genocide for loot. The less important they seem to be in the scheme of things, the less will I be reminded of myself, or see in them the human face, or hear the voice of my brother's blood calling to me from the ground.

At this point I am capable of doing a great deal of harm to other people without feeling much pain or regret. My capacity for identifying with other people still operates, but now it operates negatively. I can no more identify with other people than I can identify with myself in depth. What I do to another, negatively, I also do to myself.

This Law of Negative Identification, as we shall want to call it, seems to be a hidden but introspectively discoverable law of human psychology. If it were not one, the thesis defended here would be correct only for people who are already sensitized to it. Instead, it seems to be applicable to everyone who is legally sane and therefore eligible for a moral analysis. Probably it applies as well to many who are not legally sane. If, in a particular case, one doesn't find this Law of Negative Identification applicable, one is probably not looking closely enough at the experience in which one thinks one has found a "counterexample."

---

*On the point, a contrast should be drawn with the reported deliberate extermination of forest Indians in Paraguay and Brazil, where the imported influence of Nazi ideology and practices has been noted. See Frances R. Grant, "Paraguayan Realities" (1976, pp. 77–80).

†Davis and Zannis make this point (1973, p. 38). For an account of the social erasure suffered by a pretendedly Navajo woman working for a white family in California, see Halsell (1973, pp. 164–78). Halsell, who is white, has also passed for black and found that the latter was much more comfortable socially.

So, operating under the Law of Negative Identification, as a corporate genocide I accomplish the compression of my identity, dehistoricizing my sense of self, making my psyche a kind of horizontal strip or band, unattached to the past or to the future, merely wrapping itself around information in the present tense. This way I *can* identify with the dehistoricized Indian. He'll be no different from what I will make of myself. (In psychoanalysis, the process is called "projection." But it is misleading to suggest that the rejected other must unconsciously represent to me some childhood traits that became early repressed in a traumatizing fashion.[4] I can begin the process of negative identification *ab initio,* in adulthood, begin it by simply ceasing to be good. Nobody need force me to begin it. This fact is, I think, also introspectively discoverable.) In sum, once I have taken this small jump, I can become truly unconscionable, as a human being. I can become a person who would cavil at nothing that I was directed to do by the company. For, in order to cavil, I would have first to decompress, lengthen, and retemporalize myself. Otherwise, the voice in the voice box will have nothing of the caviling kind to record.

So the corporate agent who has taken the small jump may feel in himself or herself no obstacles, nor sense any from the philosophic, religious, or literary traditions on which people draw when they try to build a self in our culture. No impediments except practical ones need be felt, none from the protests of the native peoples, none from their silences, none from the common future, none from the land. The agent's insensibility, if achieved, will be a crashing, a stunning, achievement. He or she will be in fact self-stunned. And members of the target *genos* risk getting correspondingly disconnected from their native sensibility, in consequence of the corporate policies the agent will pursue. They risk becoming victims under the Law of Negative Identification.

It would be prudent not to underestimate the malice or the drive of such a type, nor to impute to it much tenderheartedness.* Tenderheartedness, if it were to be found, might be a residuum from the past, still accidentally lodged in the personality. It would be nothing to count on. On the other hand, genocide would certainly not be the main plan, for this type. Genocide could be renounced, and speedily. Greed is fickle, in regard to its undertakings. Protests from local

---

*Richard Arens writes: "Heavy private American investment in Paraguay and substantial aid to the government in power coexist with a policy aimed at the extermination of an entire forest Indian population. There are also American military bases throughout the country. These facts, no doubt, bear on the silence of the American press and of American officials." See Arens (1976, p. 4).

townships could reach the press, and state assemblymen.* Then again, good pragmatic management can by itself steer toward responsible trusteeship in the community and the environment. Darwinian profiteering, by corporations or their subsidiaries, is no longer advocated in the influential management textbooks. (See Gluck, 1979, ch. 13.) Nor does a struggle red of tooth and claw belong to the picture that enlightened contemporary businessmen have of their own roles.†

Just as we saw that compensatory good deeds can rebound on the character of the corporate weekend philanthropist, to improve it, so it can happen that enlightened corporate management policies can work to remind employees to identify more coherently and democratically with other employees and with the community, and as a result they can become in fact and in time good people.‡ As with the weekend philanthropist, this is backward character building, or character building by behavior modification. One can, if the authors cited are to be believed, now sell one's soul to the corporate hierarchy and hope to get it back in good working order, in consequence of updated management techniques. However, if on the other hand the corporation is cast in a more Darwinian mold, owing to the dangerous nature of its product or the political weakness of the local community, this sort of backward character building by corporate behavior mod would not occur. So a would-be good person ought never to count on it.

The goodness and the wickedness of the corporate genocide are a function of external factors—but that fact is itself a description of moral collapse. If I have taken the little jump referred to earlier, there is no telling in advance how wicked I may become. There is nothing

---

*See McMullen (1981) for an account of how, in 1981, local communities in New Jersey successfully lobbied to ban uranium mining for seven years, partly influenced by representatives of Indian communities that had had no such success but could describe the ecological and health consequences of their defeat.

†The self-image is now of a "trustee of social resources . . . system regulator . . . productivity catalyst . . ." and of "agents of change . . . motivating others to be creative, imaginative and innovative . . . mediating . . . external claims made upon the organization . . ." and providing internal leadership. So results of internationally conducted studies of businessmen's role perceptions are reported by Keith Davis and Robert Blomstrom in *Business, Society and Environment: Social Power and Social Response* (McGraw-Hill, 1971, pp. 72ff), as summarized in Gluck (1979, pp. 369f).

‡For a description of such enlightened management techniques, see David K. Hurst's "Of Boxes, Bubbles, and Effective Management" (1984). Hurst finds corporate corruption to be a by-product of rigidly hierarchical, secretive, "hard strategy box" management. See esp. p. 85.

in the nature of what I have done that bespeaks limits. If the corporate policies happen to be enlightened, I will be on my good behavior. If the corporate policies are still unenlightened but visible to an informed public, then sooner or later I may have to conform to what an informed public will demand. If I can keep the public misinformed, or maintain the cover of invisibility provided by despotic regimes or provided by legal thickets within otherwise democratic regimes—I may go the distance. I am an instrument particularly fitted up to do long-term harm for the sake of short-term gains. The spectre of genocide would not slow me down, assuming I allowed myself to become cognizant of it.

So far, the main reason I am not set down here as the pure type of the genocide is that I will abandon genocide also if there are more effective ways to rise in the corporation. In the carrying out of some company policy, genocide may become psychologically important to me because of the Law of Negative Identification, which we have already noted. But for my purposes it is not an end in itself. I could give it up. A promotion and a raise would be more important. With those, I could get me a new dark suit, well tailored. Besides, as a result of external constraints, from the public, special interest groups, regulatory commissions, I am usually lucky enough not to get mixed up with anything truly awful. I come to these pages through outlying districts, through far-flung subsidiaries. I neither ask nor want to be here. At least, so I tell myself.

Something odd has happened in our attempt to get out of the confusion that beclouded our moral assessment of Pizarro. With the conquistador, there was a question of whether an individual can escape the value frame of his culture, even when he's engaged in a type of genocide. Pizarro's guilt is widely acknowledged, yet it is partly obscured for us by time and cultural distance. If he had conscious choices, we do not easily guess what they could have been. He seems to us—when we look at him closely—not so much an object lesson in how not to behave, as an object lesson in how not to pick a culture and a time and a social class from which to come. But of course, nobody picks his culture, time, or class before he is born, so far as we know. Nobody is to be judged morally for what he cannot help, by the same token. So the object lesson becomes a nonlesson—a sarcasm. In frustration, we turned to our own time, where we were more at home, and the values seemed more familiar. What we discovered, to our surprise, was that the faceless corporate flunky came off somewhat worse than Pizarro, not because he always does worse, but because he is open for anything. He is simply *available*, for good or evil. His plasticity is extremely scary and suggests a man on whom only external constraints can weigh heavily.

Pizarro was born, grew to manhood, and went to the great costume party of his age, pressed there between cultural messages, normal ambitions, and his own gifts. Our man in the dark, well-tailored suit would seem to be ready to travel, briefcase in hand, to *any* sort of party to which the corporate hierarchy was willing to send him. Having taken the small jump that we witnessed, the cool, economic reason that he applies to the company's options will be the same that he applies to himself. But, since we witnessed the small jump, we noticed his freedom. We can therefore find *his* culpability, if not Pizarro's.

(I would like to try using the "he or she," in tribute to recent more liberal hiring practices, but the "he or she" is still, I am happy to say, more likely to be "he," if we speak of indirect corporate genocide.)

In addition to the fact that the corporate genocide comes off somewhat worse than Pizarro, we have run into a different but equally unexpected finding. If the corporate genocide has culpability at all, it is very great culpability, deserving the title of "wickedness." We had expected to go down a slope in this chapter, which would lead from badness to wickedness in the agent, and at the same time, descend parallelly from alloyed to more "pure" or legible types of genocide. This correlation seemed roughly to obtain in the first case, but not to maintain itself in the second case.

The impulsive genocide wanted personal safety through power. He was not complicated. He could be moved off his road, if personal safety and power flowed elsewhere, in his changing assessments of their assumed fluidities. He seemed almost to be in a Hobbesian state of nature, where he was under pressure incessantly to choose between short-term gains. Perhaps he was under genetic constraints that forced him to be impulsive, or childhood influences that pushed him in that direction. Still, it seemed he could be appealed to, if one happened not to be afraid of him, and could match his candor. He lacked the conscious self-command, fixity of purpose, and encompassingly destructive vision of another's good that belongs to the truly evil. So, while we noted that the type of genocide that he committed was alloyed (not an end in itself), we noted correlatively that he was more nearly a "bad" man than a "wicked" one. Still, he deserved condemnation, where the mere victim of impersonal forces would not. This became obvious when one dealt with him and observed that he could have done otherwise, and could yet in the future do otherwise. The good was not out of his reach, nor was it utterly alien to him.

Condemnation might even get him to *see* that. To condemn him was to attempt to humanize him.

The genocide for loot is involved in a type of genocide that is one grade down, not quite so alloyed, *more nearly* the pure type. The pillaging of another culture is tied in with the deprecation of it. One does not walk up to a member of *one's own* society and win a general round of applause by snatching his L. L. Bean satchel. In order to make such a deed look respectable, nay, even honorable, one must first establish somehow that the victim is worth less than we are worth—doesn't share our values because his are lower on an absolute scale of values, and therefore he isn't worthy of our concern. Such an establishment of values to the detriment of the other culture may be privately and subjectively brought about in silence by the corporate genocide, as he operates behind the scenes. Or it may be done bravely, face to face, army to army, sword in hand and pennants flapping, as in the case of Pizarro, and his men, and his personal chaplain. Either way, the deprecation of the target *genos* seems to belong to the project of genocide for loot, as it did not necessarily belong to the project of impulsive genocide. So, although this is still an alloyed type of genocide (alloyed since it could be given up if the price were right, and since it is certainly not done for its own sake at the start), it is more nearly a pure type than the first type.

The trouble with our classificatory scheme, then, does not so far lie in the classification of types of misdeed, but in the classification of types of agent. As a misdeed, genocide for loot is only one grade down from impulsive genocide, down in the sense of less alloyed. But as a perpetrator, *the* genocide motivated by love of loot seems to plunge much farther down toward the base of the slope. Because he shows conscious self-command, fixity of purpose, and vision of another's good, he deserves to be classified as "wicked." Or so at least it would seem. Those who have to deal with him know he is disciplined, will get the job done if the loot requires it, and that he has a wealth of information at his command. He either does know, or else has the means of knowing, what he has done to another's good. Yet we have some residual sense of unease about putting him right near the base of the slope. We are not perfectly clear in our minds about his freedom. But why should this unease, about his (or Pizarro's) *exact* degree of culpability, be so particularly troubling and puzzling in the case of genocide for loot?

It has to do with the very factors that make this a more pure type of genocide. This type of genocide makes a direct call on the supports offered by the values and frame of reference of the genocide's culture. Hence the perpetrator seems more strictly embedded in his culture, and his culpability looks correspondingly harder to assess. To a human being, loot is not so primitive a good as is the venting of his impulses. On a desert island, for example, loot would be quite worthless. By its very abstractness and connection to other prestige values, loot attracts us insofar as our culture's other values also press down upon us. (For some primitive cultures, the desire for great wealth is not authorized and would be looked upon as incomprehensible, very wrong, or possibly mad.) So the question of whether the agent could have acted otherwise arises in this case with particular force, since we do not know *a priori* how much each agent is a cultural product. And the task of moral assessment is fraught with all the additional difficulties that come when the agent stands partly outside the frame of his culture, stands where one culture presses against the boundaries of another, stands in the stream of history.

What the corporate genocide would say in his own defense is that he didn't make up the world in which his company can get a free hand to ruin the land of another culture, and he can't unmake that world by his own power. He can't unmake it physically. He can't unmake it morally and spiritually. He was born into it. If he doesn't continue, one way or another, "in the American grain," as William Carlos Williams used to call it, he'll end up sleeping in the subway, *beneath* the American grain. In his own defense he would say we have let our emotions run away with us. Certainly he is no worse a man than Pizarro. Certainly he was no freer. Certainly "a man cannot free himself from the world of his education."*

Just when did our culture's history make of him someone who *would* jump the way he did when pressed? When and how did the prestige values that pressed down upon him assume all their present shape? Since primitive cultures do not exhibit the genocidal tendency, as a rule, since other primates closely related to us are aggressive only "as necessary," since warfare with a defensive purpose is to be distinguished from genocide, genocide emerges as a cultural product, not an innate tendency.† So we had better go back only so far as our own culture extends, or its antecedents, if we want the background rationale for the corporate genocide's decisions.

Such a rationale was provided by our Puritan divines, men such as Increase and Cotton Mather, or Samuel Nowell, who maintained—on the level of rhetoric at least—that Indians in the New World were to be treated like the Amalekites of old.

---

*Defense Counsel Dr. Friedrich Bergold, *Nuernberg Military Tribunals, United States of America Against Erhard Milch*, Case No. 2, "The Milch Case," vol. 2, p. 378.

†I am indebted to Daniel Lev for summarizing these points for me in helpful discussion.

The Puritans believed, among other things, that they were the "true Israel." It is not a point worth disputing, certainly not in the present context. But nobody, including the despised but unforgotten original claimants to the true Israel title, believed that in the seventeenth century they were still hearing loud and unmistakable voices from on high. Nobody thought the Lord's genocide command had been renewed in its original unequivocal mode. The trouble with scripting one's parishioners into an archetypal history, where they are not culturally derived from that particular history, nor attached to an unbroken tradition of reflection and commentary on it, is that the congregation is stirred into moral disquiet by what they may sense is—for them at least—partly a made-up story. That moral disquiet has perhaps remained with us. Meanwhile, in another part of the large and complex religious culture of the West, the original claimants to the true Israel title had long since reinterpreted the genocidal commands so that they would no more constitute a precedent than did the divine command to Abraham to sacrifice Isaac. Exegetes are of course free to do that with a Biblical command or example. One has some responsibility for what one decides to construe as a precedent.*

At any rate, our modern corporate genocide, from the U.S.A., can draw on the Puritan precedent, if he chooses, as a part of his background rationale, but if he does so he will be leaving all its clustered confusions unanalyzed.

That background rationale was given another twist by the successors to the Puritans, for whom the notion of an impersonal, natural law bringing the races into "tragic" conflict had replaced the theological conceit. The newly supposed natural law had a eugenicist cast—quite a few decades before the work of Charles Darwin or of his cousin, Francis Galton. A superior race had, on this supposition, ineluctably brought forth an advanced civilization. A savage race had, with equal fatality, brought forth its traits of wildness, cunning, cruelty, and occasional nobility. In the coming clash, the inferior race was *destined by nature* to be entirely subdued, or to "vanish"—possibly by the road of extermination. So went the biologized version of the

---

*That people scripturally prohibited from entering the assembly of the Lord could not be barred from converting to Judaism and being thus eligible to be taken in marriage in later, Talmudic times, is evident from the ruling in Brachot 28A to the effect that Ammonites and Moabites could not be so disqualified any longer. The reason given is that, since Sennacherib mixed up the nations, there are no more pure races. I am grateful to Scott Novins for the reference, and to Peter Miller and Milton Schubin for helpful discussion of the question.

Puritan (and in its Puritan form, impenetrably occult) claim about the true Israel and the Amalekites.*

The biological part of the background rationale was, however, at least as confused as the theological part. Although being more advanced (because of the shake-out of natural law) is like being in a state of grace in that it is not wholly or necessarily an earned condition, there are still external signs of *advancement* that upon challenge one should be able to produce. Railroad trains and telegraph wires are fine external signs; Jeffersonian rhetoric is fine too; Longfellow is fine; but they are none of them as trustworthy evidences of *moral* advancement as are fulfilled promises. Otherwise, if the moral aspects of advancement are left aside, the question of who is the more civilized and who the savage will get less and less clear, as one scoops up one's ill-gotten gains and stumbles to keep up with one's culture's delinquents.

When all this is said, against that part of the corporate genocide's rationale which is culturally supplied, something mitigating must be added. There must also have been what one might call a "Hegelian" aspect to the background rationale. Now, Hegel would have claimed that the domain of the ethical is internal to a culture, or to some cultures. For Hegel, the ethical cannot override the demands of cultural self-defense that can arise in a clash *between* cultures. For example, in cultural self-defense, our culture might want to maintain that it could not keep up its normal pace and continue to deliver its expected benefits without railroads. Railroads required that vast tracts be cleared of buffaloes and therefore of buffalo-dependent, hostile Indians. Again, in cultural self-defense, our culture might claim that nomadic cultures, which depended partly on hunting, required a share of the earth's surface disproportionate to the number of their members, and that a greater good might befall a greater number if that land were distributed to European immigrants, who could feed vast numbers of people from all over the world, by intensive farming and the profits from manufacture. In both examples, the culture's self-defense is seen as benefiting humanity, and the culture's default on its self-defense would be seen as a loss to human welfare overall.

Here the argument itself has forced me into a corner, and no amount of moralizing can get me out of it quite unscathed. It must

---

*On the Puritan analogy between Indians and Amalekites, see Slotkin (1985), pp. 53–62. On Jefferson's biologization of the conflict, see Slotkin, pp. 73f. On its nonnegotiable or "tragic" irreconcilability, see Custer's "The Red Man" (1858), quoted in Slotkin, p. 380.

be admitted—I must admit—anyway *somebody* must admit that there is
something to the Hegelian claims. That is, there is something to all
three such claims. On the first claim, it must be admitted that the
historical has a kind of sovereignty over the ethical, obliging each
contending culture to win, insofar as it can do so while preserving the
good life for its members. It is not obliged to annihilate itself and
mankind in order to win. It is not obliged to turn itself into a ravening
beast in order to win. (In fact, it is obliged not to do that.) But it is
obliged to try to win, *ceteris paribus.*

If a mutually acceptable "win" can be negotiated between the
contending cultural parties, fine. Sometimes, it cannot be. In such
cases, universal imperatives are partly suspended, albeit not so completely nor in such a way that one could never recall them or put
them into operation again. For the time being, the good life has found
its outermost boundaries. In the state of war, one's ethical sense has
little to be preoccupied with except confining damage to the necessary
and keeping in view the relative worth (for the good life) of the two
contending cultures. One might conceivably go over to the other side,
because one had decided that the opponent culture contained more of
the good life, or less of the bad life. But such an about-face would be
immensely tricky morally, since it would involve the painstaking
renunciation of many prior commitments. Even without that painstaking self-review, cultural treason can turn out for accidental reasons
to have been the right decision. But if such a decision is made on blind
impulse alone, it cannot be the decision of a *good person,* as following
from his goodness. (But in practice these are extremely delicate
questions, hard to assess from outside, hard to assess from inside.
One can only state in a general way what the right assessment would
have to look like, if one could get it.)

On the second and third "Hegelian" claims, it must again be
admitted that more people were benefited by undercutting the
economic base of Indian culture than would have been by leaving the
virgin land uncolonized, and that this has been found to be so virtually
every time that city culture has taken over land from nomadic culture.
Indeed, it is partly in consequence of concerns that are now surfacing
within our culture, for wilderness conservation, for protection of other
species, for preservation of the ecosystem, for mutual respect between
groups that are ethnically identifiable, that the white assault on Indian
culture is coming more and more to be felt and acknowledged as
immoral.

That the new concern for aboriginal rights has cultural boundaries
drawn around it becomes clearer if one imagines conservationists and
Indian advocates confronted with the chance to repeal the last three

hundred years, and to make entire restitution. Of course I cannot speak for anybody else's family, but had my paternal grandparents been confronted with the chance to leave their house on 2nd Street in Louisville, Kentucky, and go back to Lithuania, I do not think that they would have been particularly interested. One's own interests as a member of a culture simply go without saying and are, as a rule, left out of coherent, high-level moral discussion. One moralizes with one hand, and keeps one's interest intact with the other hand. Even to point out with too much emphasis the double game is by implication to line up with General Custer on the one hand, or with mystical dropouts from the culture on the other. It seems to close out the discussion, with a sarcastic punctuation mark. Almost, it is bad form. Yet there *is* a double game, whether or not it is bad form to say so. Doubleness is not removed by pointing out that the worst encroachments were done on the Indian long ago. Space and time are not all that opaque. They do not really block our moral view, though they may limit (to our benefit and the Indian's detriment) *some* of the legal possibilities for redress of Indian grievances.

It begins to look as if our contemporary corporate genocide, busy destroying the Indian for the sake of the loot, is identifiable as such, to himself and to us, largely because *our culture has changed.* His ancestors, whether Puritan divine, patriot-statesman, or rough soldier-frontiersman, were no doubt somewhat confused about God and natural law. (We are no doubt somewhat confused about God and natural law ourselves, but just how confused we are may be more apparent to our descendants.) But the cultural ancestors were *not* confused about what was involved in cultural self-defense. About that, they were and are right on the money.

In the course of trying to assess the exact degree of culpability of the corporate genocide, we looked into the background rationale that the culture had made available to him, as in the sixteenth century Pizarro's culture had supplied him a background rationale. The background rationale for genocide in our own culture comprised theological supports that were, we thought, ill-founded, and not justifiably used to constitute a precedent; it comprised a biological theory of culture that, in its day, had been ill-considered and inconsistent with the very claim of moral advancement that it was fondly supposed to bear out.[5] But it also could draw on the reasonable belief that cultural self-defense is a prerequisite of the good life and that—in the Hobbesian state of nature that in many respects still subsists between cultures—often the best defense is an offense.

We have come aground on deep confusion. Unless we assume that it is reasonable for entire cultures to assume the posture of Tolstoyan nonresistance both to external and to internal threats, we must concede that it will in principle be reasonable for cultures to place other cultures in the severest jeopardy, or to practice genocide in the broad sense of Lemkin's definition.* Before we go further, in our attempted assessment of genocidal guilt, let us make sure that we were forced by the argument to come aground here. Let us call back to mind typical arguments that are used for the purposes of condemning genocide as broadly construed, and condemning it wholesale, and see whether our qualified endorsement of the Hegelian view can survive in the face of all these condemnations. (The project is hardly gratifying to our moral self-complacency, but I do not see how it can be dodged at this stage of the proceedings. Surely what is needed here is *not* one more display of moral self-complacency.)

As usual, it is Lemkin, with his beautiful passion for justice and his elegantly comprehensive legal culture, who gives the most direct and clear statement of the case against genocide broadly construed.

> We conceive that nations are essential elements of the world community. The world represents only so much culture and intellectual vigor as are created by its component national groups. Essentially the idea of a nation signifies constructive cooperation and original contributions, based upon genuine traditions, genuine culture, and a well-developed national psychology. The destruction of a nation, therefore, results in the loss of its future contributions to the world. Moreover, such destruction offends our feelings of morality and justice in much the same way as does the criminal killing of a human being. (1944, p. 91)

Lemkin cites the Versailles Treaty as evidence of an international consensus to recognize national and religious groups as entities having rights and requiring protection (1944, p. 91). Hannah Arendt, however, *blames* the Versailles Treaty for replacing the rights of man by the rights of recognized national groups, and thus inadvertently creating a whole new class of stateless and rightless persons, namely, those whose nationalities were not singled out for mention by the treaty. In addition, Arendt points out, the Versailles Treaty did not include provisions for the enforcement of the rights of those minority groups it did recognize (Arendt, 1951, ch. 9).

As this indicates, Arendt is not implying that national groups are not valuable in themselves nor deserving of protection. What she has uncomfortably reminded us is that nations may not feel they can

---

*See Irving Louis Horowitz's *Taking Lives*, for the distinction between genocide in the broad sense and holocaust (1982, pp. 15f). The point is that there *is* a distinction.

afford to single out for mention and protection all their subordinate *genē*. She has also urged upon us the claim that cultures, whether nationally embodied and protected or not, are placed in the service of human rights, not placed to override human rights for the sake of their own aggrandizement. But all these moral-sounding pronouncements that can be drawn out of Arendt's text are really just preliminary sorting operations. We still do not know why a *genos* has rights, or how far it may go in defending its rights.

In the passage just cited Lemkin has written of the world's "intellectual and cultural vigor," and of each culture's "future contributions to the world." Monroe Beardsley, who does not hold that a culture's right to survive is indefeasible, writes that absent "the most stringent conflicting moral demands," demands which for some reason cannot be furthered by negotiation, members of cultures have the right to continue their cultural practices if they choose to do so. The rights of cultures are, in Beardsley's view, based on the necessary conditions for becoming a moral agent, and on the access of all humanity (possibly its "right of access," though Beardsley does not say this) to what "the rich diversity of its boundless talent has created."[6]

We can summarize this. To make a person cultureless is to deprive him of an important piece of the good life, even if one is not necessarily thereby depriving him of life itself. To diminish a person's access to his culture is to render his striving for the good life that much more arduous and bitter. Insofar as persons are made less able to be good, the human world is also made less able to be a good world. But the qualifications on this are as important as they are confusing, morally.

Not every cultural practice that the culture may see as essential to its integrity does actually conduce to a good life. Thus one may do something that to a culture is "genocidal," and the results be somewhat more conducive to a good life than if one had left the genocidal thing undone. For example, in *The Genocide Machine in Canada*, Robert Davis and Mark Zannis cite the Canadian government's suppression of the potlatch ceremony as an example of a genocidal practice (1973, p. 65). And so it is, in the broad terms of Lemkin's definition. Yet, Orlando Patterson's *Slavery and Social Death* notes that "it was during the potlatch ceremony culminating in the ritualized exchange and destruction of property that the murder of slaves became a veritable carnage . . ." (1982, p. 191). So, insofar as "genocide" prevents the massive damage to self and others that results from what we have here called the Law of Negative Identification (under which the other is regarded as the same kind of storyless nonentity that I have already let myself become for myself), this instance of genocide is a good thing, and prevents a bad thing.

One can, of course, rush about amending Lemkin's definition, so that genocide henceforth means *only* holocaust. But not every great massacre is genocidal, and not every genocidal practice leads to mass death. One will simply have to work out a more differentiated consciousness of these human realities, if one is to get the applicable moral categories into play.

To sum up: there are cases where a culture is in itself—and so far as the good life goes—morally acceptable, but a rival culture may *correctly* see its survival and ability to continue to bestow benefits on its members as tied in with the partial undermining of the targeted culture. In such a case (we may take the American story as such a case), the victorious culture retains an acute responsibility toward the offended culture and its members, to assist them toward as much autonomy, cultural dignity, and restitution of lost goods and status as may comport with the common good and safety of the offending culture. If such responsibility to make restitution is not noticed and accepted, the offending culture places its members under the Law of Negative Identification, a law corrosive to the stories of each one of them, and therefore to the goodness of the world.

There are also other cases, where actions that are in the broad sense "genocidal" are nevertheless provisionally admissible. For example, in the case of cultures that include morally pernicious practices, harmful to good character and to a good life story, the moral requirement would be to get those cultural practices and beliefs delegitimated and undermined. It would not matter how central those practices and beliefs were to the culture, how important to its morale, if the culture's practices and beliefs made the good life unlivable for its members.

It should be noted, however, that if the "genocidal" assault on such a practice has a *moral* basis, there are constraints on it analogous to those that operate whenever we try to thwart another's will for his or her own good. Ideally, it would be more respectful of the moral agency of the culture's members (and of the ethical opacity of the river of human history) if one stood back and let the culture's reform come from within. But even such reform-from-within often involves a partial dilution of the culture by external influences, as filtered through its internal reformers. And one should not underestimate the trauma of even the "gentlest" movements for internal reform, involving as they must assaults on the culture's self-confidence as to its hold on truth and on goodness, and attendant displacements of the most tenacious power relations. Western culture has undergone many such reforms-from-within, and they were mostly traumatic in the extreme.

At the same time, as the history of the West probably shows, if the assaulted culture includes any significant elements of goodness, it can in principle withstand and emerge stronger from attacks on its immoral practices, whether these attacks come from within or without. So it does not seem to me necessarily *wrong* for a moralizing reformer to enter a culture and proselytize for a repeal of some of its practices, however central these might be, if the practices appear inimical to human goodness. Evidently it is an extremely consequential thing to do. But studied avoidance of the task of being an influence is also consequential and includes its own brand of condescension. In sum, nonviolent external influence, or violent cultural self-reform (as in the American Civil War), is not in all cases wrong.

But what about *violent* external influence, with a moral basis (as opposed to a moral pretext)? This too is "genocidal" in the broad sense, particularly where the practices violently interfered with are central to the assaulted culture. Let us take the case where the Canadian government, from a cultural standpoint external to that of the Kwakiutl, outlawed the practice of potlatch, and let us assume for the sake of the argument that Patterson's description of potlatch, as a practice involving the large-scale slaughter of slaves, is by and large the correct one. Here we have delegitimation of a central cultural practice (and associated beliefs), a delegitimation *imposed* by one culture on another, with the aid of the "genocidal" culture's own laws and armed force. This does not seem to me wrong either, but the context creates uneasiness.

Ordinarily it is to be supposed that each person should mind his own business, or at most should help mind the business of his particular culture. If somebody on the other side of the globe is doing the wrong thing, there is something on the face of it suspect in my dropping my own affairs and sallying forth physically to prevent him. Whether or not justice is, as Plato said, minding one's own busi-ness—we at least hold suspect the fairness of someone who cannot mind his own business, because he is violently minding another's. So it can be supposed that the task of violently suppressing immoral practices in another culture does not ordinarily fall to the person who is minding his own business, and that any other sort of person is not entirely fair minded.

What usually happens, however, is something more complicated, from the standpoint of a moral analysis. The targeted culture has attracted the *interested* notice of, say, some Western culture. It has land that attracted interest, or mineral wealth, or a possible work force, or a market, or a strategic location. For that, or some similar selfish reason, its business has become important to us while and because we are minding our own. That's how we happened to get involved. That's how the Canadian government, for example, happened to find that minding the Kwakiutl's business was part of minding its own.

It is usually thought that if wrongs are to be reproved, or stamped out, the moralizer should not have a particular interest in undermining the alleged wrongdoer. Yet this is just what happens when the Canadian government outlaws the potlatch ceremony. The moralizer, who is backed by police powers, is yet not disinterested. In such a case (which is the usual case—the banning of Hindu suttee by the British might be an instance of the same kind), should we, despite the interested relation in which we stand to the targeted culture, go ahead and outlaw its immoral practices? (Of course a designated judge should not stand to profit by his own ruling. I do not speak of direct conflicts of interest, only of whether or not we should endorse and support and carry out a ruling that is "genocidal," in that it bans a practice on which a targeted culture partly depends, in cases where there is some indirect benefit to our own culture in the undermining of that culture.)

I think in that case *we should*, where otherwise the harmful practice would continue, and we should even though the very use of force will be in itself damaging and embittering. It is true that it would seem that in such cases we are either failing to mind our own business, and being unjust, or minding our business only too well, and being hypocritical. We are not deeply or solely concerned for the humanness and welfare of these strange people. We are more concerned for our safety, or for the loot. Hypocrites should not impose their morality on other people. If we are hypocrites, then either our morality is not a very good one, or—if it (the professed standard) is a good one—then *we* are not the ones who can be found worthy to impose it on other people. For that it needs clean hands and a pure heart.

The trouble with this pretext for backing down on the potlatch or the custom of suttee is that we are not so easily got clear of hypocrisy. The backing down may be fraught with its own hypocrisy. The charge of "hypocrisy" has a familiar ring to it. It rings of repressed nature giving its usual riposte to repressing conscience. That good manners, reliability in intimate relations, professional honor, and civic responsibility may all be deeply hypocritical in the sense of burdensome, does not make them any less morally correct and desirable. Too often the person who charges "hypocrisy" has an interest of his own to press—revoluntionary (and a "hypocritical" revoluntionary can still *count* as a revolutionary, still count as doing the best he can, even if caught in the contradictions of capitalism)—or he may have an interest in pulling down the moral—never the technological—superstructure of civilized life and romping around in an imagined original savannah, blessed with high tech. Nothing more swiftly conduces to *that* than showing how "hypocritical" and tied to his selfish interest is the moralizer. (The revolutionary's hypocrisy can be scientifically explained away. The moralizer's hypocrisy is supposed to undo him totally.)

Yes. We are all tied to our selfish interest. But we must try to make accurate judgments about our stories and their ramifications in the stories of others, all the same, although we *are* caught in the contradictions of history.

In sum, there are cases where "genocidal" practices as broadly construed must be allowed morally. These may include cases where the justification is cultural self-defense—although here one is under an obligation to be as accurate as one can in making the political judgment, and to reduce and repair the resultant harm as much as one can. There are other cases where the justification is moral. In both cases, violence is sometimes allowable as a last resort, although persuasion is clearly the better way.

It is true, as Lemkin writes, that a culture has, in all its phases, a right to life, as does an individual, other things being equal. And it was no part of Lemkin's purpose to note, in *Axis Rule in Occupied Europe*, his massive treatise on genocide, that, in the human community, nobody's right to life is unconditional. Nevertheless, that too is true. And no culture's right to life is unconditional.

In cases where one has a moral basis for interference with the customs of another people, one usually has some selfish business with them as well, which gives one an interested relation to them. One's moral obligation will be, then, dual in such a case. One has to repair the damage one has done, to dignity, autonomy, goods, and status, so far as one can without severely compromising the well-being of one's own culture and people. One has also to negotiate—or, in the worse case, impose—the moral restraint. (Head-hunting is illegal and punishable, human sacrifice is illegal and punishable, slavery is illegal and punishable, and so forth). And, in doing this, one seldom has clean hands. If one had clean hands, one would ordinarily not be in a position to do it. Nevertheless, one ought to do it, if one can bring oneself to the point.

Are we really forced to take this view? What is the alternative, for a culture? There are those whose concern with the motivational roots of genocide goes so deep that it leads them to call for abrogation of most of the defensive-offensive measures by which cultures now preserve themselves. They maintain that genocide cannot arise without sustained failures of empathy, and social practices that conduct to failures of empathy. "Legitimate violence always provokes illegitimate violence," argues one such writer, who goes on to advocate preventive abolition of the police, of capital punishment, of war, and of social distance between such groups as the marginal, the mentally ill, and the establishment.[7]

In practice, however, a commitment to the good life involves a real, serious, unsuppressible commitment to the survival of the culture in which we have come to envisage and reasonably to articulate the good life for ourselves. At the present time, a commitment to the survival of our culture must include a provisional endorsement of "legitimate violence," which is that violence that is—as things presently stand between men and nations—so far needed for the culture's defense of its members in the context and framework of its self-defense as a culture. Those who propose that we drop out of the life of culture, or that the culture drop out of its own life by abandoning measures for its own defense, have rightly seen that there is a connection between the life of culture and the potential for war between cultures. They want to avoid genocide, however broadly construed, and they want to avoid it at all costs. But the costs will include dropping their commitment to the good life.

If repressive or violently repressive measures against other cultures are sometimes legitimate acts of cultural self-defense, or of moral self-assertion, then the question arises: under what conditions do such acts become so legitimated? The question is one for political as well as for moral judgment. The person who has to make such a decision must know what in his culture, or anyone's, is worth defending, or worth opposing, for the sake of the good life, and this is a moral sort of knowledge. If it's a question of self-defense, the one who judges must have a realistic sense of when his culture's life is being jeopardized, and that is a political-military sort of question. One can be wrong, obviously. All sorts of opportunities for self-deception ring the politician. But a good faith mistake about when we are in jeopardy belongs to the character of human life in history. It is not by itself the act of an evil person, or even necessarily of a bad one. Neither does one become a good person simply because one has never had to make such decisions.

We are getting very uncomfortable—*because this is the way that Nazis talk.* Well, many of them had read Hegel, Schopenhauer, Nietzsche, Fichte, and God knows who else. Oh yes, Luther and Kierkegaard.[8] Their statements in their own defense at Nuremberg read—many of them at least—like a succession of commencement addresses at a private, well-endowed, no-longer-strictly-denominational college in the Midwest. Not everyone who talks this way is a Nazi, or even implicitly, latently, and "logically" a Nazi. Nazis did not have a commitment to what has here been called the good life, nor had they any aversion to what has here been called evil. Indeed, the Allied conquest of Germany, the Nuremberg trials, and the denazification programs could have been classified—had the Reich lasted a few more generations—as "genocidal" in the broad sense here being partly defended. The men in the prisoner's dock were not entirely wrong to have called this "victors' justice," nor to have been amazed at being made to submit to a bunch of foreigners' rules. What had become the victor in Germany, however, was among other things the possibility of a good life. About getting to be a Nazi, more will have to be said later. Meanwhile, we are not there yet.

If there is in principle something legitimate about some genocidal practices in cultural self-defense, and if their legitimation must await a case-by-case judgment that is political as well as moral, then how finally may we proceed to assess the moral guilt of the modern-day corporate genocide? (Recall that with his assessment will come clearer the moral assessment of anyone who practices genocide for loot, Pizarro included.)

It is unlikely that the corporate genocide, dumping toxic waste on an Indian reservation for example, believes the theological business, though it will probably be all right with him if anyone else believes it. Besides, it is hard to invoke the Bible to sanctify projects of turning productive territory into wasteland. On the whole, the Bible seems respectful of scenery, and of local craft life, even of local gods, provided one does not turn to worshipping them oneself. So a corporate genocide who invokes the theological part of the background rationale that the culture has in storage could be called cynical, morally open to anything, up for grabs, and "wicked," still.

If the racial rationale were reached for by the corporate genocide, it could hardly be done in good conscience at this point in our culture's history. If there proved to be such a thing as absolute genetic superiority along racial lines, the superiority could be expected to show its worth by incessant acts of kindness, consideration, and promise-keeping—both as regards the letter and especially the spirit of interracial, intercultural promises. Nobody can honestly claim to be superior at the same time and in the same respect as he acts like a brute and makes other people miserable and desperate. If in the past people were better able to bring off this self-deceptive sleight-of-hand, it is not to be supposed that anybody can bring it off today, for any continuous period of time. An aboriginal susceptibility to alcoholism is no more a sign of absolute and general racial inferiority than was an earlier susceptibility to smallpox. To view these epidemics with smug complacency, or to have complicity in the spread of them, and then take advantage of the consequent cultural devastation, is not to have given oneself an occasion for any racial self-congratulation. A natural weakness in another is not an authorization from nature for me to bring about his doom.

But what of the "Hegelian" rationale, the one we agreed to let pass, because cultural survival and flourishing still depended on it? To repeat the Hegelian point: cultures have a duty to their members, both to survive as cultural wholes and to continue to provide culturally promised and approved benefits. That duty may lead cultures to clash with each other, in roughly two ways. (1) The clashes may occur because the wherewithal for the good life is itself a scarce good, when there is only room for one of two competing cultures to live some approximation of it on a given territory. The clashes may thus occur because the good life requires some raw materials, markets, labor sources, defensible frontiers, that one culture can get only at the expense of another, negotiations not being always feasible. (2) The clashes may further occur because one culture's practices are absolutely offensive to the *morale* and life stories of another culture, the morally offended culture being here assumed to provide for its members the greater opportunity to live reasonable and self-corrective life stories. In the case where the target culture has given moral offense to the potentially "genocidal" culture, it often happens that they are (or will soon be) also in competition for material goods. That fact complicates and sobers the moral assessment but does not change it fundamentally.

How much of a smokescreen do these "Hegelian" considerations provide to our corporate genocide? None of them excuse the business of making land unlivable, or turning coherent cultures into derelicts. That cannot benefit an aggressor culture over the long pull, if history is what we mean by the long pull, and if history is framing the conflict. When material advantage is taken of a culture that has rough moral parity with that of the aggressive culture, or moral superiority to it, and the reasons are found in (1) above, a responsibility is immediately incurred by the aggressor culture. The latter must repair the damage, or compensate for it, so far as that can be done compatibly with the aggressor culture's overall aims and needs. It is always assumed that these aims and needs correspond to or allow for a reasonably self-corrective life story, which is to say a good life. (Where the aggressor culture's predominant aims preclude the good life, its aggression is then wrong absolutely, that is, corrosive to the good life of its members and its victims. This remains true, even if over the historical long term some good may yet be pulled out of it. There are few wrongs so evil that good may not be pulled out of them. Nevertheless, one wants, paraphrasing Thomas Mann in the Joseph stories, to have a care for one's story [1936, p. 774].)

In the moral case (2), where one culture imposes its will on another for the sake of the good life, the corporate genocide will have a very hard time stretching such justifiable interventions to cover the sort of irreversible undermining of economic foundations that he is hastening to bring about. He can of course say, "Well, economically forced relocations have traditionally included forced transfer of Indian children to boarding schools, where the immoral practices of their tribe get delegitimated. So what I am doing can be seen as having a moral tinge to it, or possible moralizing consequences." That is what we can picture his saying, perhaps saying it to himself. He can *say* that. But it is not the case that a culture is entitled to capture children and disrespectfully or randomly discredit the practices, values, and beliefs of their parents. Likewise, it is not the case that anyone, culturally authorized or not, has the right to convince children that their parents have no legitimate claim to an economic base in the world. So one thing should not be confused with another.

If one is taking the time to think clearly, these confusions either do not arise, or at least they cannot persist. If one means anything reasonable or plausible by history, natural law, or theology, then neither history, natural law, nor theology can authorize these confusions. If one does not mean anything reasonable by history, natural law, or theology, then there is a reason for this. The reason is that one has stopped trying reasonably to work out one's own life story. One is then—because of the Law of Negative Identification—open for anything. The only reason one has not done worse is that the culture and its institutions will so far not permit worse. Where one can get away with it, however, one will go the distance. So one *is* wicked, at least in potential, and has deserved some of the name. The loot is ill-gotten, inglorious.

The pieces are now in place for a comparative assessment of the corporate genocide and Pizarro, vis á vis each other, and in regard to their respective places on the slope of genocidal guilt. It seemed earlier that Pizarro was not so bad as the corporate genocide, although they both practiced an alloyed type of the evil that is genocide: genocide for loot. Can we equalize the outcome of their assessment at this point? Once again, another look at each man, then.

It is true that the corporate genocide wears a suit. He plays tennis.

He looks like anybody. He is not, to judge by appearances, a war-movie Nazi. (Real Nazis were not necessarily like the ones in the war movies either.) But, if the accoutrements of normality were taken away and the deeds with their intentions were left to stand un-adorned, one would see an agent whose distance from "the worst" is maintained only by contingencies external to some of his motivations and dispositions. (By "the worst," we mean perpetrators of holocausts—here, the desk men.) The real difference between him and the worst is that he is merely potentially what they are already in actuality.

However, this difference is not an insignificant one, given the fact of freedom. Between the potentiality and the actuality room is always left for a turning-around of intentions and practices. Some of that turning-around potential inheres in the very motive of loot. Since the genocide is in the present case merely instrumental, one instrument can always be changed for another, with no change in the goal. And some of the turning-around potential is contained in the cultures that produce these types. If the culture is not itself hellbent on holocaust, this is because many social norms still hold that are better than that, and that work on the corporate genocide, to keep him conformed to those rules of conduct that are reasonable and self-corrective. This means that in the social organism in which we find him embedded, the corporate genocide has many opportunities to turn around. The wickedness is there all right, but there in potential, most of the time. For it to be fully actualized, a steep descent is still necessary. If we combine this factor of potentiality, within a culture that is better than that, with the factor of alloy in the type of genocide performed, we will find the corporate exemplar to be not so far down on the slope as we feared, at first. He still has some way to go.

But where is Pizarro now, with his headful of invidious social and theological distinctions, his blinkered ambition for glory, his confused conviction that his looting was somehow bound up with his victims' salvation? Can we give him a grade, on the same scale as the corporate genocide? How can we lift out the moral part from the rest of the muddle?

The loot question and the religion question come interconnected. Religious conversion of another people, without brute force and cultural conquest to back it up, is not genocide. Religious, moral, or ideological conversion backed up by brute force is, in the broad sense of Lemkin's definition. Yet a culture is generally not found to lend force and numbers to the conversion project, where there is nothing *in it* materially for the culture or some of its influential members. So, without saying the Marxists are right—they are not right since loot is itself partly a prestige value, tied in with the culture's ideal formulations of what a man or woman should be like, and anyone who can get a *predominantly* materialist doctrine out of this is playing with words—we admit that where there is cultural or religious "genocide," the loot is generally found changing hands too.

Pizarro's religious project is excusable, since he may have thought he was called upon to control the damage that another people was doing to its own chances for living the good life. He can be excused for taking over the Christianity that had come down to him as tradition, and building his ambitious life projects on it as foundation. That's what it means to be a plain man.[9]

His ambitions, too, are excusable. At least, we are not in the best position to judge them. But, even allowing for the partially extra-ethical standpoint of "history," no people has license both religiously to delegitimize and materially to despoil another people, without then doing everything that belongs to getting the victimized people back on its feet and on the way to a self-maintaining and self-corrective or good life again. It is at the point where Pizarro fails to notice this obligation that we begin to sicken of him. Even his contemporaries sickened of him.

Both Pizarro and the corporate genocide think they can make up the rules for themselves as they go along. Both are restrained from holocaust by constraints in a culture that refuses to sanction that, and they will continue to be so restrained, as long as the culture is looking. Both would give up the genocidal project if the loot could be better secured some other way. I believe that the differences between them could be resolved into the chemistry of impulse, a chemistry we have already analyzed in our earlier inquiry into the impulsive genocide. That is, one could appeal to either by reminding him that he is in jeopardy with regard to certain prestige values in the culture (the honor of a Castilian, the good P.R. of an American firm, the menace of a possible recall to Toledo to stand trial, the threat of a tribal lawsuit), and whatever the irreducible differences in the openness to appeal of either man, these differences too could be traversed if one understood how the chemistry of each man's impulses was adjusted to the rugged lay of the land.

In each man we find a disposition to give up his story absolutely, and without looking back, but that disposition still hedged about by each man's intent to remain respectable in a culture not absolutely destructive of the good life. Each man has an undoubted potential for the worst. But each keeps his distance—on impulsive grounds perhaps—from the base of the slope. So the outcome of the moral assessment of each can finally, if roughly, be equalized.

The Ideologue

There remain cases of genocide to consider that come nearer to the pure type, or in fact are it.

We refer to the type of genocide, widespread in our time, that is conducted under an ideological umbrella, and to Nazi genocide as an arresting specification of that general type.

Let us look first at the genocide who has the general features of the ideologue, but not the Nazi specification of them. An ideology is not present, nor is an ideologue present to entertain an ideology, every time anyone has far-extending convictions, or convictions that pretend to be systematic. An ideology is not present, neither is an ideologue, every time someone holds beliefs whose consequences he does not or cannot now wholly foresee—for otherwise every belief would be an ideology. When a belief serves to rationalize other motives, not so ideal-looking, of which the believer is at present unconscious, that fact alone does not serve to identify the belief as an ideology, nor the believer as an ideologue. Otherwise moral progress (which occurs whenever one uncovers less-than-ideal motives in oneself) would be something that never occurred, and one's claim of it would reduce to a hypocritical simper. (When one is asked to define "ideology" in any of the above-mentioned ways, one is asked in effect to write the Marxist a blank check, in whatever currency held one's commitment to ideality, and he will cash it where he wills—later.)

Despite the popular claim that one has only biologic and economic life and—ideology, the belief that there is also a place for reasoned argument in the setting of one's private and public course in life is a well-founded one, for which there is plenty of evidence. If one attempts perseveringly to act on the latter belief, one will gradually gain in skill, and that gain includes a rise in one's ability to detect previously unconscious motives and the previously unforeseen boomerang effects of one's consciously well-intended acts. With the general rise in ability will come a proliferation of the habits of self-correction. An ideologue acts differently from an honest man or woman, and the process of becoming the one differs increasingly from the process of becoming the other. I don't think that the point needs to be belabored.

Insofar as the notion of ideology bears on the concept of genocide here under examination, there are certain features of ideology that need to be brought together now. By an ideology we will here mean a substantially incorrigible view of history, whose adherents will be found to substitute the practice of terror against dissidents, and state-orchestrated dissemination of fictions, for any principled responsiveness to reasoned objections or factual counter-examples (Arendt, 1951, pp. 363, 391, 417). As objections and counter-examples are clearer in the context of a culture's traditional values and practices, an ideologue will work to obliterate this traditional context in favor of another, from which to consider all values and deeds: the context of "history" (Arendt, 1951, pp. 311, 314, 317). We have already made somewhat reluctant and embarrassed reference to "history" here, noting that there are boundary situations where a culture pitches into a struggle with another culture, setting aside for the risk-fraught nonce certain ethical constraints. The name we gave to the condition or context in which such boundary conditions obtain was "history." Now we can note that the ideologue takes that presumptive context to be his primary context, his native land.

For the ideologue, "history" is to cultures what for the Darwinian "nature" is to species: the context in which the targeted groups can be dispossessed, dispersed, economically undermined, or killed out-right. The ideologue is willing to bring a license from "history" to his culture to do that, and to speed up the process, and to use every means to legitimize it, both in the eyes of the dispossessors and the dispossessed.*

"History" also licenses the ideologue in two other ways: he may obliterate the record of what he has done (the memories die with those who could have made a weapon of them);[10] he may remove from all these actions, his own and those of his victims, any trace of a moral assessment (Arendt, 1951, p. 375; Solzhenitsyn, 1974–78, 1:24, 76, 174ff).

The notion of "history" is, then, functionally very important. It sanctions lies and predations, which ordinarily take place under what we have called the Law of Negative Identification. It erases the record. It discounts in advance moral assessment. But moral assessment—as we have undertaken to read moral language here—is nothing but the self-corrective review of all else that the ideologue has effaced. Moral assessment *is* the self-corrective review of the record. Without it, stories don't happen. By means of it, stories are allowed to run their courses, and their agent-subjects are reminded to stay on guard lest their stories veer off their courses. If the ideologue erases moral assessment, then, programmatically, he erases the story itself, which is to say he erases good itself, in character and in human experience.

---

*Stalin's view that the proletariat's right to secure its power overrides any small nation's right to self-determination is quoted in Robert Conquest's *The Nation Killers* (1970, p. 117).

How bad is he? After all, we have practically all been there. (Not to the point of genocide, of course, but we know what it means to supply a rationale for almost anything, in the name of an ideology. It is the commonest thing in the world, in our twentieth century.)

Taken by itself, ideology is no worse than any other failure of moral nerve. Ordinarily, when ideology comes in to smother the neurophysiology of moral experience, something has already occurred that was either blameworthy or at least difficult to make story sense of, in the terms that formerly gave significance to one's life. In Merleau-Ponty's account of the moment when ideology burgeoned for him, what couldn't be made story sense of was that he and his friends had had to knuckle under to the German occupation forces, at least in daylight, and also that they had been obliged to dehumanize the individual German in their minds, to make him the Enemy, insofar as they'd meant to resist him by violent means and by subterfuge. Instead of registering the pity of this, and the sorrow of it, and doing his duty quietly, Merleau-Ponty tried to rise above the sorrow, and the duty, and the pity, into "history"—that plane of would-be experience where it was hoped that the exploitation of man by man would be done away with—at the cost of stepping up the pace of the exploitation in the short term.[11]

Now, this sort of moral strategem is an everyday occurrence. Sometimes "history" provides the crutch to lean on, sometimes religious zealotry, sometimes an obsessive love affair. Whatever one uses, or even if one uses no crutch at all, zestful clear-sightedness remains hard to win one's way to, and harder yet to sustain. The ideologue is in moral default, not so much when he first reaches for a crutch as when he hardens his grip on it, in the face of countervailing evidence, and insists that the corrective data be redefined away. At that point, what is actually (and paradoxically) being rejected *is* history, history without quotation marks.

One's own time began at a place and a moment that was neither of one's own choosing nor, originally, of one's own describing. One found oneself there, amidst a set of happenings and an interpretive vocabulary, and one's self is what ensued in the working out of one's own grasp on all that. The time of one's life flows backward toward a point of origin, and forward, irreversibly, away from that genesis point. Each experience adds its voice and sedimentary weight to that forward flux of time. It is not in one's power to make what happened into a nonhappening, although one may still choose to travel against the current of what has indelibly happened so far.

Instead of reckoning with all this directly, the ideologue makes up a story. *It is not his own*, whatever else can be said about it. It replaces his genesis point with one belonging to a collectivity, belonging to people who are elsewhere, spatially distributed through the population at large. It replaces the key dates of his personal life, marking the sequence of times when his understanding of the circles around him thickened, with another chronology, applicable to other circles, not coinciding with his own. Every other impiety of which he will be capable will be preceded by the filial impiety, and that by the impiety toward his own story, on which he will impose a closure that is utterly premature.

For the ideologue, the wider story of his culture and the human race will not come into his own story by way of showing its ramifications and derivations; it won't be discovered, or discovered anew, in the course of self-inquiry; instead, his own will become trivially or stereotypically illustrative of a generic story, a doctrine. (But if history is not finally the human inquiry into people and their stories, then it is *about* nothing.)

So, the ideologue begins, as a type, not when the crutch of pseudo-history is first reached for, but when the disillusioning events, or series of refuting instances, are not faced. *Now*—how bad is he, in the first place, and how shall we assess him when he becomes genocidal?*

The line dividing the generic ideologue as *incidental* genocide from the pure type for whom genocide is a fixed and explicit goal is a line that can be drawn on paper, although in real life the one type shades into the other. (Indeed, in real life, as scarcely needs to be said, all these abstract types shade into one another. But their separation into abstract types facilitates the moral analysis of the compounds that are to be met with in the real world, as any appropriate abstract analysis will do.) As a type, then, the generic ideologue does not need a rationale tailored to the specific injury he is inflicting. This is so whether he is busy with genocide, or with some minor assault on the story of another. Any individual will do to fill an arrest quota (Arendt, 1951, pp. 404–13; Solzhenitsyn, 1974–78, 1:71). Any nation or group can be construed as testing the consolidation of party power, and requiring therefore to be eliminated (Solzhenitsyn, 1974–78, 1:24f, 27–41, 51–68; Conquest 1970, p. 12). Any act destructive of social cohesion can be demanded for the purposes of showing party loyalty.

---

*Against some of the substantive claims about history made by certain ideologues, and against the view that ideology itself is determinative in genocide, Irving Horowitz notes that there is no detectable causal correlation between particular socioeconomic structures and genocide as a policy; likewise, there is no ascertainable correlation between any particular ideology, or even nonideological beliefs, and genocide as a policy. See Horowitz (1982, ch. 3).

What has been called for by the generic ideologue is the destruction of history in general. One starts from the history that radiated out from one's own genesis point. The destruction proceeds to encompass the history of other individuals and one's own *genos*. In the course of such things, the destruction will take in other *genē*. While the destruction of history, as a process, may seem for a time to favor one class or race over another, the seeming favoritism is opportunistic. Some groups must be made to feel they are being helped by this process, or it could not proceed, not even for a season. However, since the possession of a coherent record is a good part of what *enables* us to be efficient and nonarbitrary in our decisions, the destruction of the historical record, and of the groups whose record it was, is a process inherently arbitrary and inefficient. It has, therefore, no inbuilt timetables or priorities that give more importance to one people over another, or to one historical achievement targeted for destruction before another. In the sense here meant, generic ideology is genocidal inevitably, but also—as regards any given *genos*—genocidal incidentally.

How bad is this, on the slope going from bad to wicked? How pure is this, as an instance of the genocidal type? Is the individual who slanders a fellow worker and gets him arrested so as to advance his own standing in the party *worse* morally than (or different morally from) the individual who oversees the brutal deportation of an entire nation out of the Caucasus or the Crimea, or—in another department—insures that nation's disappearance from official maps and reference books?

There is an odd mix in such an individual, of impulsive primitivity (like the genocide of brute impulse, the genocide of ideology is afraid—terribly, *realistically* afraid—of getting the same thing done to himself), and of ideological appeal to "history." Correctly conceived, world history is an abstract, limiting idea, approached at the boundaries of nations, where individuals and nations agree or do not agree to conduct themselves with each other in ways that each would demand inside its own territory. History is that condition between nations where the social contract can be extended or retracted with much greater fluidity than it can be within the borders of a given nation. History is also the imagined single repository, in which are unevenly clustered the longer memories and anticipated projects of the human race. Historians investigate these, from one standpoint or another, with one purpose or another. However, as the ideologue reconceives it, "history" is falsely converted into an entrenched, positive state of affairs, that can be appealed to as giving purpose and sanction to innumerable abrogations of nationally real and internationally possible social contracts. "History" really becomes the Hobbesian state of nature, writ large and authorizing everything. A brute who believes that he is *authorized* is a far worse type to deal with than a simple brute. Ask any Cambodian survivor about that.

We are finding, as we get close to it, that the Nazi stands for us at the bottom of this slope, as its human marker. So our questions about the moral assessment of the genocide as generic ideologue have become, whether we willed it or not, a question of the following type: are these people as bad as the Nazis? From the broad uplands of the generic ideologue, we have Solzhenitsyn who says they are worse. Some SS men report that the Russians were better, being acquainted at first hand with German slave labor and death camps that they themselves ran, and subsequently with Soviet slave labor camps where they worked as prisoners.* How is one to analyze such a question?

In order to simplify the question, let the Stalinist accomplice to terror (and to mass-terror-become-genocide) stand in for all generic ideologues. The remoteness of the posthistorical ideal of a classless society from the procedures being used to realize it lends to the Stalinist accomplice a certain intellectual and moral imprecision. Given such an appeal to "history" as his, everything is retroactively predictable; nobody is or can be at fault. All are accomplices to the impersonal process that is supposed to sweep all before it. Thus, while Stalinist apparatchiks share with Nazis a propensity for villainous-outgroup/pureminded-ingroup dichotomizing—a propensity also found in American cases of wartime atrocities and antisocial outbreaks[12]—in the Stalinist case, the particular group or individual targeted does not seem to matter very much. Solzhenitsyn reports no step-by-step processes whereby a whole people is singled out for ridicule and hooliganism, deprived of work, isolated from civil society, systematically starved, and then set upon and murdered. Rather, what he reports are "waves" of scapegoating, happening with speed and ferocity, falling with such arbitrary finality on the suspect and the

---

*Thus Solzhenitsyn remarks of an Orthodox Christian clergyman who had been in the hands both of the Gestapo and the MGB: "He was tortured by both, but the Gestapo was nonetheless trying to get at the truth, and when the accusation did not hold up, [he] was released. The MGB wasn't interested in the truth and had no intention of letting anyone out of its grip once he was arrested" (1974–78, 1:145, n. 1). Contrast with this the opinions of the SS Hauptscharführer interviewed under the code name S2 in Dicks (1972, p. 105). "'No, no,' he exclaimed, 'the Russians were fairer than the SS'—he had never seen a Russian guard strike a prisoner; executions were always on a written verdict of the courts martial"; and there had been a successful uprising after Stalin's death.

nonsuspect alike that no member of that society could feel safe or know by virtue of what his future was jeopardized. In all this there is enormous imprecision of result, enormous imprecision of motive.

Possibly in consequence, the records are not kept in the Stalinist cases, as they were in the Nazi cases, by and large. Solzhenitsyn finds this retrievability of the record (which made possible eventual trials of war criminals in postwar Germany) a moral element missing from the Stalinist canvass, and I think he is right (Solzhenitsyn, 1974–78, 1:175–78). On the other hand, both he and former SS men who have been interviewed report opportunities for moral resistance and a development toward humanization that seemed to be far less tolerated in the Nazi camps and concentration points (Solzhenitsyn, 1974–78, 2:560f, 578, 604–17; Dicks, 1972, p. 150).

If the Soviet system was relatively more porous to humanizing incidents than the Nazi system, the record on that point is not always a clear one, surely. Solzhenitsyn reports as a general rule that the man who had given up every earthly consideration, who did not care for his family, his name, his health, his dignity, his freedom, his personal exemption from physical torment, or his life, who cared only for his spiritual purity, could sometimes walk away from the interrogation a free man. Such a man, willing to die, willing to lose all, would refuse implacably to produce the signed confession—and the interrogators would decide not to lose their time with him (Solzenitsyn, 1974–78, 1:130f). But this report from one of its chief detractors does not by itself make the Soviet case a better one than the case of the Nazis. An exceptional man like Pastor Karl Ernst Gruber could also report (Eichmann Trial, Session 41) stopping an impending Nazi medical experiment by his moral resistance, expressed with simplicity and force.

> When he told me that his grandfather was a priest, I said, "A man must be ready for everything in life." I said that according to my belief his grandfather is in the World of Truth and sees and knows what his grandson does, and he has no peace and no rest . . . . One has to be ready for everything, but I was not ready that all of a sudden this Dr. Rascher referred to me as "sir"—and released me from that . . . experiment room . . . brought an ambulance . . . examined me . . . and said that I was no longer fit for arrest and detention.

(Dr. Grüber also attributed his release to efforts made on his behalf by his wife and others on the outside.) Perhaps in both cases, it was a lucky hit—the right man and the right tormentor colliding and hitting it off. Even Jews occasionally had such moments, when by giving voice to their fully resistant spirits they were able briefly to deflect the intentions of their Nazi persecutors.[13] So the question of whether the human spirit had a better field for its resistances among Nazi than among Stalinist tormentors is not decidable in advance for individuals.

That said, there is an overwhelming weight of malice connected with Nazi operations, as practiced in detail toward individuals and step-by-step *en bloc* toward *genē*, not found in Solzhenitsyn's accounts of ideological brutality. It may be that the positively numbing malice of Nazi practice and the keeping of careful records go hand in hand. Something determinate was intended for the victims of Nazi genocidal ideology, and this may be contrasted with the something massive, impersonal, and imprecise that was intended for the victims of Stalinist generic ideology—even where the latter led to genocide. What alone seems fairly precise in the Stalinist case are the brainwashing techniques, but it has not been practicable literally to subject a whole *genos* to these techniques.[14]

Let us take the imprecision of the generic ideologue, imprecision of motive and result, as a given, and try to draw his moral portrait sketch. We have here a man (it was usually a man) of brute performances, against individual prisoners or large masses of people, raking in the benefits that accrue to a man in his position, having good cause to be scared for his life, and professing himself convinced that nothing he does will enter the memory of man—but that instead "history" will absolve him.[15] Is this man different when he denounces a coworker from what he becomes when he oversees a whole people's deportation? Hardly. The only difference is in the degree of coarsening effect that his cumulative assaults on the stories of others will—by rebound effect—have on him.

Where does he stand, then, on the slope going from bad to wicked? As we ascertained earlier, he has given up on his own story and—by the Law of Negative Identification—given up on the stories of others, and he has authorized himself to do *anything*. So he is "wicked" in potential, no matter what he has actually done. Also, there would probably be a felt gap (dealt with by him in a shamefaced and/or polemically blustering way) between the professed rationale for all the suffering being inflicted, and its reality. The children are playing, and playing for a pretended reason; he is one of them; only these are not toys they are playing with, these are people. One can get angry and nasty when this is pointed out, or one can shrug and say, "We know it; but we can't help it." Either reaction is close enough to the musculature of what is happening to be a realistic reaction, on its own state-of-nature terms. A "realist," assuming a brutal caste to his realism, would be a bad man to deal with. A realist who is trained to believe his brutality authorized by a mystifying abstraction called "history" is worse still.

Yet, in our portrait sketch, there is some room for the generic ideologue to feel impulses of kindness. If *all this* will be forgotten, if no one will find the bones, if no one is being blamed for it in a precise way, not victims, not victimizers, then—moment by moment—perpetrators and victims can even forgive each other. What else is there for them to do? God's love, or some other mythos nursed in the shattered community, can bathe all the killing fields. There is nothing to stop it. There is no one to make a reckoning.

In sum, Solzhenitsyn is both right and wrong to claim that the generic ideologues of the Gulag process are worse than Nazis. They are worse, in that they have inscribed themselves within a framework that permits no moral assessment. Not even the names are recorded. There is nobody here to be held accountable. If one wants moral development for oneself personally, and if, being a patriot, one wants such a development for one's native land, then this is the worst of situations. But it is not the wickedest. For that, it needs conscious targeting of the story in one's victim, and of the culture from which such stories take their sense and plot. It needs the full resources of memory and record keeping, to insure that consciousness will pervade the entire scheme. It needs a false-witness machinery, which will be the obverse of an obsession with rectitude and with purity. It needs a negative obsession with goodness, in sum.

In such a case, one has not merely made war against history as such, in the style of the generic ideologue. Rather, one has turned it inside out and made a great effort henceforth to read it backward. Here the lie is more tailored to its target. Here one is consciously *in pursuit* of the stories of others, to destroy them. If possible, one wants the victim to be observant that that is done to him, and to register the whole fact consciously. Further, one wants to make the stories that one has mutilated unreadable by posterity too—or rather, remembered but *mis*read. Here the targeted *genos* is fully embraced by a conscious destroyer, so that its practical needs, its values, and its intentions can be attacked on all sides. It is only if one can do all that that one has a "good enough" story sense to be fully wicked and—in the pure case of the Nazi—genocidal without alloy.

CHAPTER SIX

Banality and Originality

Arendt and the Trials

ONE OF THE curious and oft-noted facts about the Nazi is the elusiveness of his character, from the standpoint of a moral accounting. Set in the lurid and transforming conditions of a terror state, the conditions of a routinized nightmare, conscience and the information on whose basis conscience must decide are alike battered out of recognition. That is, for example, the contention in Arendt's *Eichmann In Jerusalem: A Report on the Banality of Evil* (1964, pp. 52, 69, 106, 110f, 175, 276f, 293f). Where a nation, with its social and pedagogic practices, has prepared in its citizens a striking tendency to become passive under external authority, this too plays its (possibly mitigating) part.* We condemn the *phenomenon* of such moral abdication. At the same time—except in cases of legal confrontation whose legitimacy is still in dispute—we cannot be confident that we have found any distinct individual agents of that phenomenon, any makers of it. It seems to be a phenomenon without causes—only effects. For this reason, it will be part of our business in this chapter to reexamine the legitimacy of the postwar trials of Nazis.

Because the banalization of the Nazi was a natural and conspicuous feature of his own defense, in trial after trial at Nuremberg and, notor-

---

*Alice Miller discusses twentieth-century Germany pedagogic practices and their bearing on character formation among Nazis in *For Your Own Good* (1980), though with a thesis about Hitler's parentage whose apparent documentation is convincingly shown to be false in the Bradley Smith biography of the young Hitler (1967, Plates 2–5 and Appendix I). Both that biography and the Smith biography of the young Himmler (1971) depict young men of no striking talents or personal qualities who failed to resolve apparent conflicts with authoritarian fathers. Neither young man seemed destined for greatness in the wicked line.

iously, at Jerusalem, we had best reserve condensed consideration of this *motif of his defense* until after we have plowed through some of the other confusions that surround him.

The prose view of the Nazi as the product of totalitarian circumstances has, however, its even more popular contrary, in twentieth-century linguistic conventions, works of literature, and in post-Nuremberg philosophy, where the tendency has been to take the Nazi to be the very prototype of evil, the one about whom the poem of evil would have to be written, if there were to be a poem about evil. If values have been pervasively relativized in our time, there is still the Nazi to force us into uneasy puzzlement about the consequences of this. (Thus R. N. Hare lets the figure of "the Nazi" bring out the last consequences of his contention that conflicts between ideals are not necessarily resolvable in argument [1963, pp. 158–72]. Gilbert Harman reserves the more poetic term "evil" for Hitler, precisely because Hitler's actions imply his refusal of "the relevant moral conventions" and therefore put him "beyond the pale" where wrongness and rightness are concerned. Wrongness and rightness, however, remain for Harman conventional [1977, p. 109]. If utilitarian arguments threaten to overthrow consideration of innate human worth and human rights, philosophers will let the sobering recollection of the postwar trials, with their evidences of Nazi disregard of human rights, serve as a conscious corrective to such arguments.)*

While the term "genocide" had, in Lemkin's definition, a meaning extending beyond Nazi holocausts, there can be little doubt that the sensitivity of the moral nerve touched in contemporaries by the very word is traceable to memories of Nazi mass murders, practiced against *genē*.

We are not sure who or what the individual Nazi is or isn't. We are not sure if anybody occupies the seat reserved in our imaginations for the Nazi. We are not sure what sort of toxicity he represents, and under what conditions, and to whom. Still, it is at least clear that our moral and dramatic landscape, the narrative look of the twentieth century, would be far different if we could imaginatively erase the Nazi from that landscape. He occupies it with us. He is a kind of measuring rod of our relation to the category of evil. The hangman's rope that did

---

*See, for example, A. I. Melden's introduction in *Human Rights* (1970, p. 7). For an example of a utilitarian defense of Nazi medical experiments, see the cross-examination of prosecution expert witness Dr. Andrew C. Ivy by defense counsel Dr. Robert Servatius, in *Nuernberg Military Tribunals*, Case No. 1, "The Medical Case," *The United States Against Karl Brandt et al.*, vol. 2, pp. 42f.

a bit of work at Nuremberg has slacked of late. But he still awaits a judgment that is inadvertently, and—whether we will it or not—also a judgment as to the nature and dimensions of our moral framework.

In May 1960 in Buenos Aires, Israeli agents seized SS Lieutenant-Colonel Adolf Eichmann, head of the variously initialed and named Gestapo Section IV D4, IV B4, and IV A4, on "Jewish Affairs and Deportations," and removed him clandestinely to Jerusalem to stand trial before the District Court of Jerusalem for, among other charges, five counts of "Crimes Against the Jewish People." It was the first time that the Holocaust had been brought to the attention of the world as a single, planned crime, of immense scope, with many stages. That there had been slaughters of terrifying magnitude and thoroughness was a fact that had sunk into consciousness with the liberation of the camps. Evidences of these mass murders had figured prominently in the Nuremberg trials, but always among others. But here a case that the planning and carrying out of *this particular project of genocide* in all its broad ramifications and details had occurred was to be made in a court of law, with the kind of evidence acceptable in a proper court of law, original documentary evidence or attested copies and eyewitness testimony, and safeguarding the right of the accused to hear the charges against him, to defend himself, and to introduce evidence that he did not do it—or evidence of an exculpatory nature.

It was one of those moments in contemporary history where the opportunity to see justice done that was opened by a court proceeding also opened a channel to conscience and stock-taking in the world. Into this moment stepped Hannah Arendt, with a report on the Jerusalem trial that—more than any other report—captured the moral imagination of the intellectual community. The thesis of Arendt's *Eichmann in Jerusalem* is threefold: (1) Eichmann was administratively subordinate and psychologically free of malevolence, or "ordinary"—a sort of boring clerk or mailman; (2) the Jewish victims were in crucial ways in complicity with their Nazi executioners; (3) the jurisdiction of the Jerusalem court and its findings were legally and/or morally questionable. This threefold thesis, or at least some of the points relevant to it, will be reexamined here.

My own reading of the trial transcript satisfies me that Eichmann took a great many initiatives of singular malignancy, both in the subjective impetus that such initiatives would have required and in the harm that these initiatives did objectively.* Nor did I discover him in

---

*A number of them are conveniently summarized in the prosecutor's account of the trial. See Hausner (1966, pp. 66f, 69, 78, 82, 95, 103, 106, 109, 114, 116, 120, 124f, 138f, 143 [this important to the question of Eichmann the so-called Zionist], 148f, 151f, 266f, 271, 334f, 338f, 381).

testimony to be ordinary. Unlike every other human voice that sounded at the trial, whether the voice belonged to someone in a humble station or a high-placed one, Eichmann's was immensely and startlingly boring. But being *that* boring is the symptom of persistent and thickly insulated untruth. It is not at all the effect of proletarian or—as Arendt suggested—lower-middle-class speech patterns. Nor is it the effect of *arriviste* speech patterns, which may sound unpleasantly on the ear but are seldom soporific in their effect on the hearer. Other things being equal, such "real people" as Arendt compared Eichmann to are often enough a little less boring than academics, and I myself have never met an academic as boring as Eichmann. In this respect alone, if in no other, he was most unusual.

Eichmann's claim of administrative insignificance, which Arendt accepted, had no more plausibility *in the light of the evidence* than had the similar claims made by the defendants at Nuremberg whose trials I read. Here in part is Chief of Counsel for the United States Robert Jackson's summary rendering of such claims:

> If we combine only the stories from the front bench, this is the ridiculous composite picture of Hitler's government that emerges. It was composed of:
>
> A number two man who knew nothing of the excesses of the Gestapo which he created, and never suspected the Jewish extermination program although he was the signer of over a score of decrees which instituted the persecutions of that race;
>
> A number three man who was merely an innocent middleman transmitting Hitler's orders without even reading them, like a postman or a delivery boy; . . .
>
> . . . A security chief who was of the impression that the policing functions of his Gestapo and S.D. were somewhat on the order of directing traffic (Jackson, 1947, pp. 156f)

The one difference from the Nuremberg norm that I did notice at Eichmann's trial was the latter's frequent claim that his signature on incriminating documents must have been *forged*. Possibly the Nuremberg defendants were too freshly captured for them to have thought of making such an implausible counterallegation. They did not know how much the International Military Tribunal had in the way of documents. They thought they would have to show how a mass forgery could have been done in that short a time. So they did tend to acknowledge their signatures. Eichmann offered no evidence at all to support his forgery defense, and Arendt herself did not appear to believe him, on that point at least.

The line that one had been a bureaucratic cipher acting by rote is in fact the only line to take if one was documentably guilty, did not care to try to plead insanity, and had before one that prospect of one's hanging that is said wonderfully to concentrate the mind. The other impression that I got of Eichmann from reading his direct testimony and the cross-examination was of a nimble, purposeful, and powerfully concentrated mind. I doubt that any ordinary man in his shoes could have maintained his sangfroid and dodged every implication of guilt as quickly and consistently as Eichmann did. To put it more simply, the man was an unconscionable liar.

Arendt's is a selectively edited and, to my reading, unrecognizable account of the trial. The task of showing how her selective editing misrepresents the defendant would, however, be an immense one, going far beyond the proper purview of this book. On the other hand, answering the question of whether *anyone* who does what a Nazi does can be free of "evil" as here defined *is* properly a task for this book. We will want to show here that no legally sane Nazi can be free of "evil" in the sense here meant. We will also want to show that the definition of evil offered in this book can account for the full range of Nazi activities and ideas better than other definitions currently on offer can do.

Arendt's case against the Jews (point [2] above) is not a report of the trial at all—which incidentally gives quite a different picture. It is largely a condensation of Hilberg's far more carefully worked through evidences, as presented in his historic work, *The Destruction of the European Jews*, which came out in 1961, after the conclusion of the trial (Arendt, 1964, p. 282). The case for Jewish complicity is one that I will accordingly try to evaluate in Arendt's source, working from Hilberg's revised and expanded three-volume 1985 edition, and comparing that study with some other materials, including testimony given at the trial. My purpose, in evaluating Hilberg's case, will not be to counter it with empirical evidences of Jewish noncooperation and resistance. I am not a historian. I have opinions here, but the dispute is not exactly on my territory. My purpose will be rather to get clearer about how moral judgment ought to work in such a case, what factors are relevant, what factors irrelevant, and what standards ought to guide the moral thinker.

The only part of Arendt's *Eichmann in Jerusalem* that can be summarized and evaluated point-for-point here is her discussion of the Jerusalem court's jurisdiction and judgment, a discussion that takes place largely toward the end of the book, in pages 254 to 279. The gist of that extremely obscure and tortuous discussion would be something like this: the perpetrators of the Holocaust were not "in essence" anti-Semites, and the victims were not in essence Jews; *since* what was victimized in the Holocaust was "humanity," the judges also ought not to have been Jews. They ought to have been representative (non-Jewish) of "humanity." Let us try to see how this gist emerges, step by step, in Arendt's argument, and try to see the worth or the sense of it. It is worth going through rather carefully, since it appears to form the *theoretical* core of an extremely influential and, I think, pretty confusing book.

Arendt begins her discussion of the Jerusalem trial's legal and moral appropriateness by reviving and reviewing questions that were raised about the Nuremberg trials. Objections to the latter had turned on the retroactive character of the laws under which the defendants were tried, and on whether the defendants were not therefore really being tried because they had lost the war—the "victors' justice" objection.*

On the retroactive or *ex post facto* law objection, the objection to applying a law to acts that were committed before the law was on the books, Arendt writes that defendants may properly be charged under new law only where—as in "crimes against humanity"—the crimes committed were "previously unknown" (1964, p. 255). If we have new crimes, then we may have new law, is her position. Accordingly she suggests that scrupulous care should be taken not to formulate new law (as was done at Nuremberg with "war crimes"), when the old language of the Hague and Geneva conventions could still have served to cover the acts in question.

If this objection to Nuremberg is just a reservation about language, and not a point about substance, then it seems a rather small point. In any case, Arendt does not compare the language of the Nuremberg trials' charter with the language of the Hague and Geneva conventions, to show what substantive deviations occurred and that the deviations, if any, could not be accounted for by *the novelty of the Nazi crimes*, thereby falling once again into line with her canons. Arendt's point, in other words, is either trivial or unsubstantiated.

A further objection to Nuremberg is that some acts, such as conspiracy to wage aggressive war, should *not* be criminalized because, according to Arendt, the international consensus does not support their criminalization.

---

*My thanks are due to Hurst Hannum, Louis Henkin, and Milton Schubin for giving me the benefit of their comments and criticisms of an earlier draft of this discussion. Mine is the responsibility for the use I have made of their comments in the present draft, and any errors here are entirely mine.

Whatever the *de facto* international support for preemptive strikes in the case of border wars, Arendt fails here to note what was special about Nazi Germany's conspiracy. It was a very big-scale conspiracy, involving deliberate fraud and deception emanating from the highest councils of the Hitler government. The conspiracy was well documented, not a haphazard or spontaneous thing. The series of invasions that followed were and *were documentably intended to be* exceptionally destructive to the invaded countries. We don't just have occupation. We have ruined economies and mass slave labor. Against an aggressive policy of this magnitude, there was surely an international consensus. In that context, Arendt's casual dismissal of the applicability of the 1928 Kellogg-Briand Pact, renouncing war as an instrument of national policy, a pact to which Germany, Italy, and Japan were signatories, seems rather hasty.[1] By contrast, it was more constructive and more realistic to view that treaty a part of the evidence for an international consensus and to frame a law that could reach the Hitler's government's *policy* of aggressive war.

Finally, with respect to Nuremberg, Arendt writes that no nation ought to nominate representatives to an international penal court if it is itself responsible for the same sort of crimes as those for which nationals of nonrepresented countries will be charged. Such a court, she charges, is politically tainted, not truly international. The International Military Tribunal, presided over by jurists from the four Allied powers, comes under this stricture since the Allies were guilty of saturation bombings of open cities, of dropping atomic bombs on Hiroshima and Nagasaki, and—in the Russian case—of shooting 15,000 Polish POWs in the Katyn Forest (Arendt, 1964, p. 256). Arendt finds another indication of the political basis of the tribunal in its quick dissolution with the breakup of the Four-Power Alliance after the Nuremberg trials.

To Arendt's final points against Nuremberg it must be rejoined that the kind of enduring, globally authoritative, international penal court Arendt calls for would presuppose a degree of centralized, worldwide political control that is—as people and nations are now constituted—realistically to be feared, because of its potentiality for abuse. As mankind is presently constituted, it is only an extraordinary emergency that could have created the temporary alliance between Great Britain, France, the Soviet Union, and the United States, and the correlative possibility of bringing to trial war criminals in the name of an "offended community," ideally the peaceful world order, that had been injured and had now to be repaired. In sum, as things now stand, Arendt's remedy would have been and would still be worse than the ethico-political disease she finds.

On the subject of Allied war guilt, it should however be noted that the Allies did not start the war, that—however prudentially unwarranted, or callous, or vicious were the excesses they committed in the use of force—their purpose was to bring to bear sufficient force to end the war. In this, there is no analogy to Germany, whose atrocities against civilians were stepped up in pace and magnitude after their military occupation was secured. Allied war crimes, such as they were, ended with Allied victory and were replaced by a benign policy toward the vanquished.* If the same cannot be said of the Soviet Union, that nation was also less subject to pressure from the democratic nations of the wartime alliance. And the Soviet Union, with its own tenuous relation to legality, seems to have been the most passive of the participants at Nuremberg, the participating nation least responsible for its coloration and for the course it took.

On the topic of "victors' justice" it might also be observed, as it was at Nuremberg, that no individual German soldier was charged with losing the war, much less tried for losing it. "The defendants are in court not as members of a defeated nation but because they are charged with crime."[2] Individuals were charged with direct responsibility for acts, such as mass enslavement and mass murder, whose criminal nature had long been recognized, both because they were crimes prohibited in national and international codes and because they were of the sort considered *malum in se*.† There was no serious question as to whether *such acts* were crimes, or could reasonably have been known to be crimes. The question at Nuremberg was whether the individuals accused of doing them had in fact done them, and whether, if they had done them, any exculpating factors—such as fear of immediate reprisal if they refused to do them, or ignorance of the harmful consequences to innocent people—could get them off. Sometimes, in individual cases, such factors were found and they got off. Sometimes they were not found. I myself did not see any signs of a rush to judgment, once the courts were in session.

Having, qualifiedly (and—as we find—overhastily) delegitimated the Nuremberg trials, Arendt returns to her consideration of the Jerusalem trial. She disputes its historic role as the first trial to treat

---

*I owe these points to Telford Taylor's Closing Statement, *Nuernberg Military Tribunals*, Case No. 9, "The Einsatzgruppen Case," *The United States of America Against Otto Ohlendorf et al.*, vol. 4, pp. 380ff.

†I am grateful to Milton Schubin for pointing out this distinction, which the law has long recognized between an act *malum in se*, that is, obviously criminal, where ignorance of the law is no excuse, and an act *malum prohibitum*, that is, not recognizably a crime absent prior knowledge that it was under legal sanction. Over the centuries, this distinction has also been used by courts to expand the law and punish conduct not previously labeled illegal by any statute.

the Holocaust "as a separate crime," asserting instead that it was a desire to capture the crime against the Jews "that had prompted the Allies to conceive of a 'crime against humanity' in the first place" (Arendt, 1964, p. 258). In further support of her claim of special notice paid to the Holocaust at Nuremberg, Arendt notes that the only defendant to be put to death for "crimes against humanity" alone was the notorious anti-Semite Julius Streicher.

As regards Allied concern for the Jews, Arendt considerably overstates the case. That the Allies made the concession of charging the Nuremberg defendants with "crimes against humanity" *reluctantly*, and under pressure from Jewish organizations, is a point documented in Hilberg (1985, pp. 1060–66). Whatever is proved or not proved by the Streicher death sentence, it cannot show that the Nuremberg trials treated the Holocaust as a separate crime, in the sense that they made particular efforts to get all the evidences of that crime into a court record for the purpose of finding criminal responsibility for the whole of it. There were of course many agents of that crime. But some were not involved merely in a segmented way. Some initiated and oversaw the entire international policy whose conscious aim was the Holocaust. What the policy was and how it was carried out was not made clear at Nuremberg. It was made clear at Jerusalem.

Against the charge at Jerusalem that Eichmann did have criminal responsibility for the Holocaust, Arendt adduces the evidence that he was never charged at Nuremberg. This was not, she notes, because he was absent, since Martin Bormann, equally absent, was charged and condemned at Nuremberg anyway (Arendt, 1964, p. 258). Eichmann, she concludes, was not charged at Nuremberg because he was not a major war criminal.

Since Arendt does not offer any evidence to show that a separate investigation into Eichmann's status was actually conducted at Nuremberg, the failure then and there to charge him would not seem to have much bearing on his status for the Jerusalem court. The major war criminals were "major" because they held the highest positions on the Nazi organizational charts. Those low down on the charts were by no means exempt from responsibility for serious crimes, however. Ohlendorf, for example, was not "major," but was found criminally responsible for 90,000 deaths. So one could do a lot of harm in the minor leagues. Since the Final Solution was a clandestine operation, it is not on the face of it implausible to suppose that the Nazi hierarchy would have confided its implementation to someone who was not in their front office.

The Jerusalem trial did, however, see testimony from Nuremberg, among others from one of the judges there. Judge Michael Musmano (who sat as judge in two trials and presiding judge over the Ein-satzgruppen trial) testified that, in the course of a Navy investigation into the fate of Adolf Hitler that he had been directed to conduct right after the war's end, he had heard of Eichmann's dominating position over "the entire Jewish extermination program emanating from the RSHA" from a number of high Nazi officials who were differently placed and not necessarily in contact with one another.

> Now, what gave versimilitude to the reply of Ribbentrop and the reply of Goering and the reply of Hans Frank and all the others that I mentioned this morning, in which they say that Eichmann was the man who headed the extermination programme of the Jews, was that they didn't select—and if they were really clever in that respect and were not spontaneously speaking the truth—they didn't select the man who might have been more obviously acceptable as the culprit, and that was General Müller who was at the head of the Gestapo. Therefore it wasn't a matter of logic; it was a matter of telling just what the facts were.

There was in any case certainly no exoneration of Eichmann that took place at Nuremberg, whether explicit or implicit. And he did have a clearly identified place on the Nazi organizational charts.

> There was introduced in the concentration camps case and also in the Einsatzgruppen case a chart of the RSHA. This chart showed that Eichmann was chief of an office for projects which on the chart were identified by one word—Jews.*

Arendt next turns to the question of the jurisdiction of the Jerusalem court. She makes no objection to an Israeli court's assertion of jurisdiction over a defendant accused of killing its nationals (the "principle of territorial jurisdiction"). In this respect, she holds Israel's right equal to the right of Poland to try people after the war for killing its nationals (Arendt, 1964, p. 259). There is, however, her objection to the language by which the court asserted its territorial jurisdic-tion—specifically, to the court's failure to define "territory" as a certain kind of codified cultural-political-historical relationship between mem-bers of a group, a relationship that can at times "become spatially manifest" but is not "spatially manifest" necessarily or at all times (p. 263).

---

*Testimony of Judge Michael A. Musmano, Eichmann Trial, Sessions 40 and 39. According to military psychologist Gilbert, Musmano was the only person (outside of psychiatrists, chaplains, and prison personnel) who was allowed access to the jail cells. On the crucial role in the extermination process that other high-ranking Nazis assigned to Eichmann, Gilbert's testimony confirmed Musmano's (Session 55).

Like Arendt, I also like to talk, in the language of German speculative philosophy, about relationships that become spatially manifest,
but unlike Arendt, I do not find that a court that has been unable
to share this taste and has resorted instead to the more workaday
language of precedent has thereby "failed" properly to assert its
jurisdiction. In any event and however she gets there, Arendt finds,
and I agree, that objections to the court's territorial jurisdiction were
"legalistic in the extreme" (p. 259).

However, Arendt interleafs her qualified endorsement of the
court's assertion of territorial jurisdiction with a rejection of the
jurisdiction that it asserted on two other grounds: the "passive personality" principle, and the principle of "universal jurisdiction." The
"passive personality" principle gives warrant to the action that a state
may take on behalf of its interest reflected in the fact that its own
nationals are the victims of a criminal act. According to the second of
these two principles, any nation can try the perpetrator of a crime
that comes under "universal jurisdiction," no matter who the victims
are, or what the nationality of the perpetrator was, or where the
crime was committed.*

To the invocation of the passive personality principle Arendt objects that the principle wrongly implies that the victims "have a right
to revenge," so that invoking it impedes taking the correct view,
which is that the body politic—not the victim or victims—is the injured
party (1964, pp. 260f). And to the universal jurisdiction principle
Arendt objects that it cannot apply to Eichmann, because it was
designed for the pirate whose "crime is committed on the high
seas . . . which are no man's land . . . outside all organized communities." Since Eichmann served under the German flag, he could
not be in the pirate category. Also, Arendt asserts, the Genocide
Convention of 1948 "expressly rejected the claim to universal jurisdiction" (pp. 261f).

Again, some rejoinders would seem to be in order here. First, the
passive personality principle does not imply, nor does it assert, sur-
rogate revenge. It is true that one of the reasons that the law has a
general concern with punishment is to *restrain* the victim's family from
revenge, revenge being of itself destructive to a community.† But it
is always the standards of the community that are affirmed in the law
and enforced by the threat of punishment, never the passions of
individuals.

---

*I am grateful to Louis Henkin for his explanation of these two principles.
†I am grateful to Milton Schubin for this point.

With regard to the exemption from universal jurisdiction that
Arendt claims on Eichmann's behalf, Eichmann's having acted under
orders from a state would not have exempted him from trial on a
charge of having committed any crime that is under universal jurisdiction. It is not true that the Genocide Convention *expressly* rejected
the move to make genocide a crime under universal jurisdiction. That
is, there is no such rejection in the language of the convention. It had
not made genocide such a crime, but—despite the fact that that option
was considered—it actually lacked the power to do that, since only
customary law (or treaties, or a universal treaty) can place a crime
under universal jurisdiction.

"Yet," as Robert Jackson wrote, "unless we are prepared to abandon every principle of growth for International Law, we cannot deny
that our own day has the right to initiate customs and to conclude
agreements that will themselves become sources of a new and
strengthened International Law. International Law is not capable of
developing by the normal processes of legislation, for there is no
continuing legislative authority" (Jackson, 1947, p. 85.) Although the
situation in which Israel acted, asserting the principle of universal
jurisdiction, was less clear in 1961 than it has since become, in the
intervening years it has become acceptable under customary law to
think of genocide as a universal crime, even for countries that have
not adhered to the Genocide Convention.*

About the kidnapping of Eichmann, Arendt is justifiably concerned,
especially in regard to the violation of international law and the
precedent that that might set. In the end she allows that overriding
considerations of justice gave Israel no alternative to this dangerous
and unprecedented act, since—even had Argentina been willing to
extradite Eichmann (which it was not), and even had the Bonn
government asked for his extradition (which it did not)—the Argen-
tinian statute of limitations had expired for Eichmann's crime.

With regard to Arendt's concern, it is probably relevant to recall

---

*I am grateful to Louis Henkin for his discussion and explanation of the process by
which a crime comes under universal jurisdiction. Illustrative of this process is the
Oct. 31, 1985, Opinion written by Chief Judge Pierce Lively, U.S. Court of Appeals for
the Sixth Circuit, Cincinnati, Ohio, in *Demjanjuk ;v. Petrovsky.* The Opinion, subsequently
upheld on several appeals, affirmed a lower court decision to extradite John Demjanjuk
to Israel for trial under the same law under which Eichmann was tried, although
Demjanjuk is a Ukrainian, and the crimes with which he is charged were committed at
Treblinka, in Poland, before Israel became a sovereign state. I am grateful to Murray
R. Stein of the Justice Department for his kind assistance in directing me to related
Opinions and materials on this and other cases where the principle of universal
jurisdiction has been upheld.

that the government of Israel did not claim any "right" to violate Argentina's sovereignty, and it apologized to Argentina for doing so. The action of the Israel government became, accordingly, a matter for negotiation and eventual settlement between the sovereign nations concerned. Meanwhile, what was claimed by the attorney general at the Jerusalem District Court was, rather, that a train of precedents in British and American courts combined to establish that "a court does not inquire into the circumstances under which a person has been brought before it; once he is physically present, the court will proceed to try him. Abduction across frontiers may become a political issue between the countries involved, but it is not a consideration for the court."*

To this argument, Arendt rejoins that the precedents did not apply because Israel did not have a "valid warrant of arrest" (Arendt, 1964, p. 264). I do not pretend to understand how this one doubtful dissimilarity makes the entire train of precedents disanalogous in all other respects, and makes it possible for Arendt to put in the place of them all what she calls "the only relevant precedent," namely, a 1935 *Gestapo* kidnapping of a German-Jewish journalist from Switzerland. Why the action of what was described at Nuremberg as a criminal organization, in furtherance of activities that overrode all law and all justice, is described by Arendt as a precedent at all, much less the "only relevant precedent," Arendt does not explain. Nor does she offer any further particulars about the Gestapo incident. So the slur remains gratuitous.

There follows a lengthy discussion of the "crime against humanity" or, as Arendt prefers to call it, the "crime against the human status." Since Germany pursued Jews not only on its own territory but wherever they existed on the globe, Arendt finds that it was engaged in "an attack upon human diversity as such, that is, upon a characteristic of the 'human status' without which the very words 'mankind'

---

*Hausner (1966, p. 312). In the trial, cases where courts had consented to try defendants illegally abducted across U.S. state lines were also cited by Hausner. With regard to extraterritorial assertion of arrest authority, overriding absolute national sovereignty in foreign countries where the case is not covered by extradition treaties, recently the U.S. government appears to have moved toward the position of no longer ruling it out, although viewing it as appropriate only for the most extreme cases. See for example, the testimony of State Department Legal Advisor Abraham D. Sofaer before the Senate Judiciary Subcommittee on Security and Terrorism, on the subject of S.1429, the "Terrorist Prosecution Act of 1985," on July 30, 1985. Sofaer also noted that, whether their seizure is legal or illegal, "the Due Process clause of the Constitution does not automatically preclude U.S. courts from trying persons forcibly seized abroad by U.S. authorities."

or 'humanity' would be devoid of meaning" (1964, p. 269). Since this was according to Arendt a new crime, involving Jews only because the prior history of anti-Semitism had made them particularly vulnerable to selection as its victims, and since the real victim was humanity, "it needed an international tribunal to do justice to it" (1964, p. 269).

This sounds fine—the part about one sole *genos* being gone and the whole earth being empty—even if it's not exactly true. (We still use the term "humanity" meaningfully, with or without any living Tasmanians.) But, as Arendt acknowledges, the General Assembly of the United Nations had already repeatedly turned down proposals to establish such an international penal court. She admits the "technical" unfeasibility of the astonishing proposal from Karl Jaspers, that the Jerusalem court try Eichmann but then declare itself "incompetent" to sentence him, but overlooks the more substantive objection to Jaspers's proposal, namely, that a court incompetent to pass sentence would also, by the same token, be incompetent to hear the evidence. Arendt's own proposal is that the Israeli prime minister "set up an international court in Jerusalem, with judges from each of the countries that had suffered under Nazi occupation" (1964, p. 271).

Unfortunately this recommendation, even if it could have been acted on absent the international consensus that had obtained in the postwar moment at Nuremberg, would not have removed the several problems of "impaired justice" that Arendt found at Jerusalem. Such a court would still have been a "court of the victors" (1964, p. 274) as was, according to Arendt, the International Military Tribunal at Nuremberg. It couldn't have freed all defense witnesses from the risk of indictment, a flaw Arendt considers "the most serious . . . in the Jerusalem proceedings" (p. 274).

This problem, that witnesses for the defense may themselves be subject to indictment, is however a feature common to any conspiracy trial. A mafioso could argue that he cannot get a fair trial because the witnesses he could produce in his own defense could themselves get arrested. The answer is, very simply, that is true.* However, Arendt rhetorically aggravates the problem when she writes that "the court would not admit witnesses for the defense" (1964, p. 274). What was done in the actual trial was to take depositions from such witnesses abroad, for subsequent entry into the court record.

Nor would the Arendt-proposed international tribunal have freed the other, avowedly victimized countries from the same anti-Nazi partiality Arendt was apparently cautious about in the case of Israel. (Unless of course the judges from those countries turned out not to

---

*I am indebted to Milton Schubin for this point.

have cared about their *Jewish* fellow nationals, which would have left the problem of a tilt toward the defendant because of shared anti-Semitism: a different problem of bias.) It wouldn't have closed the gap between political "neutrality" and judicial "impartiality" that Arendt possibly did not notice when she advocated the additional inclusion of "neutral" countries in this international court. So it is hard to see how an international tribunal could have escaped Arendt's moveable condemnations, even supposing that it could have surmounted every practical hazard.

Arendt of course recognized that there was in fact no functioning international court empowered to try individuals for crimes under international law. Partly in response to the ineffectiveness of the Genocide convention since its unanimous adoption by the General Assembly in 1948, the U.N. Commission on Human Rights authorized its sub-Commission on Prevention of Discrimination and Protection of Minorities to prepare a report on "the question of the prevention and punishment of the crime of genocide" (Whitaker, 1985, para. 3). To date, two such reports have emerged, one by Nicodème Ruhashyankiko in 1978, and a revised and updated one by B. Whitaker in 1985. Both the 1978 report and the 1985 report agree that the following problems hinder punishment of the crime of genocide: there is no international penal court; the 1948 Genocide Convention does not place genocide under universal jurisdiction; by giving jurisdiction either to a (presently nonexistent) international penal court or to a "competent tribunal of the State in the country of which the act was perpetrated" (Whitaker, 1985, para. 56), the crime goes practically unpunished, for such acts are usually committed in states whose governments themselves bear responsibility for them. The Whitaker report further notes that "it was partly the failure to make progress internationally that caused Israel to take unilateral measures to seize and try Eichmann" (para. 57). Finally, both reports *urge* that genocide be considered a crime under universal jurisdiction. This change, recommended in the two reports and anticipated at the Jerusalem trial, is by now well under way, and addresses the problem more practically than did Arendt's proposals at the time.

Arendt goes on to make the following general criticism of the letter and the spirit of the Jerusalem trial. "At no point . . . either in the proceedings or in the judgment, did the Jerusalem trial ever mention even the possibility that extermination of whole ethnic groups . . . might be more than a crime against the Jewish or the Polish or the Gypsy people, that the international order, and mankind in its entirety, might have been grievously hurt and endangered" (Arendt, 1964, pp. 275f).

This seems to me to misrepresent outright the spirit of the trial. As to its letter, in a fifteen-count indictment, counts 6, 7, 9, 10, 11, and 12 were for "crimes against humanity." Count 8 was for "war crimes." Counts 13, 14, and 15 were for "membership in criminal organizations" (i.e., the SS and Gestapo, as was charged against defendants at Nuremberg). The remaining first five counts of the indictment were for "crimes against the Jewish people." But even here, attention was paid to the international order and to the interests of humankind. The judgment of the court, "which was confirmed by the Supreme Court of Israel," spelled out "that 'the crime against the Jewish people' had been defined in the relevant Israel law in the same terms as in the 1948 Genocide Convention because it was not a crime under that law alone but also an offence against the law of nations" (Ruhashyankiko, 1978, para. 188).

In deciding to try the case, the court also affirmed what Arendt denied: that it could be impartial. But Arendt's point about impartiality is rather an elusive point. If, as she claims, the Jerusalem court could properly try people for crimes against Jews, on the same basis that Polish courts could try people for crimes against Poles, surely the ground of the propriety in both cases would be that Jews, like Poles, could be impartial. No one is expected to be impartial with regard to the crime itself. On the contrary. Impartiality, and abhorrence for the crime, are perfectly consistent with one another.* What is expected of a properly constituted court is that it will be willing impartially to review the evidence and decide on the basis of the evidence whether Y is or is not guilty beyond a reasonable doubt. If, as Arendt concedes, Israeli judges could in principle impartially review the evidence bearing on the guilt or innocence of someone accused of "crimes against the Jewish people," then she ought at least to have shown *why* their impartiality was to be placed in question where the accusation was "crimes against humanity." The first crime is a particular instance of genocide, and genocide *is* one of the "crimes against humanity."†

---

*I am grateful to Milton Schubin for this observation.

†For the definition of "crimes against humanity" in Control Council Law No. 10, see the prosecutor's summation in *Nuernberg Military Tribunals*, Case No. 1, "The Medical Case," *The United States Against Karl Brandt et al.*, vol. 1, p. 913. The first uses of the notion of genocide in official documents and indictments are reviewed in the Ruhashyankiko report (1978, paras. 22, 23, and notes). According to Telford Taylor, the expression "crimes against humanity" first appears in modern history in a joint manifesto issued by England, France, and Russia during World War I, denouncing the massacres of Armenians as "crimes against humanity and civilization." (Taylor, panel discussion on "International Law and Crimes Against Humanity," New York Academy of Medicine, April 6, 1986. Panel moderator was Professor Louis Henkin, and the co-panelists were Judges Abraham Sofaer and Marvin E. Frankel.)

There would seem to be no difference in the degree or quality of the impartiality required of the court, just as there is no difference in the principle involved, except the difference of species to genus.

Arendt's last point concerns the "helplessness" of the Jerusalem court to grasp and understand the point of Eichmann's ordinariness, that he was one of a "new type of criminal, who . . . commits his crimes under circumstances that make it well-nigh impossible for him to know or to feel that he is doing wrong" (1964, p. 276). To repair this failure, Arendt scripts an alternative judgment, and one that would be from her standpoint ideal.

Arendt's ideal judgment admits that Eichmann has *not* been found guilty of criminal intent beyond a reasonable doubt. That, I take it, is the purport of its projected "difficult, though not altogether impossible to believe" admission that Eichmann "never acted from base motives . . . never had any inclination to kill anybody . . . never hated Jews . . . could not have acted otherwise and did not feel guilty" (Arendt, 1964, p. 278). One would think that, having admitted *that*, the court should have awarded Eichmann an Iron Cross and two tickets to a resort on the Sea of Galilee, but no matter. We pass on. The court is to find Eichmann guilty anyway, on the ground that his obedience constituted support for mass murder, since "in politics obedience and support are the same" (p. 279). This sounds rather like a page from the Vyshinsky trials, where the notion of "objective guilt"—the guilt that comes from one's having bet on the wrong horse, and being then called to account by the other horse—had such singular utility. In Western criminal law, on the other hand, where the defendant is thought to be called to some kind of a moral accounting, compelled obedience, or obedience to superior orders whose harmful results weren't apparent, would be found to be exculpatory. However, the court had precisely *not* found Eichmann's defense along these lines a plausible one.

Arendt's ideal judgment is to wind up by sentencing Eichmann to die on the ground that he and his superiors arrogated to themselves the "right to determine who should and . . . should not inhabit the world." Since he and they did that, the judgment is to continue, "no member of the human race can be expected to want to share the earth with you" (1964, p. 279).

There is an ambiguity about this "can be *expected* to want." Is a moral or legal standard for invoking the death penalty being appealed to here, or are the results of a poll being anticipated? If the latter, one should remember that people are not properly sentenced to die because some other people may possibly not want them around. In Eichmann's case it was certain that some of his fellow mortals did indeed want to "share the earth" with him. Arendt herself reports active sympathy in the Arab press (1964, p. 13) and worldwide appeals for clemency (pp. 249f). If we were to consult the popular sentiment alone, Eichmann might just possibly outlive us all. In some sense, he already has.

We are led to conclude that behind Arendt's conceptually and politically remote "humanity" was an all-too-proximate Jewish experience, being strenuously discerned as anything but. If it is granted that Jews are, *qua* Jews, *qua* German Jews, Polish Jews, Israeli Jews, etc., fully human, the Holocaust—perpetrators and victims—fully human, the precedent series of anti-Semitic acts in Western history (dissociated from the Holocaust by Arendt, but given detailed linkage to it by Hilberg, her chief historical source here)* fully human, then the whole contrived antithesis between particular Jew and outraged humanity falls away. Other things being equal, "Israel or any other nation . . . may undertake to vindicate the interest of all nations by seeking to punish the perpetrators of such crimes" (Lively, 1985). In sum, it is not so easy as all that to throw the legitimacy of such trials into chiaroscuro. If the trials are legitimate, then the moral discourse to which the trials have supplied the attested evidence can now proceed. We are left alone with our moral problem, to be faced in its particulars, without preciosity.

The Paradigm Case

Nevertheless, facing it remains quite difficult. It is not a question of no sooner said than done. Philosophical, political, and ordinary usage has already placed the Nazi in our moral landscape as the most legible or purest case of genocide, and incidentally of evil itself. But the Nazi's outstandingness in evil, or outstandingness in the evil of genocide, has also been challenged. And, although popularly the Nazi is grouped with the Jew as the victim who suffers the fullest impact of him, there have also been questions raised about the outstandingness of the Holocaust as a case of victimization by the evil of genocide.

---

*Arendt (1964, pp. 267ff). Cf. also Arendt's *The Origins of Totalitarianism* (1951, pp. 8ff, 14f, 25, 29–39, 42–45, passim), where the flow of anti-Semitism through nineteenth-century and twentieth-century pre-Nazi Europe is analyzed into atomic episodes, without significant motivational interconnection. For Raul Hilberg, by contrast, canonical or secular precedents can be shown for every Nazi decree or negative stereotype except those having immediate bearing on the extermination itself (1985, pp. 11–12). For Arendt, the connection between anti-Semitism and the Holocaust is accidental. For Hilberg, it is virtually logical (1985, p. 9).

(I will ascribe "outstandingness" in evil, rather than "uniqueness" to the Holocaust, so as not to set off a rockslide of epistemological quibbles.) Finally, we have already alluded to questions raised about the integrity of the Jewish victims, or the "purity" of their victimization. Holocaust victims have been charged with various kinds of moral default, ranging from passivity to complicity, charges that make it hard to see them clear, for the purposes of a moral analysis. If we do not know where the victim *as* victim begins, we will not be able to make out sufficiently clearly where his victimizer in turn begins. Before we can take a fresh look at the Nazi, we must take another look at all these objections.

Douglas Lackey is one of those who take philosophical objection to the view, associated with Emil Fackenheim and others, that the Holocaust is an extraordinary or unique case of evil, requiring categories, or a quality of meditation, different from its predecessors and successors to date.[3] It is wrong, Lackey argues, to consider the Holocaust extraordinarily evil in virtue of its perpetrators' evidently erroneous *belief* that Jews were not members of the human species. An erroneous belief, Lackey points out, isn't worse morally (though it may be worse in its consequences), than, say, weakness of the will in resisting what are correctly believed to be immoral desires.

Against that kind of objection, Emil Fackenheim has urged that, in going to exceeding great lengths to inflict mental as well as physical torment on their Jewish victims, the Nazi genocides went beyond what even their eugenicist beliefs could have authorized or justified. Berel Lang has additionally pointed out that the large-scale use of systematic mechanisms for concealment, euphemism, and destruction of the evidence bespeak a consciousness that the moral or at least the criminal line had been crossed. These mechanisms don't suggest that the perpetrators earnestly and in good faith believed what they said they believed.[4]

In support of Lackey, it could however be rejoined that the Nazi resort to mental and physical torment of their Jewish victims had the pragmatic purpose of instilling in the executioners the requisite *relish* for what was earnestly believed to be a eugenically necessary job. In further support of Lackey, it can be argued that the Nazi use of concealment and euphemism was a necessary concession to the (as they believed) unscientific prejudices of ordinary people, whether of the contemporary or future generations.

For the sake of the argument, let us grant that (despite many evidences of Nazi bad faith) there were Nazis who felt genuinely convinced at the time, and who therefore felt sincerely aggrieved later that they should be condemned morally for their *beliefs*. Granting this,

a distinct moral problem does emerge. The problem has to do with
the relation between damagingly erroneous beliefs, held in alleged
good faith, and moral responsibility. But to notice the problem is not
to decide in advance the outcome of the inquiry it must provoke. It
is to be recalled that *these* erroneous beliefs were damaging in quite
marked ways (I think of the punctured canisters of Zyklon B on
exhibit in the visitors' lobby of the United Nations, and the guide who
said to me, with the gently emphatic accents and demeanor of a
survivor, "15,000 people a day!"*). It is also noteworthy that the moral
responsibility that ordinarily might have devolved on the mistaken
Nazi "believer" appeared to be shiftable by him in indefinitely many
indistinct ways.

> Accused [Eichmann]: . . . There is truth here and honour. And Loewen-
> herz [Dr. Joseph Loewenherz, director of the Jewish community office in
> Vienna], I must say, was a very dignified and decent person.
>
> Q: And you started the negotiations with him by slapping him in the
> face. True or not true?
>
> A: I must say that if I first slap a person in the face and then I apologize,
> this is a private matter between the two people. [Eichmann Trial, 90th
> Session]

In view of the two above-noted aspects of these particular erroneous
beliefs, it may be that further inquiry into the puzzling syndrome of
them can take us straight to the center of the knotty relations
between erroneous belief and evil. Let us not dodge the invitation to
that inquiry by fixing on the distracting fact that in the majority of
human cases, which are the ordinary cases, an erroneous belief doesn't
make its owner a worse character than an incontinent will would
make him. On its face, the Nazi case doesn't *look* like an ordinary case.

What we are proposing to talk about here is the bringing to be of
worsened characters. Now it can be argued that, since the worst
consequences don't necessarily result from the worst characters, Nazi
characters weren't strikingly worsened by the results of what Nazis
in good faith did. Thus it might belong to Lackey's point to say that
if, in consequence of a mistaken belief about something technical, one
inadvertently starts a terrible fire or an industrial accident, ordinarily
these consequences would not provide a fair measure of one's charac-

---

*Mrs. Rosa Goldstein, of the International Auschwitz Committee, Brussels, Jan. 29,
1986. The exhibition, "Auschwitz—A Crime Against Mankind," was organized by the
International Auschwitz Committee together with the Auschwitz State Museum in
Poland.

ter. But here we are talking about a close and continuously renewed and readjusted correlation between the planned infliction of suffering on Jews and the actual suffering that did accordingly result. (Whether or not Jews were believed to be human beings, nobody denied that they were sentient creatures and could suffer. They were even thought to be unusually intelligent, and capable of mental suffering.)

So, even if one were to take a strictly utilitarian view of character, as that which makes likely certain pleasurable or painful experiences, it would have to be conceded that character was worsened when a man habitually bent his efforts to bring about painful experiences. If, additionally, one regards the team factor as morally significant (as Lackey does not in this article), then one has to reckon in not only the effects on individual character, but the effects on the character of the social organism in which all these perpetrators were smoothly combined (See Hilberg, 1985, pp. 994, 1013.)

To this one might rejoin, still on behalf of Lackey's overall point, that, despite Nazi use of utilitarian rationales from time to time, their fundamental beliefs were not utilitarian and cannot fairly be evaluated by a utilitarian standard. That is to say, Nazis did not equate the good with the greatest pleasure (or the least pain) for the greatest number of sentient creatures, each sentient creature to count for one. Rather, they equated the good with greatness, or historical dominance itself, with no one to count at all except the dominant.

We come back to our earlier sense of the matter. What is a problem, and what will have to be investigated, is whether such a belief as that actually crosses a line, entering a tundra where belief itself, *qua* belief, may count as a moral wrong. In any case, we cannot decide that question prior to a painstaking further inquiry. That inquiry will be the task of Chapter Seven, "Thinking like a Nazi."

Lackey also argues that the Holocaust got its "terrible poignancy" because it was preventable. For example, it would have been prevented if Hitler had been assassinated. He reminds us that an act is no worse *morally* because it is in this way preventable. But, although a preventable forest fire started by a careless camper is ordinarily thought to be a great shame, it is not ordinarily thought to be poignant *morally*. If we are permitted to lodge moral claims against the perpetrators of the Holocaust, it is because most of them could have acted otherwise, not because some of them could have been assassinated. What is morally poignant, if that is the word, in the Holocaust, is that against its fires are silhouetted failures of *self*-prevention on the part of the arsonists.

Other ways in which the Holocaust's outstandingness has been queried have to do with its similarities to other holocausts. Since those

who stress these similarities must *also* do the "dangerously unbecoming . . . moral bookkeeping" (Horowitz, 1982, p. 194) they deplore, let
us too swallow any aesthetic compunction about unavoidable bookkeeping and just get on with it. Moral bookkeeping is out of order if
one is deciding how much horror to feel and how much *compassion* to
expend. (There is no way of quantifying that, and no reason to impose
a limit. One expends as much as one has.) But moral bookkeeping is
quite in order if one is estimating with what kind and degree of evil
one has to deal. For example, when courts of law have before them
a ranking as to the severity of offenses, we don't find that they have
lapsed into moral bookkeeping of the unbecoming sort.

   It will be convenient, if a bit rough and ready, to take Irving
Horowitz's arguments in *Taking Lives* as typifying the move to equate
the Holocaust with other holocausts. (See Horowitz, 1982, ch. 11). If
it turns out that there are other such arguments, not covered by
Horowitz, then they may of course escape the rebuttals here being
offered to Horowitz. Be that as it may, my reading of Horowitz makes
it evident to me that his ethico-political concern is with getting victims
of all ethnic persuasions to ally with each other (p. 199). If an alliance
between all victims everywhere were the concern, moral bookkeeping
would be tactically imprudent and humanly tactless. But I do not know
that the alliance is imminent. In any case, whether or not it is, the
moral bookkeeping will have to go on. We can do it in the next room.*

   That said, the bookkeeping is partly a matter of estimating the
percentages of a *genos* destroyed, also the absolute numbers, also the
lastingness of the biological and cultural damage done, also the
amount of free malevolence behind each such significant case of
genocide. On most of these scores, the Holocaust appears to emerge

---

*It is interesting to note that in the *debate* over the Whitaker report, the observer
from Turkey said, "There is no analogy between the holocaust of the Jews and the
events of 1915" (U.N. Sub-Commission, 1985, para. 28). Similar disclaimers for the
1965 and 1972 Tutsi massacres of Hutu were entered by the observer from Burundi
(paras. 13, 30), and for the 1974 massacre of Aché Indians by the observer from
Paraguay (paras. 42–49). So, in the day-to-day politics of genocide, reference to the Nazi
and the Holocaust as the extreme or paradigmatic example often seems hard to avoid.
Even the stomach-churning remarks of the observer from the Soviet Union, turning
the paradigm on its head (paras. 81–85), did not, for all that, cease to make use of the
Nazi Holocaust of the Jews as a paradigm. Its *service* as a paradigm is noted in William
Shawcross's *The Quality of Mercy: Cambodia, Holocaust, and Modern Conscience* (1984,
pp. 15–18, 45ff, 93, 192). I am grateful to Elsa Stamatopoulou, of the New York Liaison
Office of the U.N. Human Rights Commission, for making the summary record of the
debate on the Whitaker report of 1985, and the 1985 and 1978 reports themselves,
available to me.

among the finalists. When it is not clearly ahead on one score alone, it moves out in front when several factors are taken in combination. Picking our way gingerly over the killing fields, let us look for these factors, separately and in combination, and make the comparisons.

On percentages, the Armenian percentages are close, but their 50 percent is not the European Jewish 60 percent (Horowitz, 1982, p. 195); Gypsy losses to the Nazis were high, but again 25 percent is not 60 percent (Dawidowicz, 1981, p. 11). Polish percentages were high, but then again between 12 and 22 percent is not 60 percent (Dawidowicz, 1981, p. 6). Unnatural death totals in the Soviet Union have been fantastically high, but even if they had been all the result of genocide, which they were not, we are not talking about 60 percent of the Russian population.[5] These are cases which, either on the side of victim, or of aggressor and victim, might be thought of as internal to Western culture.

There are also cases of non-Western, intertribal destruction, or cases where a Western culture has encountered an aboriginal culture and wiped it out, as happened in the confrontation between British settlers and the Stone Age Tasmanians in the late nineteenth century. These are cases which, on the score of percentages and lastingness of the damage, do overshadow the Holocaust. (See Horowitz, 1982, pp. 18ff and references, pp. 21f, also pp. 50–64.) But the absolute numbers are either not comparable, or, where possibly comparable, did not pile up as a result of a unitary, deliberate operation.[6] And one feels that an outburst of butchery based on lust for loot or power, and racial contempt, is somewhat different, in terms of the quanta of free malevolence it summons, than the meticulously planned Nazi Holocaust that drew on the effective resources of two thousand years of theological contempt, *as well as* lust for loot, power, and racial contempt. Both the Holocaust's meticulous planning and the affective resources on which it could draw suggest greater free malevolence, insofar as such a thing is open to objective comparisons. Even the Cambodian black page of auto-genocide involves estimated percentages of something like 40 percent. Forty percent is not 60 percent. If one talks about the percentages of all Jews, rather than European Jews, then one can get them to match, in this and the Armenian case of course. But the absolute numbers are still not comparable.

If one is talking about a clear case of *genocidal* holocaust, as opposed to mass death alone, or ethnocide alone, the front-runner character of the Holocaust is more salient still. Certain kinds of Cambodians were targeted by the Khmer Rouge (Shawcross, 1984, pp. 29, 40f, 54), and in certain places and times (p. 36)—however absurdly and evilly—but not all Cambodians. Outside of Constantinople and other large cities,

Armenians in Turkey were targeted for slaughter, not all Armenians on the face of the earth for liquidation. "Several hundred thousand" survived the deportations. Exceptions were sometimes made for religious converts.[7] The unhappy Armenian women who were impressed into Turkish concubinage were not then butchered, for example. At least, not so far as is known.

In the history of human conflict, wars of extermination, or wars involving mass death and ecocide, may, at certain times and places, have been customary. This is assumed, for example, in the Whitaker report, whether rightly or wrongly. However, once restraints came to be accepted in the context of developed civilizations, certain "regressive episodes" then stood out, and became appalling. Morgenthau provides a convenient, if abbreviated summary of them, in the context of his particular reflections on the Armenian massacre:

> I am confident that the whole history of the human race contains no such horrible episode as this. The great massacres and persecutions of the past seem almost insignificant when compared with the sufferings of the Armenian race in 1915. The slaughter of the Albigenses in the early part of the thirteenth century has always been regarded as one of the most pitiful events in history. In these outbursts of fanaticism about 60,000 people were killed. In the massacre of St. Bartholomew about 30,000 human beings lost their lives. The Sicilian Vespers, which has always figured as one of the most fiendish outbursts of this kind, caused the destruction of 8,000. Volumes have been written about the Spanish Inquisition under Torquemada, yet in the eighteen years of his administration only a little more than 8,000 heretics were done to death. Perhaps the one event in history that most resembles the Armenian deportation was the expulsion of the Jews from Spain by Ferdinand and Isabella. According to Prescott 160,000 were uprooted from their homes and scattered broadcast over Africa and Europe. Yet all these previous persecutions seem almost trivial when we compare them with the sufferings of the Armenians, in which at least 600,000 people were destroyed and perhaps as many as 1,000,000. And these earlier massacres . . . have one feature that we can almost describe as an excuse: they were the product of religious fanaticism. . . . Undoubtedly religious fanaticism was an impelling motive with the Turkish and Kurdish rabble who slew Armenians . . . but the men who really conceived the crime had no such motive. (Morgenthau, 1918, pp. 321ff)

Among these appalling regressive episodes—whether regressive chronologically or morally—should be counted those cases in which whole cultures, and sometimes whole peoples, have been wiped out by civilized Europeans, who were unrestrained by any feeling of identity with their different-looking, different-acting victims.

In the meantime, and partly in the middle of the stream of these appalling regressive episodes, the culture of the West has come increasingly to be, if not world culture itself, then at least a dominant element in the world. Reflecting on the crimes committed during the Nazi regression, Lemkin found in them *a pattern* that could be best analyzed in terms of a new concept, for which he supplied the coinage "genocide," and the analysis. He found that the Nazis did not merely destroy cultures and peoples on their way to accomplishing something else. He found that such destruction was in the forefront of the Nazi intent. With two other "experts in the field of international and criminal law," he worked with the secretary general of the United Nations to draft the Genocide convention.[8] Eventually, in a watered-down form, that convention was unanimously adopted by the General Assembly in 1948. So Lemkin's reflections on a regressive episode within Western culture had helped to set in motion the process by which a certain kind of appalling regression came to be recognized as a crime in the whole human world.

The point is not usually made this way, but still it might be said that, through the agency of Lemkin and others, the Holocaust and related Nazi crimes against other *genē* have been made to have a gentling and a moralizing effect on the conscience of the world. It is not an accident that the Nazi Holocaust is paradigmatic. Rather, because we now know what "genocide" is, we can see its horrors elsewhere than, and subsequent to, Auschwitz. We have a framework and a word that permits us to see the more than half a million of Indonesia, the more than one hundred thousand of Uganda, the one-to-three million of Cambodia. It is far too hasty, and historically superficial, to expect an alliance between victims. It is enough if they, or some of them, can now *see* each other. Once one can see, one can think, or at least start to do that.

So the Nazi genocidal endeavors should be understood as morally pivotal events in the internal drama of Western culture, and—through the influence of Western culture on the world—pivotal events in the still-to-be-agreed-upon "history" of the world itself.

Now, among the Nazi genocidal endeavors, the endeavor against the Jews does stand out. Other peoples were gassed en masse at Nazi killing centers, but they were not targeted in toto. Exceptions were made for German Gypsies, Aryan-looking Poles or Poles not belonging to the Polish elite, Russians not identified as communists or soldiers. If such targetings, for example of all Slavic peoples, were sometimes discussed among the Nazi brass, if plans were even on the drawing boards, if preliminary measures to prevent reproduction by separating the sexes or by means of mass sterilizations were imple-

mented in part against Slavic peoples, the holistic vision and the
steady follow-through were not present that were present for the
Jews of Europe. No Pole or Russian, attempting to escape the Nazi
net, tried to pass for a Jew. No Pole or Russian, inmate in a concentration camp, asked to wear the yellow star. (If perchance a saintly
person, unknown to me, did ask, he was not thinking to get better
treatment thereby.) In the aftermath of the Nazi crimes against *genē*,
no moralist has asked of the culture of the West, in its religious
component, that it reflect on the status its theology has assigned to
the Pole or the Russian.[9] It is a fact, and a fact about the culture of
the West, that whatever was said by the Nazis to menace non-Jewish
genē, was easier said than done. But what was said to menace the *genos*
of the Jews was almost as easily—and almost as thoroughly—done as
said. That, of course, the Nazis were counting on. So there is, it
would seem, an "appalling regression" that is, as it were, embedded
in the culture of the West, and that came to light in the Holocaust.

Viewed in this light, what characteristics belonged specifically to
the Holocaust? It means something that Jews were an internal, ancient, and highly influential element in the culture of the West. What
it means is that minimal identification with them, as also human, was
already in a measure normal to Europeans, and had to be massively
undone—repealed by many separate and combined measures. If I fail
to recognize you as human and kill you as I would an animal, my
failure is deplorable and horrid. But in one sense it may also be viewed
as impulsive and instinctive. What this means is that an animal might
do the same, with an outsider.[10] Once I learn better, I may come to
behave myself, and act instead like a human being, "expanding the
circle"—as Peter Singer would say—within which I can feel identified
with others who don't look like me. (The same Australians whose
forefathers destroyed Tasmanians a century ago may read about them
today with interest and compunction.) But if, culturally and historically, I have long recognized you, albeit with profound ambivalence,
as fully human (e.g., as still capable of being saved by God if you meet
certain conditions), and I then take measured steps to implode that
recognition, my attack against you and against what counts as human
in myself cuts much deeper. What were those measured steps?

The operation comprised, first, *defining* Jews for the purpose of
isolating them from the economic, social, and higher-cultural communities into which they had been absorbed or vitally connected, and
second, progressively *depleting* their physical, economic, and political
strength by all the measures to disconnect them from the social
organism, followed by all the measures to crowd them into a few
holding areas where rapidly they could be further reduced by starva-

tion and epidemics (adequate food and medicine being simply and deliberately withheld). Third, with would-be resisters forced to comply in consideration of families and whole communities held hostage, the operation was concluded by transporting them to killing centers for killing on an assembly-line basis, with last effects and body products to be utilized in the Germany economy.* An operation like *that*, we do not find anywhere in the history of the West, or indeed in the history of advanced civilizations. (We do not look to the holocausts of the primitives, if any, since they lacked the technology that is the practical counterpart of such a sustained purpose.) For free malevolence, there has been nothing like it.

Add to this that the Western governments, opposing Nazi Germany and fully aware of the Holocaust, failed to take and even blocked perfectly feasible concrete measures either to thwart it in part, or to rescue some of its victims, and we do indeed have virtually "the whole culture of the West involved in the Holocaust," by commission or conscious, crucial omission.† We are not talking about overblown *metaphors* for commemorative sermons here. We are talking about data for the intergalactic anthropologists. And if the Holocaust had the active or passive "consent" of the culture of the West, then, in the long run and retrospectively at least, that "consent" is passed along to diffuse into the culture of the whole human world, whose inhabitants will be obliged to ratify it actively, or ratify it passively, or refuse it. Enough said about the paradigmatic character, or outstandingness in the genocidal line, of the Holocaust.

The Right Way to Act

The Nazi, who brought it about actively, remains hard to see clear, however, as long as the picture of him is blurred by the superimposed picture of the alleged complicity of his victim. If the victim *was* in complicity, then we get instead the picture of an odd sort of morbid human interaction, a shared sickness, an epidemic if you like, where

---

*For this overview of the matter, and the meticulous documentation as regards its details, I am most recently indebted to the revised, three-volume edition of Raul Hilberg's *The Destruction of the European Jews* (1985). On the Holocaust's counterutility to the German war effort, see pp. 377–81, 440–44, 463f, 535, 538, 780f, 803, 918, 1006f.

†Documentation for the charge about the British and American governments is generously supplied in David S. Wyman's *The Abandonment of the Jews: America and the Holocaust, 1941–1945* (1984). In Wyman's account, the context, both for U.S. government resistance to the pleas of Jewish leaders and for the muffled notes of those appeals, is partly found in the voter anti-Semitism of the period (pp. 5–15, 57f, 107f, 116, 266–76, 327, 337f). The context, of course, does not remove the responsibility on either hand.

clear lines between poisoners, carriers, and felled members of the healthy population can no longer be drawn. If anti-Semitism is some kind of an illness (and possibly it is—an undiagnosed kind, a cultural morbidity), well, we do not blame people for their maladies. Not as a general rule. A responsible physician will withhold praise and blame alike from his patients.

The problem of Jewish complicity needs, I think, now to be viewed in the widest possible context. We have said that there is no such thing as "history," or "world-history," if by history is meant a single, universally agreed-upon narrative making collective sense of the stories of all individuals in their respective *gene,* and of all *genē* together. The myth of such a common narrative, already emplaced, is what gives ideologues their spurious authorization to overthrow real stories, of real people and of real *genē.* Nevertheless, such a universally agreed-upon story is not logically impossible. It is what happens, writ small, when any two individuals, who have lived a certain course of experience together, agree as to the factual content of what happened and as to its significance. Such agreement *can* come about, without any necessary sacrifice of the uniqueness of the parties, or the indissoluble otherness of each one's particular perspective. If individuals can do this (and if doing it is crucial to the ratification of their experiences), and call the doing of it "friendship," then larger groups might in principle also do it. In utopian or millenarian vision, what is at best pictured is all individuals and all *genē* getting a sort of shared (in the Quaker sense) "sense of the meeting," and getting it in an unforced way. This state of universal, unforced friendship, lifted free of empty platitudes, embedded in each person's real story, may be a kind of "regulative ideal" horizoning the goodness of each of us. When one thinks of how difficult it is for any single person to get his own story straight, one has a dim notion of the real obstacles that will delay indefinitely the actualizing of this regulative ideal. But, as long as we know that this ideal is what we are talking about, we *can* talk about "world history."

In the context, then, of "world history," what should we suppose was really happening in the course of the Holocaust, from start to end? At the very least, here was a whole people seeking to erase another people from its history, and from world history altogether. The German people worked as a team to get this done, and to let it get done. They looked away at the right times and they pitched in at the right times. The implementation of Nazi orders affecting Jewry required the active or passive consent of virtually all of the adult German population (Hilberg, 1985, pp. 993–1007). Whatever economic gains the targeted people could have voluntarily offered the genocidal people were feared, precisely because they might have deflected the genocidal people from its course (pp. 1006f). On the other hand, whatever spoils the targeted people could *involuntarily* have yielded up to the genocidal people were relished, precisely because these were evidences that the planned genocide was indeed running its course (pp. 947–61). Set in the world-historical context of German ambitions with regard to Jewry, plundering the strengthless dead loses its base character. Rather, the fact that one *can* do it becomes proof of the success of the original mission.

By the same token, appeals from Jews that reflected a Jewish experience were refused as such and *because* they might convince and, convincing, deflect the genocidal people from its course.*

In the light of the same German intent, Jewish professions of patriotism and loyalty were not to be evaluated case by case, pragmatically, on the principle that the "disloyal" should be rooted out, but the services of the loyal retained for the Reich. Rather, the whole German system of justice was bent, and bent itself, so as to prevent such case-by-case evaluation. In line with this, the obviously harmless were not separated from the potentially harmful (Hilberg, 1985, pp. 93, 423 and note 12, pp. 450–54, 678, 997).

It is in this context alone that we can fully understand how there might exist, side by side, high-level Nazi exhortations to world-historical "idealism," apparently unfeigned expressions of regard for individual Jews (more frequent of course from those Nazis who found themselves in Allied hands after the war), *and* systemic tolerance of a sadism that stopped just short of cannibalism, in the implementation phase of the destruction of the Jewish people.† Viewed at the highest level, from the world-historical summit, what was wanted was merely the erasure of one people by another. These aims were couched in terms broadly Darwinian and markedly amoral. Analogies were often drawn with struggles between other species in nature. In the same

---

*For example, at his first anti-Semitic meeting, one Nazi recalled being almost persuaded by a protesting rabbi, whom the audience finally threw out. "That evening had shown to me the danger of Jewish intelligence." See Theodore Abel's *Why Hitler Came into Power: An Answer Based on the Original Life Stories of Six Hundred of His Followers* (1938, p. 226).

†On official tolerance of sadism among concentration camp personnel, see Hilberg (1985, pp. 904f). Detailed examples abound in survivors' eyewitness testimony and in memoirs. On utilization of the body products from condemned and dead Jews, see pp. 954, 959, 966f, 976ff, 983. For the view that cannibalism is the expression of unsublimated rage, I am indebted to Eli Sagan's *Cannibalism: Human Aggression and Cultural Form* (1974), where this comparison to Nazi utilization of body parts from the slain is drawn (p. 140).

malice-free Darwinian spirit, but for the sake of the race's upgrading, below-average Germans could be done away with too.* In Hilberg's paraphrase of a typical exhortation from Hitler, "They [the Jews of Hungary] had to be treated like tubercular bacilli that threatened a healthy body. That was not so cruel when one kept in mind that even innocent creatures like hares and deer had to be killed in order to prevent damage" (1985, p. 817). If hares and deer have to be killed by their natural enemies, which sometimes include men, the actual killing of hares and deer is harder to do if it is felt by the killer to be distasteful, and he fails to relish his killing. And if (as is not generally the case between species in nature) one species sets out deliberately to exterminate another and not let one member of the target species escape alive, then additional relish will have to be summoned, in order to get that harder job done. So the sadists among us are *needed*. Let them not drive us all beserk. That said, they are still the leaven in the mass.

If a eugenicist theory pretends to find itself in the very script of history, and we who hold the theory lose a battle for historical dominance—why then, no hard feelings. We have simply misread the script. Someone else was supposed by nature to win. Perhaps the very people we opposed. Why not? There was never anything personal in it. We were simply trying to do nature's bidding.†

It is in the light of this *sliding* requirement—of an impersonal nonmalicious commitment to a world-historical script on the high end of the scale, and sufficient passion to get the real killing done on the low end—that we can *understand the flexibility* with which the general run of Nazi bureaucrats could remain docilely behind their desks and favor euphemisms over straight talk, or else take to the field and become truly savage there.‡

---

*On euthanasia, see Hilbert (1985, pp. 872f). German clerical and civilian protests eventually halted the program, however.

†On the Nazi racial theories as applied to Jews, see Hilberg (1985, pp. 482, 739, 817, 946). On justifying the destruction of the Jews so long as it is done high-mindedly, without personal "corruption," see pp. 1009f, 1021. On the swift relinquishments of these racial-historical commitments in the face of German defeat, see p. 988; also Dicks (1972, pp. 219f). Gustave Gilbert, who was a military psychologist assigned to the Nuremberg Prison, testified: "So I let it be known that I was Jewish and they, in turn, did not seem to react to this, beyond making it clear that they never had anything against Jews personally, and that this was all silly ideological nonsense. . . . Streicher, for instance, decided that since the Jews were fighting courageously to make a homeland in Palestine, he wanted to 'lead' them" (Eichmann Trial, 55th Session).

‡On the interchangeability of desk men and field men, see Hilberg (1985, p. 1011). "You have on your hands a most dangerous person," wrote Hungarian psychologist L.

It was not a case of misguided Hegelian desk men, with a dash of Darwin and Nietzsche in their formula for history, who then combed prisons and the violent wards of insane asylums until they could put together a raggle-tag bunch of sociopaths who would do "history's" work. The point was that the same man could and would do both. The absolutely protean character of Nazi zeal is what is so striking about it.

Everything functioned as if this was indeed, as it was self-styled at the time, an act of the national will—if there ever was such a thing in the world's "history." Orders did not have to be given. Far-reaching interpretatons and creative implementations welled up from every stratum of the national life. The omissions and the lookings away, the differentiated (not blanket) failures of empathy, were all functional—as they were intended to be.

To that world-historical context in which alleged Jewish complicity has to be viewed, we should add two other important factors. One we have already mentioned and concerns the world. The other we have not yet mentioned and concerns the internal character of Jewish culture.

As regards the world, there was the fact that rescue was largely unavailable from the lands and peoples surrounding the victimized Jews. "Where were we supposed to go," said the guide at the United Nations exhibit on Auschwitz, pointing to a map. "The North Sea?"* The distribution of such rescue reports as were made was largely invidious where Jews were concerned (Wyman, 1984, pp. 338ff). This seems a point crucial to the correct evaluation of the Jewish responses. In Denmark, which might be said to have offered a "control" on the Holocaust experiment where the effectiveness of Jewish leadership is concerned, the Jewish community went smartly to its own aid, full on the mark, having people and lands available for its rescue (Hilberg, 1985, pp. 558–68).

Szondi, analyzing Eichmann's test results, which were sent him without identification of the subject. See Hausner (1966, pp. 6f, and cf. p. 310). This, side by side with Eichmann's much-discussed ordinariness. Cf. also the interesting contrasts between the "soldier's language" in captured Nazi documents, and the world-weary, almost over-civilized reflections by the same Nazis in the dock. See, e.g., *Nuernberg Military Tribunals, The United States of America against Erhard Milch*, Case No. 2, "The Milch Case," vol. 2, pp. 531, 613, as contrasted with p. 650. Note also Eichmann's "After all, one must remember that the jargon employed by soldiers is different from that of clergymen or doctors" (Eichmann Trial, Session 90). What is interesting is that *the same man* could employ either sort of "jargon."

*Mrs. Rosa Goldstein to the author, Jan. 29, 1986.

Since Jewish culture has been, for thousands of years, permeated by religious convictions and traditions, it is appropriate to consult these components of the culture, even when attempting to analyze the passions of secular Jews. Religiously, the culture has entertained the conviction that God has a relation to man such that His preferences express His Providential purposes. This is not astonishing for any revealed religion. Any prophet or saint or disciple would be thought of as singled out by God for the expression of God's hidden but benign long-range purposes. What is emphasized in Judaism, however, is that a whole *genos* has been so singled out, as such a vehicle. This faith is sometimes misdescribed as a species of ancient racism, but it is not, since (*a*) anyone who is willing to take the trouble to meet Halakhic requirements is eligible to "convert," which is to say to enter the *genos* as a new member in good standing, and (*b*) the rabbis have long since ruled that there are, for good or evil, no more pure races (see p. 138 above, note). Nor is the divine preference felt as damaging to other *gene* since a righteous Gentile is ruled eligible for salvation equally with a righteous Jew.* It is certainly not a license to conduct oneself less ethically toward the non-Jewish neighbor (in whom even the Amalekite comes eventually to be comprehended, as in Baba Mezia 112a), for that also would defeat the benign providential purposes.†

The Providential purpose is to recognize man (and get him to recognize himself) as capable of holiness in his physical, national, and international setting (as opposed to a purely "spiritual" setting), and to accomplish human redemption *in that setting*.[11] (The belief that man is ineligible for salvation in consequence of Adam's sin is foreign to Judaism, however central it may be to the Christian doctrine of incarnation. Judaism does not see God as holding that terrible a grudge against Adam's sons and, perhaps for that reason, has a tight and continuous grip on its cultural conviction as to the benignity of God's long-range purposes. This may also be one way of explaining why Judaism has not managed to see its own face in the mirror that Christianity has traditionally held up to it.)

In any event, Jewish thought pictures the good life (i.e., the divine vocation) for the Jewish people in human history, and not primarily

---

*"There are also righteous people among the nations of the world who do have a portion in the world to come" (Tosefta Sanhedrin 13:2). "The righteous amongst the Gentiles is as the high priest of the law" (Baba Kamma 38:a). I am grateful to Ora Hamelsdorf for the references.

†I am grateful to John Bacon for tracking down this reference.

in a supernatural, other world. This is not because Jewish thought was originally naturalistic. It is because the Jewish religious commitment *is* to history. There are no precise eschatological blueprints for history, as fundamentalist or secular millenarism has them. There is no militant wing of Judaism, committed to organizing cadres for a Jewish world takeover, as anti-Semitic imagination has it.* The story of history is pictured rather as a hidden story, for God alone to see as a whole and to unfold, and for man to enact bit by bit as the divine intent becomes clearer. Man is not supposed to take the bit in his teeth and run with it. Still, the scene where the divine purposes are carried out is thought to be the human scene, where there are many individuals, each one safely embedded in his nation. That is the situation now, and we will find that situation at the end of time too. We will find it because it is basically a good situation. God likes it that way.

That being the Jewish religious frame of reference, any live occurrence of anti-Semitism does not merely strike a raw nerve, evoking its antecedents in the long train of such incidents. It also recharges a profound theological anxiety, from which only the most pious are wholly free, an anxiety on behalf of God's purposes. And for the secularized Jew, for whom God's purposes are quite out of it, it remains a given that justice and mercy *must* be done in human history. To take the extraordinarily long view remains second nature. It is not even necessarily a conscious thing. But an urgent sense of concern for mankind, and—in the same breath and by the same token—concern for or about the Jewish people, gets manifested by the secular Jew in all kinds of ways, big and little. Both concerns have a common, theological essence. What the Holocaust struck at, then, was the system of meaning internal to Jewish culture.[12]

That being the world-historical context, German, non-German non-Jewish, and Jewish, how shall we view the alleged "complicity" of the Jewish people in their own destruction?

Hilberg, perhaps the most articulate and historically careful spokesman for this view, cites a number of evidences of Jewish complicity. They vary in scope and moral gravity. Included are fatalism about the end (Hilberg, 1985, pp. 841, 969) and mass compliance (e.g., with ghettoization) without actual force having to be used (p. 773). They further include giving administrative assistance to the Germans in

---

*This should go without saying, and would have, had I not noticed that there were more catalogue entries for *The Protocols of the Elders of Zion* in the New York Public Library, in more languages, than for any other text that I came across.

supplying lists and other information (pp. 187, 434f), and in manufacture and distribution of such instruments in the isolation of the Jewish people as yellow star armbands (p. 216). They include cooperating, often under armed threat, by self-denigrating words and gestures (pp. 456, 471). The include providing assistance in actual roundups (pp. 460, 463f). They include popular opposition to the armed resistance movements (pp. 385, 500, 503 and n. 69, p. 504). They include blindly self-deceived reliance on German information (pp. 459, 696, 1040), and blocked awareness or fatal absence of awareness (pp. 314f, 707). They include decisions by Jewish leaders to withhold information from the rank and file on misguidedly humane grounds (pp. 461, 639). They include sectarian divisions between potential resistance groups (p. 385). Included too are instances of self-aggrandizement of the leadership at the expense of the community (pp. 580, 589) or ready use of class and wealth distinctions to favor the privileged in the struggle for survival (pp. 218, 230, 262f, 439, 448f, 577, 778). Of all the accusations, the most grave concern the activity of Jewish leaders in the Selection of successive detachments of Jews for Nazi deportation to the death camps. That Jews were also put to work in the killing centers, in readying the condemned and stripping the dead, is sometimes mentioned, but less often recently, since it has somehow become common knowledge that actual concentration camp inmates were up against overwhelming force.

Let us take these charges one by one, not of course to assess the conduct of individuals (that would be a case-by-case matter, and a matter either for evidence in a court of law or for the God's-eye view), nor certainly to array on the other side the many well-attested instances of Jewish resistance at every point of the Nazi operation and from every stratum of the community. Our purpose is rather to try to see the *moral* sense of these charges, as they are applied to human behaviors of which a moral assessment is due.

Perhaps my own biases should be stated at this point. My childhood was colored by the knowledge that there was a man across the sea named Hitler, who had got under way a project "to kill us all." If he won the war, he would come over here to our walkup apartment on Park Avenue and 86th Street, and simply finish the job. Since that outcome was by no means unimaginable in Yorkville, many of my preoccupations were horizoned by the question, "Would we all behave well *when that happened?* Would we go through that furnace *in the right way?* Would we die correctly, as one should, rather than incorrectly, as one shouldn't?" It was a childish conviction with me (the conviction seems subsequently to have been shared by many adults) that one had to behave *correctly* during one's Holocaust. Courage is grace under pressure, and all that.

Our question is, then, what is the right way to act during one's Holocaust? Let us take the wrong ways alleged by Hilberg (or some of them), and consider these one by one. The reader will be the Jew, and I will be, if you please, the philosopher.

Fatalism. You are the Jew, standing somewhere on the map of Europe. A whole people, armed and effective, wants to erase you from history. The surrounding peoples, some of them also armed and effective, having some conscious relation to your place in their history, stand by and they let it happen. Fatalism, under the circumstances, strikes *me* as a form of sanity. A preliminary form, to be sure. But you may not get much beyond the preliminaries. Meantime, to be sane, you must see that this is indeed happening, and not deny it. To understand that it "is" happening is also to understand that it "will" happen. That is, there is precious little you can do to stop it. *Except,* of course, hope and expect that the Allies will at least win the war and, by dint of doing that, take you off the back burner.

Anticipatory Compliance. In the somewhat ritualized struggles between male wolves in a pack, it is sometimes found that baring the throat, or making some other gesture of anticipatory compliance, will deter the victor from moving in for the kill. Analogous gestures of disarming submission are met with in other species. The instincts to make such gestures go very deep. There are few among us who, finding ourselves to be weaker in a natural struggle (e.g., between females and males, children and parents, weaker and stronger schoolmates, subordinates and bosses), have made no gestures of anticipatory compliance.

The more ferociously it seems we are menaced, the more we may hope or reason that it is the aggressor's primitive "needs" or "fears" which must have prompted him to threaten us, and that we ought merely to redouble our efforts to allay those needs and fears. After all (in the Nazi case), the aggressor is not merely moving to tear us apart boisterously and laughingly (though he does that too). Overall, he is moving to tear us apart with moral seriousness, with enraged *accusations.* If we can only prove to him that he need not hate us, or fear us, or absolutely despise us by his own moral lights, perhaps, perhaps, he will desist in time. He will not go the whole distance.

Now, in this kind of judgment there is a mixture of animal instinct and the common sense of the species. It is no more than an extension of the judgements we make for our survival every day. (Hannah Arendt, for example, told me of having been menaced by a young mugger in an elevator. Without a second's hesitation, she told him not to be afraid, just to calm down, that he would get his money. He did, got the money, and decamped forthwith. Her survival instincts, for quick compliance, had been sound and sure, and they worked.

When I had asked her, earlier in the conversation, how she personally had managed to understand in time that the Nazis would be resistant to normal human appeals, she cited not her instincts but her *political theorist's* grasp of German culture, her educated realization that the Nazis were an element unlike any other.)

If survival is possible and desired, and escape impossible, then ordinarily this judgment (for anticipatory compliance) is the one to make. Nor is the compliance to be understood as gratuitously "anticipatory." The Nazis made no secret of the disproportionate violence of their reprisals. In these situations they always held hostages. Noncooperativeness was interpreted as active resistance and was punished in the same way, namely, by killing a disproportionate number of other Jews.* The *morality* of thus indirectly causing their deaths is unclear to me. A split-second practical judgment, hard to make in an armchair, is what is involved.

Administrative and Executive Support. This has the same basic motive as anticipatory compliance, except that often enough it is given in response to even more direct and credible threats.

Popular Opposition to Armed Resistance. This has the same motive as administrative support and anticipatory compliance.

Self-deception. As a Jew, you want to live the best life you can, in history, in the human theatre. That your values have been so patterned that the reach toward the transcendent is rerouted, as it were, toward immanence, is something of which you may or may not be consciously aware. But that patterning is shared by other members of your culture, across the spectrum from extreme orthodoxy to assimilationist humanism. Of a sudden, important numbers of your fellow actors in the human theatre, actors within other cultures but on the same stage, want you out of it. Out of it, with all that was Egypt, and with all that was not Egypt. Out of it, without a footstep left on the sandy floor. This desire, to have you out of it, gives evidence of its existence on many hands—but you persist in deceiving yourself as to the real character of these evidences.

Now it is over. You have survived, although a great many of your fellow Jews did not. You survive, having been, it seems, as horribly hated and as callously neglected or disdained by members of brother cultures as it is possible for a human being to be. You are now told

---

*For an example of the actual cost to the uninvolved of other people's resistance, see Dawidowicz (1975, p. 328). For an example of the threatened cost of noncooperation, see pp. 282ff. That such threats were incessantly carried out was made clear by eyewitness after eyewitness at the Eichmann trial. The line between active resistance and passive noncooperation was not respected by the Nazis, despite Arendt's contrary suggestion that Jews should have acted as if it would be (1964, p. 124).

that you should not have deceived yourself about this. You should have known that confiscation of goods and jobs, and concentration—the ripping out of phones, the prohibition on talking to Gentiles—all that meant that you would be ripped out of the social organism. You should have known that those were death trains, not bound for resettlement areas. You should have known that those were gas chambers, not showers.

But in fact you *did* know. Not-quite-consciously, it is charged, you knew. And there is your real moral lapse. That you did not bring it all up to consciousness. That you tampered with your fatalism. That you were therefore in bad faith. By contrast, the killers seem models of psychic transparency. They *knew* what they were about. You alone give an unpleasant opacity to this psychic terrain.

As I was penning these lines, in a museum café, two middle-aged women tried persistently to enter and take seats, having been told by the young manager that the café was closed. They did nevertheless sit down at a table, promising him that they would stay only "two minutes," and that they would order nothing. They sat surrounded by other patrons, who were finishing their cups of coffee and so on at a leisurely pace, while the staff cleaned up. I saw the thwarted young manager pause and then gather himself up for a more concerted try. He strode to the women's table and told them that he was *ordering* them out. Unmoved, they smilingly remonstrated with him. In support of the young manager, other waiters came over. A security guard was summoned and added her point. At last the two women left, to the sounds of mimicry from the staff who, from the look of them, were possibly in the arts. What the two women had not been able to believe was that—in that small, diffuse, informal community ruled by the café staff—*they were not wanted.*

For good people, the thing is the more implausible as it becomes more global. Good people have a necessary residuum of optimism that enables them, so to speak, to get their goodness done.

Such a thing is conceivable (always presupposing your goodness) only if you believe, being for example a Hassid, or a Bundist, or a Zionist, that, as Elisha said, "they that be with us are more than they that be with them" (II Kings 6:16). Membership in some such outgunning or outnumbering community, supernatural, international, or national, makes it psychologically possible to see clearly that you are not wanted in another, more restricted or eccentric community. (See Dawidowicz, 1975, chs. 12 and 13.)

But imagine that, for one reason or another, you are not able psychologically to postulate your membership in that kind of an outnumbering community. (It must be admitted that, in the 1933–1945 case, such membership would have had to have been an article of faith, not an evidence of things seen.) What would follow, from your inability to postulate such membership, would be the admission that all your good works and all your affections would come to nothing, would be kept in no human repository.

It is a central contention of this book that such an admission is radically incompatible with human goodness.

Sectarian Divisions. There were, however, partisans—people who were able to take up arms, partly because they had beliefs, political or other, that permitted them to "see," through the veil of counter-examples, "the chariot of Israel and the horsemen thereof" (II Kings 2:12). Nerved by such beliefs, they could assume the overpowering risks of combat. This was especially possible morally in situations such as prevailed in the Warsaw ghetto in April of 1943, where the older hostage population had been largely deported and there was nothing more to lose. To those who survived such a combat, it was possible briefly to know the unbelievably acrid serenity of a warrior in the defeat of his *genos*.

> I went from bunker to bunker, and after walking for hours in the [Warsaw] ghetto, I went back toward the sewers. . . . I was alone all the time. Except for that woman's voice, and a man I met as I came out of the sewers, I was alone throughout my tour of the ghetto. I didn't meet a living soul. At one point I recall feeling of a kind of peace, of serenity. I said to myself: "I'm the last Jew. I'll wait for morning, and for the Germans."*

It is, however, charged that the whole partisan movement was weakened and delayed by internal disunity. (See, for example, Hilberg [1985, p. 385], on conditions in the Vilna ghetto.) Is the requirement of partisan unity a realistic one, on the whole? It seems to me not realistic. The corrective that it would seem to be imagining is the Jewish people as a fused, unitary will, with the hands of its energetic youth on the triggers, and the bodies and minds of its elderly committed to a Gandhi-style noncooperation, at all costs.

Let us try to imagine such an organism, such a fused, unitary will. Since the thought is extremely promising for the politics of the future, from the Philippines to Poland, there is a temptation to try to read it back into the situation of the Holocaust. Certainly Gandhi himself tried to do that. An innovative political thinker like Adam Michnik, applying quasi-Gandhian principles to the Polish opposition movement, advocated changing the system from within by applying "open-

---

*Simha Rottem, "known as 'Kajik,'" interviewed in Claude Lanzmann's documentary film *Shoah* (1985, pp. 199f).

ness, truthfulness, autonomy, and trust" in direct local actions to remedy social problems created by the Communist government. What Michnik advocated began a grassroots movement that eventually gave rise to Solidarity.[13]

In the preliminary phases of the Holocaust, however, we have a situation where the whole population of a given country (whether Germany itself or a German-occupied or a puppet country) has been issued identity cards, on the basis of which alone people can go to their jobs, shop for food, ride the public tramways, use the telephone, et cetera. If Jews are to evade the identification system, they will first of all need false cards. For that alone, secrecy, deception, dependency, and mistrust are essential. The *morality* of it is also open to question, since to get such false cards one must needs endanger the whole Gentile network (assuming one can be found) that is working to produce and supply them. If there are any documentary evidences of one's existence accessible to the Germans and their helpers, evidences such as graduation certificates, medical records, employer's files, and the like, then one's failure to be present at population checks will also be visited on one's neighbors and family. If one is to be fired from one's job because of one's Jewish origin, it is for one's employer to noncooperate. One can hardly try to force the door. Or, if one does try, one can expect to be beaten to a bloody pulp and one's family shot. And so it went, for every phase of the German process of isolating, concentrating, and deporting for death the Jews of Europe. The weapon of nonviolent noncooperation is extremely interesting, and much can be hoped for from it. But in this case, the ones who had to use it were the non-Jews of Europe, on behalf of the Jews. (Where they tried to, it had some effectiveness.) Because *their* lives were still needed for something, by the Germans. Jewish lives were not needed. Love is a powerful, magical force. But it doesn't turn bullets into flowers, Zyklon B into fresh air.

If nonviolent noncooperation requires, as a precondition, that the *genos* practicing it be permitted at minimum to live, violent resistance can proceed absent such permission. It can also proceed in the atmosphere of secrecy, deception, dependency, and mistrust that the Holocaust imposed. It nevertheless must be reined in by the consideration of inevitable reprisals against the masses of nonviolent civilians. We are in the process of learning that all the fire power in the world doesn't stop a fanatical killer from destroying civilian hostages. The Jews of Europe did not have all the fire power in the world.* Where

---

*See Che Guevara's *Guerrilla Warfare* for one account of "what the guerrilla fighter needs to have" (1961, p. 17). In most cases the Jewish guerrilla fighter had not one item on Guevara's list.

they had any, they still had to wait until either there were no significant numbers of nonviolent hostages left to be slaughtered, or, for them and the hostages remaining, it had become crystal clear that death was certain in any case.

Still, it is charged, the partisans would have been more effective had there been a single, or a unified partisan movement. Of course the lack of one strikingly refuted the anti-Semites' belief in diabolical Jewish unity. But no matter. *Dis*unity is the issue now. The youthful partisan movements had their roots in prewar commitments to secular political movements, socialist, communist, or Zionist. (There were Jewish capitalists too, but they were a more sedentary lot.) Of the three, only the Zionists were peculiarly fitted to understand the problem instantly as a *Jewish* problem. But even among the Zionists, there were tactical and left/right divisions. But imagine the opposite. Imagine that there had been a single collective unconscious, a great roar in the throat of a tribe reaching for its gun. We no longer have Jewish culture, which has cultivated in its members intellect and personal diversity. We have left the plane of Jewish history, and entered instead the plane of the comic book.

As the meaning of Allied nonrescue sank in, a growing transfer of hope and energy to a looked-for Jewish nation could be observed among Jews who had not been directly affected. (See Hilberg, 1985, pp. 1047–52. Cf. also Wyman, 1984, pp. 120–23, 160–77.) It was even more striking among survivors.

> Maybe today it seems miraculous, but it was sufficient to draw a Star of David on a sheet in ink and pin it to a broomstick, and put this into the hands of two or three hundred people, every one of whom looked like a walking skeleton; this would give them a focal point and they would concentrate in a building . . . they would then refuse to leave that block.*

Looking back now, two streams can be surmised to have flowed into the hope and the energy. The one was religious. The other was political and practical. On the religious side, from time to time God—as Abraham and the prophets were well aware—has had to be reminded of His covenant, and His covenant wrested from the very ashes.[14] A Jewish state functioned as such a theological reminder. For God, and for the believer alike, it saved God's honor. On the natural level, it was the only *practical* moral that could possibly be drawn. That Jews

---

*Testimony of Aaron Hoter-Yishai of the Jewish Brigade, Eichmann Trial, 73rd Session.

did unite, at least sufficiently to put that lesson into effect three years after the smokestacks shut down at Auschwitz, rather does show a "unity of the partisans" that is—considering the vital disunities characteristic of Jewish culture—itself almost unearthly.

If the lesson about practicality isn't clear, it should on reflection be clear enough that an Israel on the map in 1939 would have been the only state in the world willing to let in the refugees while the Nazis were still allowing emigration, and willing to bomb the crematoria once they were in operation.[15] But one did not have to be a postwar Jew to draw lessons of this kind from the holocausts that have befallen stateless persons. Solzhenitsyn, trying to account for the extraordinary brutality with which Russian POWs were treated by their Nazi captors, notes that the Soviet government was not making use of any of the accepted intergovernmental means to negotiate for their safety (1974–78, 1:219), and that it had essentially abandoned them, arresting any who returned (pp. 237–43). So the Russian POWs, whom the Nazis gassed and shot in their millions, were in the practical condition of stateless persons. In a similar vein, Ambassador Morgenthau tries to explain why the xenophobic Turks only deported Greeks, while they massacred Armenians. "The Turks showed this greater consideration not from any motive of pity. The Greeks, unlike the Armenians, had a government which was vitally interested in their welfare" (Morgenthau, 1918, p. 325).

In sum, the partisans were united sufficiently, at least for the only purpose they found that was clearly practical and culturally meaningful.

Self-Aggrandizement, Corruption, Class Privilege. "The world," Léo Bronstein used to say, "prefers a murderer to a petty-petty thief," indicating as he said so the aesthetically plausible but morally abysmal "purity" of the murderer.[16] We should perhaps take some care not to share the world's preference. But here again, the context has to be borne in mind for the purpose of a moral analysis. If what you "buy" with your bribe or payment to the extortionist is sufficient food for your own child, while another child starves, and the *fair* result would be that both children got to be equally malnourished, and you have greater natural affection for your own child than for another's—and there is no actual and coherent army of the beleaguered Jews, allocating strictly equal rations and duties, able to enforce its orders and to deliver release from the present state of nature—why, then the claims of natural affection do have some natural right.

It is to be remembered that the Nazi machinery had already broken up the old organizational lines of traditional Jewry and, more significantly, had broken Jewish communication lines with the outside communities, of other Jews and of non-Jews. (This included communication through participation in the wider work of the world, communication by speaking, writing, telephoning, use of public transportation, and the like). Concomitantly, "Jewish Councils" were formed at gunpoint. In spirit and purpose, these were not "Jewish" and they were not "councils." They were formed as part of the German destruction process, to distribute the inadequate rations and laughable medical provisions to terrified people, recently rendered jobless and crowded into unfamiliar, often walled-off, concentration areas for Jews. The "Jewish Councils" were also to distribute the work cards that were the tormented community's only means of staving off deportation, and to transmit the orders by which that community could learn what its kidnappers wanted of it. We have gone over these points, and also the point that at every stage noncooperation was interpreted as active resistance and was met by overwhelming force. In these circumstances, personal corruption was probably a sign of some kind of natural health. The organism was fighting back—not by fair means but by any means available. ("Prisoner's dilemma" reasoning doesn't apply here. All the prisoners were going to be killed whatever they did.)

However, there were paths open to those who wanted to escape personal corruption—and we have looked down some of them. There were the partisan groups, dedicated to a political redemption, and you could join them if you were young and/or able bodied, and if you had no more family being held hostage. There were also the pious, which only a certain prior acculturation would have placed you among, and for them it was rabbinically forbidden to save your son's life if the life of another's son would be forfeited in consequence.[17]

Both kinds of self-exemption from corruption were *willed* departures from a real and prevailing state of nature, in the light of an unseen "world to come." But even if you were in a position to make such metaphysical wagers, they could not be made at every juncture. If a crust of stolen bread came into your palm, presumably you would want to share it with your best buddy, not crumb it into equal bits for the whole barracks. (Cf. Primo Levi's "Last Christmas of the War," 1986.) And given the metaphysical wager, on the coming classless society, or Zion, or God, there could not be Kantian fairness in getting there. If the biological *genos* in whatever future form it would take needed the young and the able, and if God needed whoever best served His Providential purposes, then, even from a standpoint of the "world to come," there was favoritism. There was a selection.

It is not clear to me that the moment-to-moment selection that natural affection performs in favor of those whom it loves is *morally* worse.

Selection. The gravest of the accusations leveled against the so-called Jewish Councils is that, at German gunpoint, they made the actual selections of those who were to be deported from the slower death of the German-made ghettos to the quicker death of the killing centers. Acting in this way, some of them saved some of their own relatives; some saved some of those who were already privileged; some saved groups they thought politically more vital; some saved, or tried to save, some of the children; some (but by no means all) saved themselves. Many who participated in the Selections withheld from the deportees the information or educated guesses they possessed as to what "resettlement in the East" really meant.

It seems to me that the moral objections taken here fail fully to picture the nature and scale of this emergency. Rabbinic casuistry was not unfamiliar with the situation of a whole community taken hostage. The traditional rulings had been to the effect that a *guilty* fugitive may be surrendered by such a community if he is demanded by name (thus absolving the community of the moral taint of making a selection among the innocents). In a still more extreme case, even an innocent fugitive who is named may be surrendered if, failing to surrender him, his death and the community's would otherwise be certain. But if there is any doubt as to the fatality of the outcome, and/or it is demanded of the community that it make a selection among innocents, then, the rabbis ruled, the whole community must rather perish. (See Kirschner, 1985, pp. 76ff, and Dawidowicz, 1975, pp. 284f.)

Now let us alter the picture that the rabbis had in view. We no longer have one town, say third-century Lydda threatened by the Romans, or a twelfth-century legally imposed "Jewish Quarter" in the Maghreb, threatened by the Arabs. Without needing to suppose that every "Jewish Council" member participating in a Selection saw clearly the scope of the German program, it will be admitted that what could be seen was, in its thoroughness, rapacity, and brutal orderliness, like nothing that had ever been seen or heard of before. If the "Jewish Council" member was not thinking, "they are going to kill us all," he was at least trying hard *not* to think that.

What were his options? He could save his own honor—but only by suicide. Noncooperation would bring down the full force of the Holocaust on his family and neighbors forthwith. Suicide is honorable—for a Stoic. But it is not usually honorable in Jewish religious thought. It is not even religiously honorable for one individual to offer his life for another single individual, since each person's life is considered to be his on trust, not a personal possession to be disposed of at will. God is not considered to allow any individual to decide that his own life is less valuable than another's (Kirschner,

1985, pp. 119ff). According to Adin Steinsaltz, the scholar was expected to try to come closer than the common man to a standard of ideal equality in the distribution of survival chances. Thus a scholar would be expected to divide his water ration in half, even where neither traveler could survive on the ration thus divided. But even the scholar is apparently not expected simply to hand his entire ratio of water over to the other traveler (Steinsaltz, 1976, pp. 203f). So the principle that one has a religious responsibility to safeguard one's own life is preserved, even in this partial exception.

In sum, the honor that is saved by suicide is pagan honor, not honor as it is understood in the system of meaning internal to Jewish culture. Furthermore, as witness after witness testified in the Eichmann trial, as memoirists and historians have alike recorded, survival was felt to be an obligation in that realm of the Jewish psyche where history and the supernatural "world to come" are indistinguishable. It was felt to be an obligation in the Kantian sense. It overrode personal inclination. The duty was twofold: to preserve some remnant of the biological *genos* considered as a divine vehicle, and to preserve the memory, incorporating the latter into human memory itself, also considered as a divine vehicle.*

Now, considering that no escape routes were provided, that the program of liquidation was encompassing and relentless, *it was clear that survival would be an accident.* Whoever could survive, however he could, had however a twofold obligation to do so. He was not to live, in the collapse of his affections and his hopes, because it felt good. He was not to keep a diary, keep his memories intact, be prepared to tell and retell the story, because it was a great pleasure to do so. Rather, he was to do all that because it was the only appropriate rejoinder to a program of erasing his *genos* from what *both he and his liquidators* understood to be world history. (It cannot be said that the Nazis ignored the big picture. It cannot be said that the Jews were, by acculturated temperament, indifferent to it.)

If I am still, according to our earlier literary conceit, the philosopher, and the reader is still the Jew, the reader might at this

---

*"In December 1941, when the German police entered the Riga ghetto to round up the old and sick Jews, Simon Dubnow, the venerable Jewish historian, was said to have called out as he was being taken away: 'Brothers, write down everything you see and hear. Keep a record of it all'" (Dawidowicz, 1981, p. 125). Cf. the testimony of Avraham Aviel, about his thoughts prior to a mass shooting: "Q. What did mother say?" "A. She said, 'Say Shamah Yisrael—die as Jews.' . . . I repeated the words after her but I had inner resistance. . . . Because my thoughts—my thought was always: 'One must survive—*überleben*— . . . and tell what happened'" (Eichmann Trial, 29th Session).

point want to ask me, indignantly: "Are you recommending that we take part in a *Selection?*" I am not recommending anything, since my recommendations would presuppose that you have been placed, ethically, culturally, and physically, in a genocidal situation. But, if you are put in a genocidal situation, genocidal without remainder, which heaven forfend, then yes, I am recommending that you take part in Selections. It may be that not everyone selected will actually be killed. Some may be used for slave labor and will somehow survive the war. It may be that not everyone whose Selection is thus postponed will eventually be rounded up and deported. It may be that some will outlast the Final Solution, one way or another. What is virtually certain is that your whole community will be machine-gunned to death in your hundreds of thousands tomorrow morning if you do not "voluntarily" participate. Your neighbors will look on. There are no forests, or, if there are forests, the young who morally *can* get there—perhaps because they have no more families to suffer reprisals—will in large numbers be killed anyway, as a result of peasant informers, or by the bullets of non-Jewish partisans. And your old and your infants cannot make their way to forests. To cooperate in Selections, is—for the *genos* as a whole—to stall. Yes, cooperate. Yes, stall. Do what they tell you. Whoever survives, will survive by accident.

There are those who study Zen Buddhism in order to learn how, appropriately, to peel a potato, or how, appropriately, to succor the homeless. There is also a minutely appropriate way to undergo one's Holocaust. The appropriate way is to survive it, or to try to.

We are of course not trying to find out about the Holocaust victims, or about any other group of people similarly picked up at random (that is to say, picked up without regard to their wishes), how many were sinners, how many saints, how many heroes, sung and unsung, and how all that interesting stuff is to be measured. We were simply trying to figure out whether, in any sense that is morally intelligible, these victims of genocide were in actual complicity with it. We have not found that they were, and can proceed therefore to the last obscuring phase of the discussion of the Nazi: his banality.

But perhaps enough has been said. We see that this was an original happening. One would have to be in quite an extraordinary condition and frame of mind, historical and psychological, to help it go through. We see that it is the purest form of genocide on record. The time has come to enter that frame of mind, that particular experiment with evil.

CHAPTER SEVEN

Thinking Like a Nazi

TO GET INTO a Nazi's head is not difficult—is easy in fact. But what is difficult is to get into that head from the standpoint of good and evil. For a Nazi is, to hear him tell it at least, beyond good and evil. This is not to say that the Nazi doesn't have his "higher" conception of good and evil. But since his higher conception is wrong, absolutely wrong, is lower, much lower, what must be found is the fact of his astigmatism, superimposed on the fact—for we must suppose it a fact—of his underlying, normal vision. We must suppose that a fact. Otherwise he floats indeed "beyond good and evil"—and we have lost him. Losing him, we have lost our moral bearings as well.

The Nazi, we must suppose, knew all along that he was in the wrong. But *how* could he have known it? He was at most a small cell in a vastly heaving social organism, a small cell in a Leviathan shot through with malignancy. He was ordinary. Oh, ordinary as hell; the mail he carried contained blueprints for gas vans, recipes (failed, as it happens) for mass sterilizations, phrenological disquisitions on Jewish skulls, but—considered strictly in his character as mailman—he was common as all get out. The most one can object to is a bit of vulgarity, and who among us, after all—excepting the strengthless dead who are acquiring the patina of our age—is not just a wee *bit* nouveau?

How can an ordinary cancer cell, in an ordinary tumorous Leviathan, *know* that it is unhealthy? It's impossible. Our Nazi also cannot know. He is softly determined . . . not to know.

There are in some quarters cases being made out of a connection between such tracts as Martin Luther's *The Jews and Their Lies* and the Nazi's general store of beliefs. Or a connection between, say, *The Protocols of the Elders of Zion*, the Russian turn-of-the-century forgery, and the Nazi's supposedly good-faith horror at what he believed was a Jewish conspiracy to take over the world and thereafter make the world perfectly terrible. But—although some would deny, or deny with qualifications, and some would affirm, that connection—in truth the connection, if it existed, wouldn't mark off the Nazi as anyone special. Who is or can be more ordinary than an anti-Semite? Who, outside of certain circles in New York, would think anything of him? What an anti-Semite is is so ordinary that it is embarrassing to make a scene over it. Please. If you can't behave yourself at a dinner party, then let's not go. Surely one can't call *this* the ground of his or anyone's *evil?* The very thought is a forced thought. Let's not force a thought. Why not drop it? Look—if you don't *drop* it—people are starting to go home early.

On the other hand, if by any chance the Nazi had not been ordinary, if he had been deeply evil, evil with commitment, it is just possible he would have acted a no different part than the one he did act. He would have acted identically to what we know about him, in the substance and in the style. How is one to disentangle his evil from his ordinariness, his mask from the thing that it covered?

What is evil, anyway? What is the deep down dark thing? Are we not all somehow implicated in what the Nazi is or was or did, just as the most unctuously ecumenical evasions would like to have us become? Is it not, after all, just impossible to describe the boundaries of the Nazi, in such a way as to take in *only him?* We need not turn the whole question over to the poets and the sermonizers, without at least having a go at it, in the terms we have so far found serviceable.

For one thing, we can find the Nazi committed to a program for the unfolding of his life that—in the senses here meant—isn't good and can't be good, at first and minimally because it isn't reasonable. Let us get clearer on this point, since the cultural literacy of many institutionally well-placed and/or influential Nazis is a puzzling aspect of their penumbra. Signing over one's overall ability and liberty to evaluate all consequential decisions that one will make in the future, signing over all this by dint of an oath of loyalty to a Leader, or by dint of blind submission to those who have taken such an oath, isn't reasonable. No one, doing that, can suppose that the essential gesture of goodness, the gesture of keeping hold of the sense-making threads of one's life, can be maintained. No, goodness ends right there, because sense-making ends right there.

It's no good taking the road of psychoanalysis here, to avoid becoming judgmental. Alice Miller, for example, will compare such a transfer of will and ego to the strategic transfer of identity-conferring power that a child may make with an arbitrary and bullying parent, making that transfer in exchange for the father's approval. But the child's action is far more preservative of his sense-making capacities than is the Nazi's. Having said to the father, "You decide what to call me, and what I ought to do," the child can still get a good view of his father's weaknesses. In noting and evaluating how the mother or other siblings get treated by the father, and how family disputes or problems get settled by the father, the child gets a pretty good notion of where fairness is being jettisoned and how the compensations are being apportioned. Evidently the soul is bartered by the small prisoner. But it is not forfeited absolutely. The child knows he is growing, will reach his full height, will break away to a measure of autonomy, financial, political, religious, and emotional. His hostage condition is not eternal, though his rage may sometimes make it feel that way.

Nobody—putting aside the comatose and those who are asleep—is *entirely* dominated by his "unconscious." A negotiation is constantly afoot between felt pressures from the unresolved conflicts and epistemic deficits of the past on the one hand, and the articulate summonses of everyday realism where, on a daily basis, we are called on to cope with the present by assessing it fairly. This incessant negotiation isn't purposeless. Far from it. One buys time; one safeguards hope; one essays manageable conflicts in the hopes of winning one's spurs and then going on to larger things. If one is not in unbearable physical pain, this sort of thing—a negotiation—is ordinarily possible even in jail, for little things, for self-respect. It's a four-way negotiation at least: between (1) the realistic or everyday self, (2) the unrealistic or unresolved self, and (3) and (4), the elements of both in the environment.

So the Nazi, transferring his entire will and decision-making autonomy to the Leader, has done something equivalent to a renunciation of his whole personal power of negotiation. If he holds fast to the implications for his future conduct contained in this agreement, his condition is considerably worse than that of a prostitute or of any sellout whom we have considered so far. The prostitute only sells her physical intimacy. The sellout only barters his integrity in the performance of a skilled institutional function. By contrast, the Nazi is in an extraordinary situation, however ordinary the mask it wears may look.

We do not know if there is a God. We do not know if there is life after death. We do not know how history will come out, or if it will. We do not really know what's around the next corner. What we do know is that we can hold on to a continuous trying to make sense of the purposes that have announced themselves as intimately important in our own lives—or we can drop it, drop the trying. What the Nazi has done, first of all but momentously, is drop the trying. He can pick it up again, as Oskar Schindler did,[1] but he has done something large. Let there be no mistake about that.

But what about the grandiose, world-historical promises that the future would vindicate the moment of transferred will and decision making? Can we fairly abstract the Nazi from the special climate of Germanic speculative musings in which he was swept along? Here is a useful restatement of that speculative tendency, from Otto Ohlendorf, Doctor of Jurisprudence and Commander of Einsatzgruppe D, responsible for 90,000 deaths.

> My generation, when it became aware of the social conditions around it, found this spiritual, religious, political, and social decay having a deep effect. There were no values for them which were not immediately attacked and opposed by different groups. Thirty or more parties fought for power in the state. . . . This generation had become too realistic in their suffering to believe that by fixing their eyes at the beyond they would find the moral and social basis for their existence at this period of history. . . . Also the dependence of every individual in the constitution and condition of the society, the nation, and the state in which he lived was far too obvious for this generation not to look for ways and means to replace the changing rule of group interests by an order which was based on the concept of totality in relation to every single individual regardless of his social status. In National Socialism we saw this idea.*

Right. Under the Weimar Constitution, the parties from left to right had been apparently impotent to control catastrophic inflation and unemployment. These conditions were popularly traced to imperial losses and harshly imposed reparations spelled out in the 1919 Versailles Treaty, after a military defeat and surrender that the average German patriot would come inaccurately to associate with the forces of post-Wilhelmine democracy.[2] If the popular view had inaccuracies, the popular view generally does. So far we see nothing exceptional.

More philosophically, Ohlendorf had learned what we can learn from Hegel and others, that no human being lives alone or is free alone, abstracted from an institutional framework and base. We learn, too, from Hegel that institutions, however enlightened, can't function

---

*Final Statement of Defendant Ohlendorf, *Nuernberg Military Tribunals*, Case No. 9, "The Einsatzgruppen Case," *The United States of America Against Otto Ohlendorf et al.*, vol. 4, p. 385. For more on Ohlendorf, see Hilberg (1985, pp. 285f).

unless, in their shape and values, they fit the experience of the people that is supposed to accept them. So the merit of institutions can't be abstracted from the historical context.

What else does the culture permit us to have learned and therefore to "know"? We know from Fichte, from Nietzsche, from the proceeds of eighteenth- and nineteenth-century speculative musings, that there is or might be such a thing as the genius of a people, just as there is or might be such a thing as the eclipse of a people. From Schopenhauer and from certain post-Darwinian patriots we learned that the flourishing of an organism or a collectivity has also its ruthless side, and that something like natural selection works to further it or to snuff it out. Success succeeds. Failure fails. Man is a part of nature. One cannot fight the great mother, nature, and win. One must instead make common cause with the instinctual drives as they make of the individual a healthy cell in the social organism.[3] Let us take all that as true enough, or true *depending on how one takes it,* and what one is supposed to mean by it. One can recognize analogues of all these eclectic notions in the self-improvement movements of the present hour.

It doesn't sound so terrible, taken bit by bit. The least one can say about it is that it includes distillates from particular experiences of Western history, distilled by very intelligent people like Jean-Jacques Rousseau and Carl Jung, people trained to think in some of the Western manners. If one were to personify Western culture, seeing it as a kind of child, and if one were to ask the child at dusk, when its pet owl of Minerva had taken flight, what it had learned that day, and the child were to answer with some such lines as those in the paragraph just above, one would feel inclined to pat the child on its shining curls and tell it that it had been a good child, that it had had a "learning experience" today, that doubtless it would have another, different one tomorrow.

Are notions like these, however compounded, sufficient to explain the Nazi commitment? Let us compare these notions, which make up fragments of the Nazi *rationale,* with some of the tendencies of the commitment viewed as a practice, and a way of being practical.

In the 1984 posthumous study by military historian Ronald Lewin, *Hitler's Mistakes,* Lewin sifts through the Leader's policies and lifts out some giant blunders of which these four are representative: (1) in what was to be a Thousand-Year Reich, where all power flowed from the Leader's will, no provision was made for a successor (pp. 39f); (2) in what was to be a far-flung empire, no benefits of any kind were to be extended to the conquered populations (pp. 35ff, 127f); (3) in a complex, military-economic enterprise of aggression and domination, free research was stifled and with it crucial help from the quarter of science and technology, whether Jewish or other (pp. 45–50, 55ff); (4) in every sector of administration, power was exercised by competing and mutually corrupting persons who substituted life-and-death struggle and intrigue for the rule of law, of principles, and of structures functionally responsive to obvious needs (chs. 4 and 6).

Now it seems to me that one can make no greater blunders than these four, especially if one is trying to run the world, and put one's own people with their national genius on top of the job. If one looks at the hare and the deer, and other Felix Salten examples from the Nazi rhetorical bestiary, one finds no blunders like these. The hare and the deer could tell Nazis a thing or two about living and letting live, and functional specialization. Similarly, and closer to home, if one looks into the schoolyard, one finds no instances of successful dominance that go on for long years on the basis of all take, no give.

Now if one takes in hand and leafs through the document that summed up Nazi fantasies about the group Nazism was designed to wipe out, the document called *Protocols of the Elders of Zion*, one finds in it the same astonishing formulas for flunking all the tests history could conceivably give a human *genos*. Had they been real Israelites, these fictional "elders of Zion," pictured in the *Protocols* as a tightly controlled, ancient, and hereditary secret society dedicated to undermining all the instruments of culture and vitality in the world so as to take it over, and dedicated to nothing else, would have undoubtedly perished together in a bunker some three thousand years ago. What rather takes one aback is that this sort of collective dementia praecox was attributed by the Nazis to what is by any objective measure one of the more successful of the human cultures. Instant success may be accidentally compatible with pervasive delusions. Long-term cultural success is not thus compatible—especially if the culture is not in a fortunate situation environmentally. A culture that is able to cope with successive bouts of adversity must be sufficiently free and reasonable to receive continuous updates about what's out there, must be sufficiently flexible and diverse to contain many kinds of suitable adaptations, must be willing to revise both ends and means within the stabilities of a vast and spacious framework of values and beliefs. If the Darwinian theory has any lessons for human history at all, they must be lessons of that sort.

Is it possible honestly to take another group's cultural success and so heavily misconstrue it? Is it possible honestly to suppose that one can get cultural success of one's own on the pattern of this misconstruing?

What is really being thought here? Is it a "theological" thought, dipped into the hatred that was originally supposed to have the deity's approval, even if God's personality was no longer being invoked in the old style by the Nazi? Is it a thought of the insulted nation, the ego writ large, whose coming into self-awareness in 1807 coincided with a defeat from a Corsican Frenchman whose Enlightenment values got accordingly discredited in the national upsurge that followed? Is it a Romantic thought, that genius—whether of the artist or of the race—knows no laws but those of its own self-expression? Is it a biologic thought, that culture is entirely a genetic product, and that one genetic product triumphs over another by tooth and by claw? What sort of a thought is it? The Nazi is not a robot after all. If we are to be enjoined by the Sunday moralist to identify with him and to find him in ourselves, we must find him there thinking. Many species show evidence of the ability to think, and not merely to respond to innate programming. And our species can think too.

What is he thinking? Let us take the possibilities listed above and run through them, starting with the eugenic kind of thought and finishing with the theological. If it is biological thinking that is abroad with him, it is certainly not a physical anthropology of the usual kind. Italians are not Nords. They are not necessarily blond. Yet they, blond and brunette, are to be allies in the Nordic conquest of the world, while only the blond Poles are to be so included. Japanese are not Aryans at all, yet they are to get honorary racial upgrading. Arabs are not non-Semites, yet they are to be included as allies in a racially based war against the Jews. Even if one were the kind of Galtonian who took every cultural variation to be passed along in the gemmules, the Nazi's tolerance of non-Nordic, non-Aryan strains suggests an inconsistency in the theory. We must not suppose the Nazi incapable of consistency. He is a reasoning being, just as we ourselves are.

What seems to be happening is that the Nazi is carrying through on important preferences and disvaluings on grounds that are not strictly or consistently racial. But let us reconcile the inconsistencies that are apparently at work here, without more ado. In the Romantic conception of nature, which the Nazi shares, the same vital principle, whether called the will to life or the will to power or described as unconscious instinctual drives, is thought to run all through nature from the molecular to the spiritual level and back again. What might be called "race" at the biological level would be viewed in "the will" as the very same substance, only a more complex extrusion of it. So, when the Nazi is in doubt as to how he shall sort out the human competitors for the scarce goods of nature, sort out who shall live and who shall die, that is, it will be relevant for him to consider their cultural and strategic affiliations, since these will show in a different aspect the same force of nature that he thinks flows also through the blood.

What is doubtless meant by "race" in the Nazi's worldview is finally *competitive force of nature*, at whatever level the force is found. So it is perfectly logical for the Nazi to rank a convert to Judaism, or a half-Jew who practices the religion, as a "racial" Jew in the full *Nazi* sense. What the Nazi surely means here is that the convert to Judaism, or the Jewishly identified half-Jew, has thrown his natural forces behind the *Jewish life force*, which has been identified by the Nazi as a competitor in a universal struggle for life and for dominance.

So, as it turns out, the Nazi *is* thinking, about biology and its social applications. We may not share his precise brand of vitalism, but we can certainly find it familiar. Even in the English-speaking world, we do find it familiar. We can pick up shards of it from Carlyle, Dickens, and others, great round amphoras from D. H. Lawrence, and mixed bits from Freud in the James Strachey translation.

Now let us consider, and try to make thinkable sense of, his Romanticism. How is it that he can justify to himself bookburning and the crushing of intellectuals' skulls on the ostensible ground that the genius of a people knows no laws but those issuing out of its own expressive powers? Surely there is a great difference, obvious since Plato at least (*Republic*, paras. 342–52), between brute power (the power to smash an hourglass, say), and functional power (the power to make the hourglass). Can our Nazi have honestly believed that one could produce more complex timepieces, or more Goethes and Hegels, by turning all power straight over to the brutes? How can one account for this apparent inadequacy in the Nazi doctrine, one that only a little reflection would have served to disclose? What was our Romantic Nazi *thinking*? (We put aside for the nonce the question of what he was feeling. Any of us, who are not too far gone down the road to sainthood, can feel the feelings. Let us try now to find the thoughts.)

Not every skull was going to be crushed, not every victorious athlete sent to Dachau, not every author or philosopher placed on the Nazi Index. Obviously, our Nazi book-lover, music-lover, composer, or free spirit did not believe that his own skull was going to be crushed, nor that no grass *of his* would grow where the horsemen passed. What then is the explanation for a certain parsimony about the seeds of future growth in the nation? Is it simply a blinkered selfishness that looked not to the future? But the whole Nazi focus was on the future. People were being called to fight and to die for that future. How do you thoughtfully aim at a creative future by undermining the very conditions that built a creative past?

The answer is that the Nazi thought to take the vital force that we sometimes call "creativity" under his human direction. Knowing it to be a great, even at times a decisive force in human affairs, he proposed to control the spigots, turning them *on* and *off*. His belief was that the creative force itself would not abate in any event, but that preeminence in creativity would belong to whoever got control of the force's stoppage and release, and constructed the channels through which it would flow. We see, now that we have looked at it more closely, that this is in a certain sense of the terms an "optimistic" belief, and even a "selfless" one. At any rate, creativity is believed by the cultured Nazi to be both inexhaustible and impersonal. Believing this, he could contemplate whole creative sectors being stoppered, if need be his own included, and yet keep his faith in a deathless flow of energy from unconscious sources. The Nazi believed he had drunk of a water that quenches all thirst.

What about the Nazi as insulted nationalist? Is there anything that runs contrary to patriotism in his delivery of the reins of his government and its administration to people who despised the Enlightenment ideals of equality under the law, world fraternity, and the opening of careers impartially to talents? On its face, it would seem so, since one thereby deprives the nation of consistent and predictable procedures, of the opportunity to justify its laws by reasoned argument, and of the services of a good many of its best men and women.[4]

In *Hitler's Mistakes* Lewin makes out a plausible case for the defeat of Nazi Germany as a direct consequence of its having assumed these characteristics. If, following Lewin again, one adds to these blunders the blunderbuss project of getting a world empire going without making any provisions for an orderly succession, and without tendering any compensatory benefits to the governed, then one would seem to be looking at a nation careening full tilt toward disaster. How can anyone claim to be a reader of the script of "history," any kind of a reader, any kind of a script, and subscribe to such a course out of *patriotism*—insulted or not?

I suspect that the answer here is similar to the answer to our previous question. The Nazi believed that national preeminence extruded from unquenchable natural sources of vital energy. Thus, one could stopper the flow here or there domestically, damn up the spring waters of other nations, and still leave the natural forces themselves to surge unabated. To unshackle the governing art from the constraints of reason was seen by the Nazi as a boon to the nation. He was releasing vital force from repression and sublimation, unbinding instinct; he was letting *it* happen. The Nazi believed that his party would promote a great adventure in explosive vitality, one that would work to the lasting invigoration of his *genos*, if not now then sooner or later.

If we can now see better that the Nazi world-intuition has its own consistency, we also see more clearly that it is something of a *willed* view. The evidence does not compel anyone to take up such a hypothesis. There is even countervailing evidence. The Nazi has decided to take it up. But not arbitrarily. He has something further in view. At the sacrifice of his day-to-day powers of negotiation, which he has turned over to the Leader, he marches in a certain direction. Where does he *think* he is marching?

Let us on to the spiritual font of the Nazi, his Jew-hatred. After all, it seems, not everything in the Nazi's naturalism was assigned equal value, even though all things may be said to be equal in the sight of nature. Some of the things thrown up by the course of nature and history are considered purer by the Nazi, closer to his ideal of beauty and health. Other things—and Jewish things especially—are viewed by him as toxic, and ugly in themselves. We place the Nazi as a man who lived to the full the logic of his hatred. But where there is hatred, there is also love, or anyway there are positive preferences, around which the boundaries of hatred can be drawn. If he is a great hater, our Nazi is also, by his own lights, a great idealist. What ideal, or divinity, does he worship, and how does that god make his will felt? Where does the Jew come into it.?

Let us first sum up the natural or the worldly elements that compose the Nazi as thinker, and that he must lay on the altar of something that goes beyond thought. His thought comprises a vitalism that supposes the same life force to run differently combined through the whole of nature, from its simplest particle to its most complex works of human art. This life force cannot ever, he supposes, be extinguished. A good long ride on its crest is given to the people that devote themselves to tapping their own sources of it, ruthlessly damning any stream from alien peoples, and making short shrift of concerns unconnected to instinctual springs.

Since the sum total of these beliefs does not fully satisfy epistemic requirements of explanatory adequacy and consistency, the believer has two choices: either keep revising his views as new evidence comes in (and that option will take him out of the Nazi party pretty quick), or lay the whole compound of beliefs about nature on the altar of *something* transcendent of human judgment, *something* that will find these beliefs acceptable. What kind of a god would want them?

A god only passingly interested in human intelligence, or intelligent choice. A god unconcerned with fairness, in the short or the long run. A god who makes no overfine distinctions between species of power, functional or brute. It's all one. Strength is strength, says this diety. Don't bother me with your precious distinctions. A god unaware of the personal essence of the individual, only taking note of those types who attach their purposes to the largest waves of natural force.

There is a question, in the long history of the West, about whether or not God exists. It is not a question about the existence of *this* god. Nobody could care deeply whether this god exists or not. This god cannot succor the weak, reward the righteous, give to human affections the supports beyond themselves that they often seem to require. He cannot make anything better than it was. He cannot deliver Daniel. He brooks no appeal.

Jewish culture can fairly be considered the mother of a concept of God about whose existence "both in the understanding and in reality" one can care. And Jewish culture is a culture toward which the Christian daughter cultures have long entertained powerfully ambivalent daughterly feelings. It seems that ambivalent Christians could be made to remember their "racial" roots, in the special sense of race here meant, and partly by these means flattered and bullied into sufficient acquiescence in the eclipse of the God-whose-existence-matters. If all the church-affiliated people on whose acquiescence the Nazi counted had been *un*ambivalent Christians, Nazism could not have lasted a day.

But what can a committed Nazi do with people whose whole culture is based on the notion of a God about whose existence one can care, whether these people vote "yes" on the question of that God's existence, or simply continue to group themselves around patterns of behavior, value, and expectation that originated in what was culturally believed to be a covenant with such a God? People like that, with their God-whose-existence-matters, are radically inimical to the people whose postulated divinity is the patron of indiscriminate and impersonal force. Those two deities *must* come to blows. The very nature of history is at stake in this clash.

But does the Nazi really believe in his god? Well, everyone's belief in his deity is in principle falsifiable. The threshhold at which belief stops varies with each individual, sometimes with different phases of the same individual's life. With some, belief is locked so deep in the heart that it will need extraordinarily improbable circumstances to pry it loose. With others, an external shock, or the awareness of a particular wager lost, can undo the belief.

At that point, when the blind favor of the god of fate is apparently withdrawn, or when the very concept of such blind favor evaporates, the Leader stands exposed as what he was all along: mortal and fallible. If, despite his magic eyes, the Leader has been fallible at every step, misguided all along, a "madman," as the Nazi will say now, then what is to be said about the Nazi's decision to transfer his will and

future decisions of consequence to the Leader? What is to be said of
the moment that made him a Nazi?

> I wasn't like those among the S.S. who laughed on hearing my death
> sentence. I went rigid with fear. In my condemned cell I began to try and
> sum up my life. I found I suddenly came back to the Ten Command-
> ments   —yes these were the rules men had made so that they could
> live together, but which my people . . . had forgotten.*

---

*From an interview with "S2," former concentration camp official "serving a 'mul-
tiple' life sentence," quoted in Dicks (1972, p. 105).

EPILOGUE

HAD THEY BEEN real men and women, all the pure types of evildoer here depicted would likely have claimed that they were not free agents at all, hence on that score that they were not being fairly shown as pure types. Their excuses would have gone on to the effect that they had become victims of unfair persuasion, whether exercised by certain individuals on them or—as in the case of the Nazi—diffused through a whole culture. What therefore remains to be said here, in connection with one's vulnerability to evil, is that the ideal story that one may try to live can become a *remote* ideal rather early, for reasons that are not clearly one's own fault, but with the consequence that one becomes peculiarly vulnerable to types and degrees of unfair persuasion.

At that point, one's goodness becomes a more obviously relative thing, relative to the confusion and disarray of the life then being lived, and it consists mainly in trying to *find one's way back* to the story that one had originally meant to live. In these circumstances, moral default would consist in dropping the Ariadne's thread that could lead one *out* of the maze that one had got into. And unfair persuasion to do wrong would work chiefly by taking advantage of one's sense that one had lost the way back to one's story, and would exercise its unwarranted control over one's mind by suggesting false leads and irrelevant turns of the plot.

We are in truth much more delicate and high-strung creatures than many of our present-day psychologies will allow. Much has been made in our current psychologies and their therapeutic applications of the power and influence of "the unconscious" over our interpretations. Evidently, therapies that subjugate the conscious powers of judgment to the unconscious, and tell the former that the cure must come from the latter, are therapies that have a limited faith in the conscious mind's powers to detect what is true. They are therefore not necessarily going to be able to tell the difference between a spiritual crisis and a crisis of some other kind. When a crisis is neither specifically somatic, nor precipitated by what Edgar Allan Poe calls "unmerciful disaster," but is spiritual, what happens is that the devices of self-interpretation and of culturewide interpretation that the seeker had been able to use up to that time now no longer seem to him or her *true*. The spiritual crisis arises out of the individual's irresistible and involuntary revolt against what he or she feels to be false. And it is at such times that the unfair persuader gets an especially favorable opportunity.

A single sensed untruth, however briefly sensed, however apparently trivial or peripheral to everyday concerns, can, if it is not faced and dealt with *as such*, generate a long succession of distorted reactions in the feeling life and the conceptual life of the individual. The trouble is not only that, as Aristotle said, "All men by nature desire to know" (*Metaphysics* 980). The trouble is, rather, that all men, women, and children by nature do know quite a good deal, at least within the purview of their everyday experience. The trouble is, they do not live a lie comfortably.

For many kinds of reasons—filial piety, fear, and concern for social survival, loyalty and affection toward elders and companions, puzzlement about what to do with anomalous information—some of what is thus primitively known must be discounted, prematurely rationalized away, put out of mind. I do not refer here to any elaborate hypothetical mechanism of denial, repression, and projection, though there may at times be some such mechanism at work. The item that can't be faced squarely need not be "repressed" into the depths of the unconscious—especially not into such a single-aim unconscious as the Freudian one. All that needs to happen is that the item get called by some other name, or given some other significance, than the one that the individual was, at first glance, privately inclined to give it.

Start this process in motion and the soul has a secret weakness. It will begin to act so as to compensate for the felt weakness, but its resultant actions will have to carry an additional freightload of insincerity, since they were not undertaken for their own sakes. The whole process begins too early, and often on too trivial a ground, for one to call it "selling out." Sometimes and to some extent one can simply outgrow it, learning gradually to stand on one's own two feet and to tell the truth, except where the truth itself would be a species of gratuitous brutality. But at other times, and perhaps more frequently when the individual has matured into an imprudent pliancy of style or character, the secret weakness is not outgrown. As in the story of the princess and the pea, the pain caused by one small untruth to which one has accommodated is felt through all the cushioning layers of adult identity.

The pain has two main components: (1) self-contempt at the accommodation to an untruth, and (2) symptomatic maladaptiveness—the sort of skewed gait that follows from a succession of compensatory "insincere" practices. When one is in this condition, all one has to meet is some external crisis, to which one's carefully acquired skills and interpretive devices happen to be unequal, for this buried sense of profound self-doubt to well up and vitiate many of the ways that one had previously told oneself one's own story. Nothing could be commoner than such a spiritual crisis. Nothing could be less often discussed nowadays on its own terms. One has to go back to nineteenth-century novels for such discussions to be given their proper amplitude.

As long as we are, as our stories go, "still young," we are as a rule much harder on ourselves in the moral judgment department than others can be on us. The opportunities opened to the unfair persuader by a spiritual crisis are opened not so much by our vulnerability to honest error in self-judgment, as by our profound and instinctive need to get what is coming to us—in the harshest sense of that expression. It may be that, in our blinkered, unbending, stern subjective sense of our own deserts, it is felt that "what is coming to us" is that worst of all penalties, a life that has turned its back on the good. The trouble is not so much that we do evil unaware that it is evil. The likelihood of doing evil unawares is no greater than the likelihood of doing good unawares. It is not harder cognitively to do the one than the other. The real moral problem is, rather, that we do evil and are persuaded to do it unaware—or unable to face the fact—that we are worth better than that.

NOTES

1. Rudolf Arnheim draws this view of the biological offices of art out of the experimental proceeds of Gestalt psychology. See Arnheim (1966, pp. 62f, 78f, 114f). More varied and detailed experimental confirmation of Arnheim's view is reported in Berlyne (1971, pp. 43–49, 112ff, 118f, 135f). Berlyne confirms Arnheim's distinction between stimuli that evoke responses because they *resemble* previously experienced objects, and stimuli that directly evoke such proprioceptive and motor responses as fear, solace, etc. (pp. 108f).

2. The example is in Richard Taylor's *Metaphysics* (1974, pp. 62ff).

3. Cf. R. M. Hare's discussion of the fanatic's quasi-aesthetic choices and consequent willingness to override human interests, even his own (1963, pp. 158f, 161, 170–73).

4. On the formalist and postmodern attacks on art's referential role, see Graff (1979, chs. 1 and 2). For Arnheim's partly sympathetic view of formalism, as an antidote to the ugliness of machine manufacture and as a return to certain "primary generalities" of perception, captured also in primitive art and in children's art, see Arnheim (1966, pp. 8f, 47ff, 330f). For the post-structuralist or "deconstructionist" view that the expressive act by its nature erases the very intention that produced it, see Derrida (1967, p. 226). For the latter reference, and her general elucidation of structuralism and post-structuralism, I am indebted to Elizabeth Gross. See also Norris (1982) for a readable account of deconstructionism, the most recent movement in literary criticism, and one that apparently takes the dissolution of formed purposes to be the motif of art and life together. For the references to Graff and Norris, I am indebted to David Novitz.

5. On repression and transference, see Freud (1925–26, pp. 267f). On the unconscious in relation to ego, id, and superego, see Freud (1926, pp. 196–204, 223–28, and 1901). For a critical evaluation of the *Freudian* basis for denying accuracy to extraclinical introspection, see Abigail Rosenthal (1977 and 1985). For evidence that true explanations of their own behavior and decisions are not introspectively accessible to experimental subjects, see Nisbett and Wilson

(1977). And for a critical evaluation that would sharply restrict the scope of the Nisbett and Wilson findings, then see Smith and Miller (1978).

6. On personal identity, see Hume (1739, I.IV.vi.). The claim that the unity of the psyche is an artifact of particular cultures gets some philological and literary help in Adkins's study of Greek psychology from Homeric to postclassical times (1970). For a philosophical suggestion that runs parallel to Adkins's, but is meant half-ironically and speculatively, see Sellars (1956, pp. 180 96). D. M. Armstrong, who maintains the contingent identity of mental events with states of the central nervous system, agrees with Sellars that "the notion of 'a mind' is a theoretical concept" (1968, p. 337) but holds that this theoretical concept is given support by the following considerations: (1) introspective consciousness "enables 'parallel processes' in our mind to be interpreted"; (2) introspective consciousness is also "nearly-essential for event-memory" and therefore "for memory of the past of the self" (1980, pp. 66f); (3) all mental events are events of a unitary thing, the brain. I am indebted to D. M. Armstrong for these references to his views on personal identity. For recent essays on personal identity, some of which deal with such metaphysical riddles as how many persons there are when the brain's two hemispheres have been surgically divided, or when an individual is so old that his memory fails, see the collection edited by Amelie Rorty (1976).

7. Richard Rorty makes the comparison in *Philosophy and the Mirror of Nature* (1979, pp. 306–11). For Moore's general disclaimers of connection between his idea of goodness and any supersensible reality, see *Principia Ethica* (1903, ch. 4).

8. In puzzling out Moore, it becomes helpful to read Franz Brentano's *The Origin of the Knowledge of Right and Wrong* (1889), which Moore cites as containing the ethical views closest to his own (1903, pp. x–xi, and cf. Moore's Oct., 1903, review of Brentano's essay in *International Journal of Ethics*). Moore notes that he became acquainted with the 1902 Cecil Hague translation of Brentano's essay only after he had completed *Principia Ethica*. No doubt the resemblances between the two works may be explained as one of those intellectual coincidences that from time to time occur. Nevertheless, the differences Moore stresses do not seem to be the main ones to note. Thus Moore claims in *Principia Ethica* that Brentano differs from him in describing "the fundamental ethical concept" (1903, p. xi) in terms Moore would characterize aesthetically. However, in the essay in question, Brentano *denies* that the intrinsically ethical criterion can be an aesthetic one (1889, p. 9). Again in *Principia Ethica*, Moore claims that Brentano differs from him in that he "denies by implication" Moore's principle of organic unities (1903, p. xi), and this point is also touched on in the Oct., 1903, review. Moore's principle of organic unities (see Moore, 1903, p. 184) is a rather obscure principle, and one hard to avoid denying by implication, at least some of the time. So Moore may be right that Brentano denies it by implication. Yet Brentano's discussion of the relations of parts to wholes in the evaluation of mixed goods bears a certain generic, if not specific, resemblance to Moore's on organic wholes. For example, Brentano applies an anthropocentric variant of Moore's method of isolation to the evaluation of wholes with mixed (good and bad) parts (1889, p. 24). The most salient

difference between the two essays seems to be that Brentano's is explicitly embedded in an Aristotelian context, where ethical criteria govern the final objects *of human preference* (rather than governing objects impossibly imagined as existing without us), and these ethical criteria are taken to be *no more and no less self-evident* than the Aristotelian laws of thought. As a result, Brentano's essay sounds at once less original and less opaque than G. E. Moore's.

CHAPTER TWO

1. Although Kant, in making freedom the same as goodness, must hold that we never freely will the bad, he does allow that we can freely choose to go after the objects of natural preference in a perverse order. Some of the perverters of the priorities Kant sternly classifies under "malignancy of the heart" (1792, pp. 344f). What Kant has not noticed, perhaps because he considers each choice discretely, is that the *order of choices* follows from a self-interpretation or implicit story, which is itself a potentially self-ratifying choice. So, to choose in a wrong or perverted order involves, though Kant has not noted the fact, choosing the wrong sort of story.

2. Max Weber might be said to be making that use of "ideal types" in *The Theory of Social and Economic Organization* (1922, pp. 92, 101, 107–11) to exemplify generic possibilities for action and relation. Weber first abstracts from the social process types of action (pp. 115ff) and types of social relationship (e.g., pp. 136–43). Weber's "ideal type" is a "fully rational" exemplification of someone acting under some of these constraints on action and relationship, with actual agents showing degrees of deviation from the ideal type. What remains unclear is whether these constraints are imposed on Weber's ideal types to a degree that is inevitable, or arbitrarily, from the standpoint of nature and history. If the constraints are imposed to an arbitrary degree, then the *rationality* of any one of Weber's ideal types would also be jeopardized, since he would not then be *as* rational as nature and history allow him to be. But, if the ideal type is *not* fully rational, then it is harder even in principle to forecast what he will do or comprehend what he has done. So Weber's instrument of analysis is blunted. It is quite likely that any morally neutral attempt to lay out such a typology will be similarly blunted.

3. For this view of the social contract as ethically fundamental, and illustrative interpretation of Hobbes, I am indebted to H. M. Rosenthal's "The Consolations of Philosophy" (1977), where the ontological commitments implicit in social contract theory have been illuminated.

4. Even moral scepticism seems to come back to the common interests as the ineluctable safeguards of social life. See Gilbert Harman (1977, pp. 69f, 148ff, 162, and, for the bases of his scepticism, pp. 7ff, 17). R. M. Hare is unwavering on this point: "Unless a sufficient number of people were prepared to assent to the moral principles which are the constitutive rules of the institution of promising, the word 'promise' could not have a use" (1964, p. 153). Cf. also Bruce Aune's careful elucidation of Kant's categorical imperative, as usable only together with the concept of a rational system of nature, which is to say, the community or the teleological world order (1979,

pp. 50–55, 65). Like Kant (but more clearly like Aristotle), Philippa Foot is concerned with individual character, and she too grounds the virtues in our fundamental interests as social beings (1958–59, p. 128; 1963, p. 80). For Foot, morality itself is founded on the expressed "concern of the community" in "actions [that] are 'passed' or 'not passed'". She determines that, if there were a society where "people were interested in each other's actions, but only aesthetically," and that society had, exceptionally, one benevolent member, "we cannot think of him, situated as he is, as refusing to 'pass' acts of murder" (1978, pp. 203f).

CHAPTER FOUR

1. F. S. C. Northrop (1959) discusses the Roman shift from law based on tribally conferred status to law based on free contract in universalizable conditions, and the influence of Stoic philosophers on this development, on pp. 49ff, 149–52, 220–29, 268, where further references are also given.

2. See George Eliot's *Daniel Deronda* (1876, ch. 16) and Mark Twain's *Adventures of Huckleberry Finn* (1885, ch. 31). The comparison between Huck's friend Jim and Daniel Deronda as offering "some point of moral authority" was suggested to me by Irving Howe's introduction to the New American Library edition of the former novel, p. xxiv.

3. Edmund Burke, "An Appeal from the New to the Old Whigs" (1791) in *Works and Correspondence*, 4:486, quoted in Kelso (1929, pp. 163f).

4. On the stereotyped nature of gestures in our species, and their correspondence to gestures found in similar contexts in related species, see the account of cross-cultural photographic studies done by H. Hass and I. Eibl-Eibesfeldt, in Irenäus Eibl-Eibesfeldt, *Ethology* (1970, pp. 462–82, and cf. pp. 444, 454ff).

CHAPTER FIVE

1. On the tie-in between virtues and a community's practices, see the valuable discussion in MacIntyrre (1981, pp. 178–82).

2. The dilutions and qualifications on Lemkin's definition that are to be found in the U.N. resolution and the chronology of that dilution process are described in Davis and Zannis (1973, pp. 9–21).

3. On Custer, see Slotkin (1985, pp. 387, 419f, 445–53). I owe this point to Davis and Zannis (1973, p. 176).

4. See Alice Miller's *For Your Own Good* for a discussion of the effects of this process when it is made into a pedagogic system (1980, pp. 7, 42f).

5. A detailed account of the eugenics movement, its theoretical basis and social influence, is in Daniel J. Kevles (1985).

6. See Monroe L. Beardsley, "Reflections on Genocide and Ethnocide" (1976, pp. 89f, 94, 96).

7. See Bernard L. Diamond, "Failures of Identification and Sociopathic Behavior" (1971, p. 133).

8. On Nazi theologicans, see Ericksen (1985).

9. Changing European attitudes toward salvation from the early Middle Ages to the late Renaissance are discussed in Philippe Ariès, *The Hour of Our Death* (1977, pp. 221–30, 262f, 300–5, 605–8). On the "chivalric parallel between immortality and fame," see pp. 211–15.

10. On memory-erasure, see Conquest (1970, ch. 5); Solzhenitsyn (1974–78, 1:24f, 176ff, 306f).

11. An account of Merleau-Ponty's journey into ideology and back is in the author's "Getting Past Marx and Freud" (1985).

12. See, for example, "Some Determinants of Destructive Behavior," by Neil J. Smelser (1971) and "Groupthink Among Policy Makers," by Irving L. Janis (1971). The correspondences between Russian and Nazi dichotomizing are in E. A. Shils, "Authoritarianism: 'Right' and 'Left,'" in *Studies in the Scope and Method of the Authoritarian Personality* (The Free Press, Glencoe, Ill., 1954), summarized in Dicks (1972, p. 267).

13. Yaffa Eliach's *Hasidic Tales of the Holocaust* (1982) includes an extraordinary collection of such stories. See, for example, "Good Morning, Herr Müller," pp. 129f, and "For the Sake of Friendship," pp. 139–43.

14. For a rundown on techniques used to force confessions, see Solzhenitsyn (1974–78, 1:103–17).

15. For a more detailed sketch, see Solzhenitsyn (1974–78, 1:144–47, 151ff).

CHAPTER SIX

1. See the discussion in Jackson (1947, pp. 14ff).

2. See Opinion and Judgment, *Nuernberg Military Tribunals,* Case No. 9, "The Einsatzgruppen Case," vol. 4, p. 462.

3. Lackey, "Extraordinary Evil or Common Malevolence? Demythologizing the Holocaust" (now published). I am grateful to Douglas Lackey for letting me see this paper in manuscript.

4. Fackenheim, "The Holocaust and Philosophy" (1985, p. 508); Lang, "Uniqueness and Explanation" (1985), in discussion following Dec. 30, 1985, Symposium on The Holocaust, Eastern Division Meetings of the American Philosophical Association. For the claim that the Nazis engaged in systemwide cover-ups, Hilberg provides extensive support (1985, pp. 891, 917, 953, 976, 979, 983, 1013–17).

5. See Horowitz (1982, pp. 213–17), for an account of some of the Russian estimates, and the not-unrelated difficulty of securing accurate figures.

6. With regard to the American Indian, in his "Reflections on Genocide and Ethnocide," Monroe Beardsley estimates that between 1776 and 1900 their total numbers dropped from over two and a half million to "fewer than 240,000. . . . Massacre, starvation, disease, deculturation are . . . the explanation" (1976, p. 97). Horowitz, however, notes a population doubling between census reports in 1960 and 1970 (1982, p. 64). Slotkin denies programmatic holocaust (1985, p. 62). Katz estimates "a forty percent death rate" but an upturn of late, and no program of genocide (1983, pp. 296ff and notes).

7. See Berel Lang's "The Concept of Genocide" (1984-85, p. 4). See also Katz (1983, pp. 305f).

8. An account of the procedural stages by which the Genocide Convention came to be drafted is in the Ruhashyankiko report (1978, pp. 8–11).

9. See William L. Reese, "Christianity and the Final Solution" (1984-85, pp. 138–47).

10. See the discussion of "kin altruism" in Peter Singer (1981, pp. 11–15).

11. See Michael Wyschogrod's *The Body of Faith: Judaism as Corporeal Election* (1983, p. 68).

12. The extreme difficulty and delicacy of the ensuing *theological* task is made evident in Katz (1983, e.g., pp. 226–42).

13. See the account by Jonathan Schell in "Reflections (Poland)" (1986).

14. See, for example, Steven T. Katz on Emil Fackenheim, in Katz (1983, pp. 208ff).

15. These two carthy points about the practicalities I owe to New York's Mayor Koch, in a speech at the U.N. Plaza on Nov. 10, 1985, to a rally protesting the U.N. General Assembly's "Zionism is Racism" resolution, on the tenth anniversary of that resolution.

16. Quoted in the author's preface to Bronstein, *Kabbalah and Art* (1980).

17. See the Robert Kirschner translation of *Rabbinic Responsa of the Holocaust Era* (1985, pp. 116–19).

CHAPTER SEVEN

1. See Thomas Keneally's account in *Schindler's Ark* (1982, p. 29).

2. A brief account of the historical background is in Shirer (1960, pp. 83–97).

3. In this connection, see Geoffrey Cocks's *Psychotherapy in the Third Reich* (1985, pp. 40f, 56ff, 101f, 161).

4. For the two points supporting the place of consistency and reasoned argument in government, I am indebted to Barry Gross's *Discrimination in Reverse: Is Turnabout Fair Play?* (1978, pp. 102ff).

BIBLIOGRAPHY

ABEL, THEODORE. 1938. *Why Hitler Came into Power: An Answer Based on the Original Life Stories of Six Hundred of His Followers.* Prentice-Hall, New York.

ADKINS, ARTHUR W. H. 1970. *From the Many to the One: A Study of Personality and Views of Human Nature in the Context of Ancient Greek Society, Values, and Beliefs.* Cornell University Press, Ithaca, N.Y.

ALSTON, WILLIAM P. 1977. "Self-Intervention and the Structure of Motivation." In *The Self: Psychological and Philosophical Issues,* ed. Theodore Mischel, pp. 65–102. Oxford University Press, New York.

ARENDT, HANNAH. 1951. *The Origins of Totalitarianism.* Harcourt, Brace, New York.

———. 1964. *Eichmann in Jerusalem: A Report on the Banality of Evil.* Viking Press, New York.

ARENS, RICHARD. 1976. "Introduction." In *Genocide in Paraguay,* ed. Richard Arens, pp. 3–18. Temple University Press, Philadelphia.

ARIÈS, PHILIPPE. 1977. *The Hour of Our Death,* trans. Helen Weaver. Vintage Books, Random House, New York, 1982.

ARISTOTLE. 335–23 B.C. *Nicomachean Ethics.* In *The Basic Works of Aristotle,* ed. Richard McKeon, trans. W. D. Ross, pp. 928–1112. Random House, New York, 1941.

———. 324 B.C. *Metaphysics.* In *The Basic Works of Aristotle,* pp. 689–926.

ARMSTRONG, D. M. 1968. *A Materialist Theory of the Mind.* Routledge & Kegan Paul, London.

———. 1980. *The Nature of Mind.* Harvester Press, Sussex.

ARNHEIM, RUDOLF. 1966. *Toward a Psychology of Art: Collected Essays.* University of California Press, Berkeley and Los Angeles.

ARTSYBASHEV, MIKHAIL PETROVICH. 1907. *Sanine.* Martin Secker, London, 1928.

AUNE, BRUCE. 1979. *Kant's Theory of Morals.* Princeton University Press, Princeton, N.J.

BEARDSLEY, MONROE C. 1976. "Reflections on Genocide and Ethnocide." In *Genocide in Paraguay,* ed. Richard Arens, pp. 85–101. Temple University Press, Philadelphia.

231

BERLYNE, D. E. 1971. *Aesthetics and Psychobiology.* Appleton-Century-Crofts, New York.

BRENTANO, FRANZ. 1889. *The Origin of the Knowledge of Right and Wrong,* trans. Cecil Hague. Archibald Constable, London, 1902.

BRONSTEIN, LÉO. 1980. *Kabbalah and Art.* Brandeis University Press/University Press of New England, Hanover, N.H.

BUBER, MARTIN. 1952. *Images of Good and Evil,* trans. Michael Bullock. Routledge & Kegan Paul, London.

BUTLER, JOSEPH. 1751. *The Works,* vols. 1 and 2. Oxford University Press, Oxford, 1849.

COCKS, GEOFFREY. 1985. *Psychotherapy in the Third Reich: The Göring Institute.* Oxford University Press, New York.

CONQUEST, ROBERT. 1970. *The Nation Killers: The Soviet Deportation of Nationalities.* Macmillan, New York.

CONRAD, JOSEPH. 1917. *Lord Jim.* Penguin Books, New York, 1983.

CUSTER, ROBERT, and HARRY MILT. 1985. *When Luck Runs Out: Help for Compulsive Gamblers and Their Families.* Facts on File Publications, New York.

DANTE, ALIGHIERI. 1321. "Paradise." In *The Divine Comedy,* vol. 3, trans. Dorothy Sayers and Barbara Reynolds. Penguin Books, Baltimore, 1962.

DAVIDSON, DONALD. 1970. "How is Weakness of the Will Possible?" In *Essays on Action and Events,* pp. 21–42. Oxford University Press, New York, 1980.

DAVIS, ROBERT, and MARK ZANNIS. 1973. *The Genocide Machine in Canada: The Pacification of the North.* Black Rose Books, Montreal.

DAWIDOWICZ, LUCY S. 1975. *The War Against the Jews 1933–1945.* Holt, Rinehart & Winston, New York.

———. 1981. *The Holocaust and the Historians.* Harvard University Press, Cambridge.

DENNETT, DANIEL C. 1981. "Reflections." In *The Mind's I,* ed. Douglas R. Hofstadter and Daniel C. Dennett, pp. 265–68. Basic Books, New York.

DERRIDA, JACQUES. 1967. "Freud and the Scene of Writing." In *Writing and Difference,* trans. Alan Bass, pp. 196–231. Routledge & Kegan Paul, London, 1978.

DIAMOND, BERNARD L. 1971. "Failures of Identification and Sociopathic Behavior." In *Sanctions for Evil: Sources of Social Destructiveness,* ed. Nevitt Sanford, Craig Comstock, & Associates, pp. 125–35. Jossey-Bass, San Francisco.

DICKENS, CHARLES. 1859. *A Tale of Two Cities.* Books, New York, n.d.

DICKS, HENRY V. 1972. *Licensed Mass Murder: A Socio-Psychological Study of Some S.S. Killers.* Basic Books, New York.

EIBL-EIBESFELDT, IRENÄUS. 1970. *Ethology: The Biology of Behavior,* trans. Erich Klinghammer. Holt, Rinehart & Winston, New York, 1975.

EICHMANN TRIAL. See *Israel v. Eichmann.*

ELIACH, YAFFA. 1982. *Hasidic Tales of the Holocaust.* Avon Books, New York.

ELIOT, GEORGE. 1876. *Daniel Deronda,* introduction by Irving Howe. New American Library, New York, 1979.

ERICKSEN, ROBERT P. 1985. *Theologians Under Hitler: Gerhard Kittel, Paul Althaus and Emanuel Hirsch.* Yale University Press, New Haven.

FACKENHEIM, EMIL L. 1985. "The Holocaust and Philosophy." *Journal of Philosophy* 82, no. 10 (October):505–14.

FODOR, JERRY A. 1975. *The Language of Thought.* Thomas Y. Crowell, New York.

FOOT, PHILIPPA. 1958–59. "Moral Beliefs." In *Virtues and Vices and Other Essays in Moral Philosophy,* pp. 110–31. Oxford University Press, New York, 1978.

———. 1963. "Hume on Moral Judgment." In *Virtues and Vices,* pp. 74–80.

———. 1978. "Approval and Disapproval." In *Virtues and Vices,* pp. 189–207.

FORTUNE, REO F. 1932. *Sorcerers of Dobu: The Social Anthropology of the Dobu Islanders of the Western Pacific.* Routledge & Kegan Paul, London, 1963.

FREEMAN, DEREK. 1983. *Margaret Mead and Samoa: The Making and Unmaking of an Anthropological Myth.* Australian National University Press, Canberra.

FREUD, SIGMUND. 1901. "Bungled Actions" and "Symptomatic and Chance Actions," *The Psychopathology of Everyday Life.* In *The Standard Edition of the Complete Psychological Works,* vol. 6, trans. James Strachey, pp. 162–216. Hogarth Press, London, 1960.

———. 1925–26. "Psychoanalysis." In *Works,* vol. 20 (1959), pp. 263–70.

———. 1926. "The Question of Lay Analysis." In *Works,* vol. 20 (1959), pp. 183–250.

GEMES, KENNETH. 1983. "Causal vs. Epistemic Explanation in Quine." Philosophy Department Seminar, Department of Traditional and Modern Philosophy, University of Sydney, May 2.

GERGEN, KENNETH J. 1977. "The Social Construction of Self-Knowledge." In *The Self: Psychological and Philosophical Issues,* ed. Theodore Mischel, pp. 139–69. Oxford University Press, New York.

GLAZER, MYRON. 1983. "Ten Whistleblowers and How They Fared." *Hastings Center Report* 13, no. 6 (December):33–41.

GLUCK, SAMUEL E. 1979. *Moral Values in Management Textbooks,* vol. 5, series 14. Hofstra University Yearbook of Business, Hempstead, N.Y.

GRAFF, GERALD. 1979. *Literature Against Itself: Literary Ideas in Modern Society.* University of Chicago Press, Chicago.

GRANT, FRANCES R. 1976. "Paraguayan Realities." In *Genocide in Paraguay,* ed. Richard Arens, pp. 69–84. Temple University Press, Philadelphia.

GROSS, BARRY. 1978. *Discrimination in Reverse: Is Turnabout Fair Play?* New York University Press, New York.

GUEVARA, ERNESTO ("Che"). 1961. *Guerrilla Warfare,* trans. J. P. Morray. Monthly Review Press, New York.

HALSELL, GRACE. 1973. *Bessie Yellowhair.* William Morrow, New York, 1974.

HAMPSHIRE, STUART. 1983. *Morality and Conflict.* Harvard University Press, Cambridge.

HARE, R. M. 1963. *Freedom and Reason.* Oxford University Press, New York.

———. 1964. "The Promising Game." In *The Is/Ought Question,* ed. W. D. Hudson, pp. 144–56. Macmillan, London, 1969.

HARMAN, GILBERT. 1977. *The Nature of Morality: An Introduction to Ethics.* Oxford University Press, New York.

HAUSNER, GIDEON. 1966. *Justice in Jerusalem.* Holocaust Library, New York.

HEIDEGGER, MARTIN. 1927. *Being and Time*, trans. John Macquarrie and Edward Robinson. Harper, New York, 1962.

HILBERG, RAUL. 1985. *The Destruction of the European Jews*, vols. 1–3. Holmes & Meier, New York, London.

HOROWITZ, IRVING LOUIS. 1982. *Taking Lives: Genocide and State Power*, 3rd ed. Transaction Books, New Brunswick, N.J.

HUME, DAVID. 1739. "Of Personal Identity." In *A Treatise of Human Nature*, vol. 1, ed. L. A. Selby-Bigge, 2nd ed., part IV, section vi, pp. 251–63. Oxford University Press, New York 1978.

———. 1751. *An Inquiry Concerning the Principles of Morals*, ed. Charles W. Hendel. Library of Liberal Arts, New York, 1957.

HURST, DAVID K. 1984. "Of Boxes, Bubbles, and Effective Management." *Harvard Business Review* 62, no. 3 (May–June):78–88.

ISRAEL v. EICHMANN. 1962. *The Attorney-General of the Government of Israel v. Adolf, the Son of Adolf Karl Eichmann* (Criminal Case No. 40/61, District Court, Jerusalem: Microcard Editions, Washington, D.C.) [unedited transcript of simultaneous translation].

JACKSON, ROBERT H. 1947. *The Nürnberg Case, as Presented by Robert H. Jackson, Chief of Counsel for the United States, Together with Other Documents*. Alfred A. Knopf, New York.

JAMES, HENRY. 1880. *Washington Square*. Penguin Books, New York, 1984.

———. 1900. *The Future of the Novel: Essays on the Art of Fiction*, ed. Leon Edel, pp. 30–42. Vintage Books, New York, 1956.

JANIS, IRVING L. 1971. "Groupthink Among Policy Makers." In *Sanctions for Evil: Sources of Social Destructiveness*, ed. Nevitt Sanford, Craig Comstock & Associates, pp. 71–89. Jossey-Bass, San Francisco.

KANT, IMMANUEL. 1792. "On the Radical Evil in Human Nature." In *Philosophical Theory of Religion, or Religion So Far As It Lies Within the Limits of Reason Alone*, First Part, in *Kant's Theory of Ethics*, trans. Thomas K. Abbot, pp. 325–60. Longman's Green, London, 1889.

KATZ, STEVEN T. 1983. *Post-Holocaust Dialogues: Critical Studies in Modern Jewish Thought*. New York University Press, New York.

KELSO, RUTH. 1929. *The Doctrine of the English Country Gentleman in the Sixteenth Century*. Peter Smith, Gloucester, Mass., 1964.

KENEALLY, THOMAS. 1982. *Schindler's Ark* [published in America as *Schindler's List*]. Hodder & Stoughton, Sevenoaks, Kent.

KEVLES, DANIEL J. 1985. *In the Name of Eugenics: Genetics and the Uses of Human Heredity*. Alfred A. Knopf, New York.

KEYNES, JOHN MAYNARD. 1949. "My Early Beliefs." In *Two Memoirs: Essays and Sketches in Biography*, pp. 239–56. Meridian Books, New York, 1956.

KIERKEGAARD, SØREN. 1843. "Diary of the Seducer." In *Either/Or*, vol. 1, trans. David F. Swenson and Lillian Marvin Swenson, pp. 299–440. Doubleday, Anchor Books, New York, 1959.

———. 1834–54. *The Journals of Søren Kierkegaard*, ed. and trans. Alexander Dru. Oxford University Press, New York, 1938.

KIRSCHNER, ROBERT, ed. and trans. 1985. *Rabbinic Responsa of the Holocaust Era*. Schocken Books, New York.

LACKEY, DOUGLAS P. 1986. "Extraordinary Evil or Common Malevolence? Evaluating the Jewish Holocaust." *Journal of Applied Philosophy* 3, no. 2: 167–81.

LACLOS, CHODERLOS DE. 1787. *Dangerous Acquaintances, Les Liaisons dangereuses*, trans. Richard Aldington. E. P. Dutton, New York, 1924.

LANG, BEREL. 1984–85. "The Concept of Genocide." *Philosophical Forum* 16, nos. 1–2 (Fall and Winter):1–18.

———. 1985. "Uniqueness and Explanation." *Journal of Philosophy* 82, no. 10 (October):514f.

LANZMANN, CLAUDE. 1985. *Shoah: An Oral History of the Holocaust, the Complete Text of the Film*, preface by Simone de Beauvoir. Pantheon Books, New York.

LEMKIN, RAFAEL. 1944. *Axis Rule in Occupied Europe: Laws of Occupation, Analysis of Government, Proposals for Redress.* Carnegie Endowment for International Peace, Washington, D.C.

LEVI, PRIMO. 1986. "Last Christmas of the War." *New York Review of Books* 33, no. 1 (January 30):5f.

LEWIN, RONALD. 1984. *Hitler's Mistakes: New Insights into What Made Hitler Tick.* William Morrow, New York.

LIVELY, PIERCE. 1985. *Demjanjuk v. Petrovsky.* Sixth Circuit, United States Court of Appeals, No. 85–3435, Cincinnati, Ohio, October 31.

McCALL, GEORGE. 1977. "The Social Looking-Glass: A Sociological Perspective on Self-Development." In *The Self: Psychological and Philosophical Issues*, ed. Theodore Mischel, pp. 274–87. Oxford University Press, New York.

MACINTYRE, ALASDAIR. 1981. *After Virtue: A Study in Moral Theory.* Gerald Duckworth, London.

McMULLEN, DAVID W. 1981. "Trouble in Turtle Island" (unpublished).

MANN, THOMAS. 1936. *Joseph and His Brothers*, vol. 3, trans. H. T. Lowe-Porter. Alfred A. Knopf, New York, 1948.

MEAD, MARGARET. 1928. *Coming of Age in Samoa*, foreword by Franz Boas. William Morrow, New York.

MELDEN, A. I. 1970. *Human Rights.* Wadsworth Publishing, Belmont, Cal.

MERLEAU-PONTY, MAURICE. 1960. "The Child's Relations With Others." In *The Primacy of Perception*, ed. James M. Edie, trans. William Cobb, pp. 96–155. Northwestern University Press, Evanston, Ill., 1964.

MIDGLEY, MARY. 1981. *Heart and Mind: The Varieties of Moral Experience.* Methuen, London.

MILLER, ALICE. 1980. *For Your Own Good: Hidden Cruelty in Child-Rearing and the Roots of Violence*, trans. Hildegaard and Hunter Hannum. Farrar, Straus, & Giroux, New York, 1984.

MISCHEL, HARRIET N., and WALTER MISCHEL. 1977. "Self-Control and the Self." In *The Self: Psychological and Philosophical Issues*, ed. Theodord Mischel, pp. 31–64. Oxford University Press, New York.

MOORE, G. E. 1903. Review of Franz Brentano [1889] in *International Journal of Ethics* 14 (October):115–23.

———. 1903. *Principia Ethica.* Cambridge University Press, Cambridge, 1956.

———. 1912. *Ethics.* Oxford University Press, New York, 1965.

MORGENTHAU, HENRY. 1918. *Ambassador Morgenthau's Story.* Doubleday, Page, New York.

NAGEL, THOMAS. 1979. "Moral Luck." In *Mortal Questions,* pp. 24–38. Cambridge University Press, Cambridge.

NISBETT, RICHARD E., and TIMOTHY DECAMP WILSON. 1977. "Telling More Than We Can Know: Verbal Reports on Mental Processes." *Psychological Review* 84, no. 3 (May):231–59.

NORRIS, CHRISTOPHER. 1982. *Deconstruction: Theory and Practice.* Methuen, London.

NORTHROP, F. S. C. 1959. *The Complexity of Legal and Ethical Experience.* Little, Brown, Boston.

NUERNBERG MILITARY TRIBUNALS. 1949–53. *Trials of War Criminals Before the Nuernberg Military Tribunals Under Control Council Law No. 10,* 15 vols. Washington, D.C. (Green Series).

PATTERSON, ORLANDO. 1982. *Slavery and Social Death: A Comparative Study.* Harvard University Press, Cambridge.

PLATO. ca. 395 B.C. *Crito.* In *The Dialogues of Plato,* vol. 1, trans. B. Jowett, pp. 427–38. Macmillan, London, 1892.

———. ca. 387 B.C. *The Republic.* In *Dialogues,* pp. 591–879.

PRESCOTT, WILLIAM H. 1843. *The Conquest of Mexico,* vols. 1–2. Henry Holt, New York, 1922.

———. 1847. *History of the Conquest of Peru: With a Preliminary View of the Civilization of the Incas,* vols. 1–2, ed. John Foster Kirk. J. B. Lippincott, Philadelphia, 1874.

REESE, WILLIAM L. 1984–85. "Christianity and the Final Solution." *Philosophical Forum* 16, nos. 1–2 (Fall and Winter):138–47.

RORTY, AMELIE OKSENBERG, ed. 1976. *The Identities of Persons.* University of California Press, Berkeley.

RORTY, RICHARD. 1979. *Philosophy and the Mirror of Nature.* Princeton University Press, Princeton, N.J.

ROSENTHAL, ABIGAIL L. 1977. "The Intelligibility of History." *Journal of the History of Philosophy* 15, no. 1 (January):55–70.

———. 1985. "Getting Past Marx and Freud." *Clio* 15, no. 1 (Fall):61–82.

ROSENTHAL, HENRY M. 1977. *"The Consolations of Philosophy: Hobbes's Secret; Spinoza's Way"* (unpublished book).

RUHASHYANKIKO, NICODÈME. 1978. *Report on the Question of the Prevention and Punishment of the Crime of Genocide.* U.N. Economic and Social Council, Commission on Human Rights, Sub-Commission on Prevention of Discrimination and Protection of Minorities, U.N. Doc. No. E/CN.4/Sub.2/416/1978.

SAGAN, ELI. 1974. *Cannibalism: Human Aggression and Cultural Form.* Harper & Row, New York.

SCHELL, JONATHAN. 1986. "Reflections (Poland)." *New Yorker* 61, no. 50 (February 3):47–67.

SELLARS, WILFRID. 1956. "Empiricism and the Philosophy of Mind." In *Science, Perception and Reality,* pp. 127–96. Humanities Press, New York, 1963.

SHAWCROSS, WILLIAM. 1984. *The Quality of Mercy: Cambodia, Holocaust and Modern Conscience.* Simon & Schuster, New York.

SHIRER, WILLIAM L. 1960. *The Rise and Fall of the Third Reich.* Ballantine Books, New York.

SIDGWICK, HENRY. 1874. *The Methods of Ethics,* 7th ed. (1907). Macmillan, London, 1962.

SINGER, PETER. 1981. *The Expanding Circle: Ethics and Sociobiology.* Oxford University Press, New York.

SLOTKIN, RICHARD. 1985. *The Fatal Environment: The Myth of the Frontier in the Age of Industrialization, 1800–1890.* Atheneum, New York.

SMELSER, NEIL J. 1971. "Some Determinants of Destructive Behavior." In *Sanctions for Evil: Sources of Social Destructiveness,* ed. Nevitt Sanford, Craig Comstock & Associates, pp. 15–24. Jossey-Bass, San Francisco.

SMITH, BRADLEY F. 1967. *Adolf Hitler: His Family, Childhood and Youth.* Hoover Institution on War, Revolution and Peace, Stanford University, Stanford, Cal.

———. 1971. *Heinrich Himmler: A Nazi in the Making, 1900–1926.* Hoover Institution Press, Stanford University, Stanford, Cal.

SMITH, ELIOT R., and FREDERICK D. MILLER. 1978. "Limits on Perception of Cognitive Processes: A Reply to Nisbett and Wilson." *Psychological Review* 85, no. 4 (July):355–62.

SOLZHENITSYN, ALEKSANDER I. 1974–78. *The Gulag Archipelago 1918–1956: An Experiment in Literary Investigation,* vols. 1–2, trans. Thomas P. Whitney; vol. 3, trans. Harry Willetts. Harper & Row, New York.

STEINSALTZ, ADIN. 1976. *The Essential Talmud,* trans. Chaya Galai. Basic Books, New York.

STERN, FRITZ. 1963. *The Politics of Cultural Despair: A Study in the Rise of the Germanic Ideology.* University of California Press, Berkeley and Los Angeles.

STROUSE, JEAN. 1980. *Alice James: A Biography.* Houghton Mifflin, Boston.

SYMONS, DONALD. 1979. *The Evolution of Human Sexuality.* Oxford University Press, New York.

TAYLOR, CHARLES. 1977. "What is Human Agency." In *The Self: Psychological and Philosophical Issues,* ed. Theodore Mischel, pp. 103–35. Oxford University Press, New York.

TAYLOR, RICHARD. 1974. *Metaphysics,* 2nd ed. Prentice-Hall, Englewood Cliffs, N.J.

TWAIN, MARK. 1884. *The Adventures of Huckleberry Finn.* Bantam Books, New York, 1984.

U.N. SUB-COMMISSION ON PREVENTION OF DISCRIMINATION AND PROTECTION OF MINORITIES. 1985. *Summary Record* (38th Session, 21st Meeting). U.N. Doc. No. E/CN.4/Sub.2/1985/SR.21 (19 August).

WEBER, MAX. 1922. *The Theory of Social and Economic Organization,* ed. Talcott Parsons, trans. A. M. Henderson and Talcott Parsons. Oxford University Press, New York, 1947.

WHITAKER, B. 1985. *Revised and updated report on the question of the prevention and punishment of the crime of genocide, prepared by Mr. B. Whitaker.* U.N. Economic and Social Council, Commission on Human Rights, Sub-Commission on Prevention of Discrimination and Protection of Minorities. U.N. Doc. No. E/CN.4/Sub.2/1985/6 (2 July).

WOLF, ERNEST S. 1977. "'Irrationality' in a Psychoanalytic Psychology of the Self." In *The Self: Psychological and Philosophical Issues,* ed. Theodore Mischel, pp. 203–23. Oxford University Press, New York.

WYMAN, DAVID S. 1984. *The Abandonment of the Jews: America and the Holocaust, 1941–1945.* Pantheon Books, New York.

WYSCHOGROD, MICHAEL. 1983. *The Body of Faith: Judaism as Corporeal Election.* Seabury Press, New York.

YATES, FRANCES. 1964. *Giordano Bruno and the Hermetic Tradition.* Routledge & Kegan Paul, London.

YOUNG-BRUEHL, ELISABETH. 1982. *Hannah Arendt: For Love of the World.* Yale University Press, New Haven.

INDEX

Addict, the, 53–56, 58
Adkins, Arthur W. H., 226 n6
Aesthetic, the, 3–5, 9, 14–16, 20, 24, 28, 68, 77, 101–2, 226 n8, 228 n4
Aggression, 62–63. *See also* Violence
Alcoholic, the. *See* Addict, the
Alston, William P., 6
Anthropological reports, 44–47, 59–63. *See also* Cultural relativism; Mead-Freeman controversy
Anti-Semitism, 168, 171, 176–77, 180, 180n, 188, 190, 191n, 195, 195n, 202, 210, 214–16, 218–19
Arendt, Hannah, 9, 197–98; *Eichmann in Jerusalem,* themes in, x, 17–18, 163, 165–80, 197–98, 198n; rights, human and national, 142–43; and totalitarianism, 154–55, 157. *See also* Nazi, the, banalization of
Arens, Richard, 132n
Aristotle, 39–42, 86, 94, 222, 227 n8, 228 n4
Armenians, 44, 119–21, 178, 185–86, 203
Armstrong, D. M., xiv, 19, 226 n6
Arnheim, Rudolf, 4, 225 n1, 225 n4
Art, 3–5, 14–15, 225 n1, 225 n4. *See also* Formalism, in art; Ideal story, and fictions; Novel, the modern
Artsybashev, Mikhail Petrovich, 11
Augustine (St.), 42
Aune, Bruce, 227–28 n4
Auschwitz, 182
Austen, Jane, 4
Authenticity, 9

Authoritarian personality, the, 159, 229 n12
Aviel, Avraham, 206n

Bacon, John, xiii, 106n, 194n
Bad, 19, 33–34, 45, 51, 118, 119, 123, 129, 135. *See also* Good, woman, the
Banality, 17. *See also* Nazi, the banalization of
Beardsley, Monroe, 143, 229 n6
Beckett, Samuel, 20
Bey, Bedri (Prefect of Police, Constantinople), 122
Bey, Talaat (Leader, Ruling Committee, Turkey), 119–22
Blomstrom, Robert. *See* Davis, Keith, and Robert Blomstrom
Bormann, Martin (Nazi Party Chancellery), 171
Brentano, Franz, 39, 39n, 226–27 n8
Bronstein, Léo, 203, 230 n16
Buber, Martin, 10
Burke, Edmund, 104–5
Butler, Joseph (Bishop), 26

Cannibalism. *See* Sagan, Eli
Carlyle, Thomas, 216
Carton, Sydney (in *A Tale of Two Cities*), 79–81
Christianity, 106n, 107, 188, 194, 219, 230 n9
Common sense, 20, 30
Computers, 10–13, 21
Conquest, Robert, 155n, 157